TAXING THE RICH

TAXING
THE RICH

A History of Fiscal Fairness
in the United States and Europe

**KENNETH SCHEVE AND
DAVID STASAVAGE**

RUSSELL SAGE FOUNDATION
New York

PRINCETON UNIVERSITY PRESS
Princeton and Oxford

Published by Princeton University Press,
41 William Street, Princeton, New Jersey 08540

In the United Kingdom: Princeton University Press,
6 Oxford Street, Woodstock, Oxfordshire OX20 1TR

press.princeton.edu

Russell Sage Foundation,
112 East 64th Street,
New York, New York 10065
russellsage.org

Jacket image courtesy of Shutterstock

ISBN 978-0-691-16545-5
Library of Congress Control Number: 2016930691

British Library Cataloging-in-Publication Data is available

This book has been composed in
Trade Gothic LT Std. & Sabon Next LT Pro

Printed on acid-free paper ∞

Printed in the United States of America

1 3 5 7 9 10 8 6 4 2

FOR MELISSA
& LAUREN

The rich shall not give more, and the poor shall not give less than half a shekel, when *they* give an offering unto the LORD, to make an atonement for your souls.

—*Exodus 30:15*

There are hundreds of thousands who have given their lives, there are millions who have given up comfortable homes and exchanged them for a daily communion with death; multitudes have given up those whom they love best. Let the nation as a whole place its comforts, its luxuries, its indulgencies, its elegances on a national altar consecrated by such sacrifices as these men have made.

—*David Lloyd George, 1916*

CONTENTS

FIGURES AND TABLES

FIGURES

TABLES

ACKNOWLEDGMENTS

Writing this book has been a great pleasure. Some portion of that enjoyment has been in wrestling with questions about politics and the economy that we find tremendously important. Another portion is working with incredibly talented research assistants, talking with our many insightful colleagues and students, and enjoying the process of learning together. We and the book have benefited from a great many friends.

We are especially grateful to the research assistants who helped us collect data for this project. Federica Genovese and Arnd Plagge deserve special thanks, as they respectively led our construction of databases on income and inheritance taxes for twenty countries over the last two centuries. They each exhibited great skill and persistence in organizing these projects and were a pleasure to work with. Michaël Aklin, Sebastian Barfort, Quintin Beazer, Laurens Defau, Aaron Egolf, Navid Hassanpour, Marko Karttunen, Risa Kitagawa, Krista Ryu, Kong Joo Shin, Rory Truex, Kris-Stella Trump, and Johan van Rijn all made important contributions to our data collection for which we are very grateful. We also appreciate advice and data that we received from Debasis Bandyopadhyay, Wantje Fritschy, Egbert Jongen, Teresa Miguel, Anton Rainer, Muireann Toibin, Daniel Waldenström, and Nico Wilterdink. In addition to the construction of these databases, we want to thank Eric Arias, Erdem Aytaç, Cameron Ballard-Rosa, Allison Carnegie, Maria Carreri, Suon Choi, Brian Fried, Nikhar Gaikwad, Saad Gulzar, Marlene Guraieb, Robin Harding, Rocio Hernandez, Young Joe Hur, Caitlyn Littlepage, Yiming

Ma, Lily McElwee, Umberto Mignozzetti, John Morgan, Jana Persky, Nick Powell, Steve Rashin, Mike Schwartz, Martin Soyland, Peter Vining, Jason Weinreb, Jack Weller, and Emily West for excellent research assistance on various other aspects of the project. We want to particularly thank Sarah Cormack-Patton for her work in the final stages of finishing the book. Finally, we want to acknowledge and thank our coauthors, Cameron Ballard-Rosa, Xiaobo Lü, Lucy Martin, and Massimiliano Onorato for letting us use some material from related papers in this book.

Our research has benefitted greatly from comments and criticisms from many colleagues. We want to especially thank Thad Dunning for organizing a book workshop for us at Berkeley. We received extremely helpful comments from Thad, Jonah Levy, Eric Schickler, Shannon Stimson, and Rob Van Houweling, who served as our discussants, as well as many other faculty and students who participated. A number of other colleagues and students read all or parts of the manuscript and provided useful criticisms and suggestions that improved the book substantially. These included Jim Alt, Carles Boix, Pat Egan, Jeff Frieden, Marty Gilens, Steve Haber, Bob Keohane, Evan Lieberman, Margaret Levi, Bernard Manin, Nolan McCarty, Jason Oh, Adam Przeworski, Ryan Pevnick, Steve Pincus, Dani Rodrik, Ron Rogowski, Michael Ross, Melissa Schwartzberg, Ken Shepsle, Jim Snyder, Sue Stokes, and Eric Zolt. We also presented the book manuscript to audiences at the Canadian Institute for Advanced Research's Institutions, Organizations, and Growth Program, FGV EBAPE, Harvard University, the Institute for Advanced Study, the University of Pennsylvania, IPEG Barcelona, Stanford University, UCLA, the University of Michigan, the University of San Andrés, and the University of Vienna.

At Princeton University Press, we are grateful to Eric Crahan for his support of the project and his excellent advice for improving the manuscript. We were also fortunate to receive advice from two reviewers that helped us anticipate a number of important questions about our argument and the evidence. We thank Karen Verde and Brigitte Pelner for all of their work in preparing the manuscript for publication. We acknowledge the *American Political Science Review*,

International Organization, and the *Journal of Economic History* for allowing us to use material from articles that we previously published in those journals.

This project would not have been possible without the generous funding that we have had for our research. We received substantial funding from the MacMillan Center for International Affairs and the Institution for Social and Policy Studies at Yale University, The Europe Center and Freeman Spogli Institute at Stanford University, and New York University. We are also grateful for a grant from the Russell Sage Foundation, RSF Project #83-08-01.

Finally, the book is dedicated to Melissa and Lauren, to whom we are thankful for many things including challenging us to think more deeply about equality. We also thank our children, Ally, Ben, Rivka, and Ezra who, while skeptical about how interesting a book about taxes might be, are pretty adamant about debating what's fair.

DEBATING TAXATION

CHAPTER ONE
WHY MIGHT GOVERNMENTS TAX THE RICH?*

When and why do countries tax the rich? It's hard to think of a timelier question today or one for which there are more sharply colliding views. We know that taxes on the rich today aren't what they were half a century ago, but how did we get from there to here? We know even less about how those high taxes of the twentieth century happened in the first place. Was it the effect of democracy, or a response to rampant inequality? Much of what is written today about taxing the rich takes the form of advocacy that is focused above all on the present. We do something different by taking a step back and showing what the long history of taxing the rich can teach us about our current situation.

What a country decides about taxes on the rich has profound consequences for its future economic growth and the distribution of economic resources and opportunities. Given the stakes, it's surprising how few comparative studies exist of taxation of the rich over the long run. Many people have asked this question only for recent decades, or for a single country. The last book to treat the question extensively was published more than a century ago, by Edwin Seligman.

---

* The online appendix, data, and replication material for all analyses in this book can be found at http://press.princeton.edu/titles/10674.html.

We argue that societies do not tax the rich just because they are democracies where the poor outnumber the rich or because inequality is high. Nor are beliefs about how taxes influence economic performance ultimately decisive. Societies tax the rich when people believe that the state has privileged the wealthy, and so fair compensation demands that the rich be taxed more heavily than the rest.

When it comes to thinking of what tax policy is best, few would disagree with the notion that governments should be—in part—guided by fairness. It is a term used frequently by those on both the political left and right.[1] How can this be? History suggests that the concept of fairness is up for grabs. Standards of fairness in taxation vary greatly across countries, over time, and from individual to individual.

When scholars write about fairness and taxation they most often adopt a normative point of view; that is, they ask what governments should do. But fairness isn't just a normative standard; it also matters for what governments do in practice because it influences the policy opinions of citizens. Ordinary people are more likely to support heavy taxation of the rich if it adheres to the fairness standards that they themselves hold. While many theories of politics assume people are concerned only with maximizing their own income, there is abundant evidence that humans are also concerned about issues of equity and fairness. These concerns don't mean that people aren't also concerned about self-interest—no one likes paying taxes—or even that self-interest isn't their prime concern. Individuals may also care about the efficiency of a tax system and whether it taxes people so heavily that they stop producing at all. Opinions about tax policy can be informed by both self-interest and efficiency, as well as fairness.

Political support for taxing the rich is strongest when doing so ensures that the state treats citizens *as equals*. Treating citizens as equals means treating them with "equal concern and respect," to use the phrase adopted by Ronald Dworkin.[2] The idea that people should be treated as equals is, of course, part of the bedrock of modern democracy. This criterion narrows the field for what counts as an effective fairness justification for a tax. It cannot be an argument that refers to how people are inherently different or how some are inherently more worthy than others. Nor, of course, can it refer to pure self-interest. Even so, simply saying that people should be treated "as equals" or "with equal concern and respect" does not allow us to proceed deductively to identify the precise tax policies that satisfy this criterion. There are multiple ways to plausibly treat people as equals in taxation, and this is what debating tax fairness is all about. We take an inductive approach and focus on the three arguments that have been the most common and the most persuasive in political debate: *equal treatment*, *ability to pay*, and *compensatory* arguments. We refer to these arguments as three ways to treat people *as equals*.

The greatest political support for taxing the rich emerges when *compensatory* arguments can be credibly applied in policy debates. This happens when it is clear that taxing the rich more heavily than the rest serves to correct or compensate for some other inequality in government action. Compensatory arguments are most likely to emerge in democracies precisely because the very idea of democracy is that citizens should be treated as equals. If the rich have been privileged by some government intervention while others have not, then it is fair that they should be taxed more heavily to compensate for this advantage. Symmetrically, if the state has asked others to sacrifice while the rich have not borne the same burden, then again taxation of the rich can compensate. Compensatory arguments push policy toward heavier taxation of the rich, but in many cases the straightest route to fairness is to remove the initial privilege in the first place. Therefore, compensatory arguments are most powerful in cases when a government is obliged to take an unequal action that somehow favors the rich.

The compensatory theory is not the only fairness-based argument for taxing the rich. Over the past few centuries, the most common fairness-based argument for taxing the rich has been the *ability to pay* doctrine. According to this doctrine, a dollar in taxes for someone earning a million dollars a year represents less of a sacrifice than it does for someone earning a more average salary.[3] Ability to pay arguments have existed since at least the sixteenth century, and they underpin the contemporary theories of optimal taxation most favored by economists.

For many, the ability to pay doctrine suffices as a reason to tax the rich more heavily than the rest. Others object to this notion. They may question how the ability to pay doctrine can be applied in practice. How much more should a rich person pay? They may also ask why ability to pay says nothing about how disparities in income or wealth emerged in the first place. Maybe the rich were just more talented or exerted more effort than others? People who criticize the ability to pay doctrine do not deny that a dollar in taxes represents less of a sacrifice for a rich person than for someone else; they simply do not accept that this is the right criterion by which to judge fairness.

In the face of doubts about ability to pay, a salient alternative is to suggest that the fairest system involves *equal treatment* for all. Both rich and poor should pay the same tax rate—a "flat tax." We use the phrase "equal treatment" to refer to fairness arguments suggesting that the same exact policy be adopted for all. Since the sixteenth century, opponents of progressive taxation have suggested that the basis of a republic is equal treatment for all, as illustrated by the norm of one person one vote. Therefore the same exact policy should be applied to taxation. The logic that equal treatment requires a flat tax is not perfect; having all pay a lump-sum tax, where each person pays the same amount, would also respect equal treatment, yet many today would consider such a tax unfair. Nevertheless, arguments based on equal treatment have carried great power in debates about taxing the rich.

Some of the earliest examples of *compensatory* arguments involve suggestions that the rich ought to pay a higher rate of income tax because the poor bear the brunt of indirect taxes on common consumption goods. The idea is that to maintain themselves, the poor must consume a greater share of their income each year. However, over the last two centuries the most powerful compensatory arguments have involved a different sort of tax—military conscription. This one simple fact goes a long way toward explaining both the rise of heavy taxation of the rich in the early and mid-twentieth century and the subsequent move away from this policy over the last several decades. The mass wars of the twentieth century were fought in a way that had a strong economic rationale but which privileged the rich along two dimensions. First, labor was conscripted to fight while capital was not. Second, owners of capital benefited from high wartime demand for their products. Heavy taxation of the rich (owners of capital) became a way to mitigate these effects and to restore at least some degree of equality of treatment by the government. This was what those on the political left claimed and what those on the right were forced to concede. It was a powerful new argument for progressive forms of taxation, and it shifted mass and elite opinion on the question of taxing the rich in a leftward direction. Other scholars before us have investigated the effect of war on tax fairness, particularly in the United States and the United Kingdom. We show that this war effect can be explained by the compensatory theory of progressive taxation and that it is a more general phenomenon across countries and time.[4]

Compensatory arguments are less credible in the case of more limited wars of the sort that the United States has fought of late. If the bulk of the population is not sacrificing for war, then how is it credible to ask the rich to pay a special sacrifice as compensation?

Finally, the choice between limited war or mass mobilization has been dependent on the state of military and related technologies. In the twentieth century the advent of the railroad made mass mobilization possible. When mass mobilization did eventually occur in 1914, compensatory arguments for taxing the rich emerged. In the twenty-first century the advent of precision weapons and drone technology means that mass armies are no longer necessary and may even be undesirable. Therefore, we are unlikely to see a repeat of the twentieth-century forces that led to heavy taxation of the rich. The compensatory theory explains why it was the wars of the early and mid-twentieth century that brought heavy taxation of the rich and not prior or subsequent wars.

Over the last two centuries, when circumstances have made compensatory arguments less credible, debates about taxation of the rich have boiled down to a conflict between the two competing visions of ability to pay and equal treatment, as well as efficiency. The outcome of this conflict has generally been for the rich to not be taxed much more heavily than the rest of the population. But, when circumstances have allowed for wartime compensatory arguments to be made, opinion has shifted in favor of taxing the rich. While those who adhere to ability to pay have continued to support taxing the rich, many of those who have preferred equal treatment have thought that the compensatory argument must be taken into account to achieve this goal. In such situations political parties of the left have used compensatory arguments to reinforce their arguments for taxing the rich. Political parties of the right have been forced to cede ground in order to remain electable.

It is also the case that political parties can and have used compensatory arguments instrumentally. If you personally are already convinced by the ability to pay rationale for taxing the rich, you may gain greater support for your proposal by making compensatory arguments that win broader support. Once external circumstances change and compensatory arguments lack credibility, then debates about taxing the rich return to a conflict between the competing notions of equal treatment, efficiency, and ability to pay.

THE RISE (AND DEMISE?) OF TAXES ON THE RICH

We can learn a great deal by studying changes in taxation over the long run. A look at broad trends can help us tease out the most important factors at play. To do this we, and the research assistants who helped us, have collected information on taxation in twenty countries, located principally in North America and Western Europe, over a period of two centuries.[5] We focus on these countries for feasibility in data collection, but the conclusions we draw apply more generally.[6] In an ideal world we would know all taxes due by a rich person and an average person in each year for each of the cases; unfortunately this is not possible. For most countries, even statutory rates of taxation are not widely published and must instead be verified by consulting original legislation. This is a time-consuming process.

We have been able to construct a unique database tracking statutory top marginal rates of income and inheritance taxation across the twenty countries. By statutory top marginal rates we mean the tax rate that would apply by law on the last dollar of income (or wealth) for someone in the highest tax bracket. This information is mostly drawn from original legislation. The top marginal rate provides an indication of what a rich person would be likely to pay. However, a focus on top statutory rates alone can provide misleading conclusions, and to deal with this problem we have also collected much additional information. First, we have the full schedules of tax rates (i.e., not just those at the top) for half of the countries. This shows whether an increase in the top rate represented a move to tax just the rich or whether it was just part of a move to tax everyone more heavily. A look at these schedules also reveals something more specific about who was being taxed. Rather than simply referring to "the rich" and "the rest," we can refer to individuals earning incomes or having fortunes of a specific size relative to the national average. What do we mean by a "rich" person? Extensive research has shown that much of the recent rise in inequality has been attributable to movements within the top 1.0 percent of the income distribution or even between the top 0.1 percent and the rest of the population. We adopt a similar categorization. Our focus on the rich also means that we are asking a question that is related to but distinct from those asked by the many scholars who have focused more generally on the politics of redistribution and/or social insurance.[7]

Second, we also compare statutory rates with effective rates of taxation. This is critical because effective rates are what people actually pay. The effective rate for the income tax is found by taking total income tax paid and then dividing this by gross income. Information on effective rates is, on the whole, not easy to come by, particularly for a broad set of countries over a long time period. We do, however, have long-run effective rates of income taxation for six of the study countries. Using these we show that top statutory rates tend to be good proxies for how much the rich actually pay. There are important exceptions to this, however, that will be pointed out.

As a way of introducing the data, figure 1.1 shows the average top statutory marginal rate of income and inheritance taxation in all twenty countries from 1800 to the present. The picture invites us to think of the world in three stages. First taxes on the rich were very low, then they rose to dramatic heights, and then they fell again, very

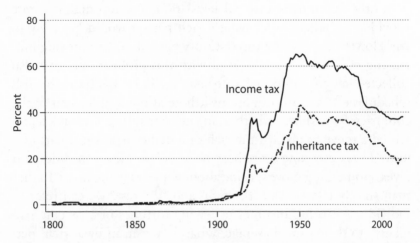

Figure 1.1. Average Top Rates of Income and Inheritance Taxation, 1800–2013.

dramatically. But a look at figure 1.1 does not immediately suggest why this was the case. The rise of progressive taxation coincided with a period of democratization across the western world. But it also coincided with an era of massive military conflict as well as other changes to the political and economic landscape. To be sure, the rich had been taxed in wars of past centuries, but all evidence suggests this twentieth-century taxation was something entirely new.[8] In chapter 5 we also show that our conclusion that there was little taxation of the rich during the nineteenth century remains unaltered when one takes into consideration a broader range of taxes, including property taxes and annual taxes on wealth.

One way in which figure 1.1 may be misleading is that it takes no account of the growth of government over time. Perhaps the rich were more heavily taxed in the twentieth century, compared to the nineteenth, because citizens demanded more from government, and all had to contribute? Average tax revenue as a percentage of gross domestic product increased from 9 percent to 20 percent from 1900 to 1950, consistent with this conjecture. However, government revenue continued to increase over the remainder of the twentieth century—to an average of 43 percent of gross domestic product—while top rates on the rich declined over this period.[9] The rich have been taxed less even though governments have increased in size. Scholars who work on public spending sometimes speak of a "ratchet" effect whereby each of the two world wars led to a permanent increase in the size of government.[10] When it comes to long-run trends in taxing the rich there has been no ratchet; the period of high taxes on the rich was temporary. We explore the role of the size of government further in chapters 3 and 5.

Another point missing from the figure is a discussion of how governments spent their money. This certainly ought to have some impact on what taxes citizens support and whether they consider them "fair." In an ideal world we would use two centuries of evidence to chart how much the rich and the rest benefited from government spending across the twenty countries. That, however, is a task that lies beyond the data that we have available. Fortunately, history has provided us with a convenient laboratory for studying taxation separately from the impact of the government transfers that are commonplace today. Prior to 1945 the governments in our study spent relatively little apart from providing basic public goods and fighting wars. Looking at taxation alone will therefore not give us a biased picture. Moreover, we show in chapter 8 that after 1945, wartime compensatory arguments applied to spending every bit as much as they applied to taxation. Therefore, a look at government spending only reinforces our main conclusions.

Combining the information on top tax rates with extensive political data allows testing of several alternative arguments about when and why governments have taxed the rich. Data on when governments expanded the suffrage, as well as other institutional details, might explain why the rich were taxed more heavily in some cases than others. We also use data on income and wealth inequality to ask whether countries taxed the rich when inequality was high.

Our analysis will go well beyond a simple examination of top tax rates and their correlates. We devote three separate chapters to asking why governments raised taxes on the rich during mass mobilization for war. This is critical because the main lesson is not that war mattered; it is instead that if the rich were taxed so heavily during wartime, then this tells us something about the broader question of fairness in taxation.

COMMON IDEAS ABOUT TAXING THE RICH

Taxation of the rich is a hotly debated topic. So it should come as no surprise that there are several theories that might explain why some societies tax the rich heavily. Each of them is inadequate for the task at hand. The very plausible assumptions underlying these hypotheses are first that individuals do not like paying taxes; second that decisions are influenced by the prevailing type of political representation; and finally that decisions also depend on beliefs about economic efficiency. The received wisdom is then that progressive taxation is natural in a democracy because the bulk of the population wants it, unless people believe that the adverse incentive effects of doing so will be too great, or unless democracy somehow becomes "captured" by the rich.

"DEMOCRACIES TAX THE RICH MORE HEAVILY"

There may be many ways in which citizens can pressure governments to tax the rich, but having the vote certainly shouldn't harm their chances of doing so. In a democracy it should be numbers that count, and the poor and middle classes outnumber the rich. Among political scientists and economists today it is common to suggest that democracies are more likely to redistribute income from the rich to the rest, and progressive taxation is one means of doing so. Current scholars are in good company in making this argument. Sometime between the years 1521 and 1524, Francesco Guicciardini composed a dialogue among several fictitious speakers debating the merits of popular government in Florence. One of the opponents of democracy spoke as follows:

> As far as methods of taxation are concerned, I can assure you that the people's [sic] will normally be much worse and more unjust, because by nature they like to overburden the better-off; and since the less well off are more numerous, it is not difficult for them to do this.[11]

Five centuries later, in a new era of expanding democracy, Edwin Seligman expressed a very similar opinion, but unlike Guicciardini, he saw this as an entirely good thing.[12] Seligman's view was that as societies became more infused with democratic ideals, people naturally favored progressive taxation because it is simply the sensible and desirable thing to do. An alternative view from this time was that within democracies, the choice for progressive taxation was an outcome of political conflict. In 1926, William Shultz suggested the following:

> In legislatures, progressive taxes are proposed by representatives from "poorer" districts, they are fought tooth and nail by representatives of the propertied classes, and usually they are passed by legislatures only when the political influence of the poorer majority of the electorate outweighs the influence of the richer minority. By means of new radical parties or radical blocs growing up within older parties, the poorer classes of the nations have come to exercise more or less control over legislatures, and in this country and abroad progressivity in tax rates is an established order. This is an incidental parliamentary victory of the poorer classes over the richer—just as the retention of proportional rates would have been a defeat—in the present veiled economic and political struggle between the two.[13]

Many subsequent scholars have emphasized the effect of universal suffrage on redistribution, and on progressive tax policies as part of the equation.[14] What does the evidence say? There is some support for the idea that the introduction of income taxation was associated with the expansion of the suffrage.[15] However, we ask not only whether governments have created an income tax, but also whether they have used it to tax the rich heavily. Chapter 3 considers a series of simple tests to answer this question, backed by more extensive statistical analyses that can be found in the online appendix to the book.[16] Though all of the twenty countries eventually established universal male suffrage, this happened at different times. If universal suffrage led to heavier taxation of the rich, then we should expect that those countries that expanded the suffrage at an earlier date also adopted more progressive tax policies at an earlier date. We examine this proposition using evidence on both income taxation and inheritance taxation. Taxing incomes requires a high level of administrative capacity. Therefore, if we see that a democratizing country fails to levy income taxes on the rich, then it might be because of lack of capacity and not because the democracy hypothesis is wrong. Historically less administrative machinery has been required to tax inheritance. If a democratizing country also fails to tax the rich through inheritance, this suggests that something about the democracy hypothesis is invalid.

The evidence shows that democracy's effect on progressive taxation has been overstated. As noted, though the expansion of the suffrage and the adoption of progressive taxation happened around the same time in many countries, one needs to distinguish between the adoption of progressive taxation and the choice of high marginal tax rates for the rich. After the basic principle of progressive taxation was adopted, many countries took a very long time before choosing top statutory marginal tax rates that we would think of today as being high. Some countries never took this step at all. One explanation for this finding is that granting ordinary people the vote didn't result in progressive taxation because they didn't want it. They may have subscribed to a version of treating citizens as equals that is inconsistent with this policy.

It is also possible to extend the analysis by looking at institutions other than suffrage. Universal suffrage might arguably only have an impact on progressive taxation when elections of representatives are direct, when the ballot is secret, and when there are not additional institutional obstacles in place to prevent a majority from expressing its will. We investigated a host of such possibilities and came up with surprisingly little. Democracy alone was insufficient to produce heavier taxation of the rich.

"DEMOCRACIES TAX THE RICH WHEN INEQUALITY IS HIGH"

Many observers remark that our current situation seems abnormal. Inequality is rising just as taxes on the rich are low and perhaps falling further. The implicit assumption behind this claim is that governments in "normal" times will raise taxes on the rich to fight inequality. There are three reasons they might do this.

The first reason is that as the amount of income or wealth of those at the top increases relative to the rest of society, voters will find it in their self-interest to tax the rich more heavily as long as the negative incentive effects from doing so are not too large.[17] Voters might also favor this choice if they subscribe to the ability to pay doctrine.

The second reason why people might demand taxation of the rich when inequality is high is if they believe that inequality of outcomes derives from inequality of opportunity.

The third reason why governments might tax the rich when inequality is high is that they fear the consequences of inequality for the political system. They fear that inequalities of income and wealth will lead to the political process being captured by a wealthy elite or oligarchy. This is a very old idea. It was a common fear expressed by the U.S. Founding Fathers.[18] It was also a view emphasized by the proponent of progressive taxation in Francesco Guicciardini's discourse on sixteenth-century Florence's progressive income tax, the *decima scalata*. Excess inequality of wealth would undermine the republic by sapping citizens of their virtue, perhaps even leading to tyranny.[19] Finally, some authors, such as Jean-Jacques Rousseau, have emphasized that extreme inequality is a danger for a republic both because the rich can overcome legal restraints and also because the poor are more likely to revolt. As Rousseau suggested:

> The greatest evil has already been done where there are poor people to defend and rich people to restrain. The full force of the laws is effective only in the middle range; they are equally powerless against the rich man's treasures and the poor man's misery; the first eludes them, the second escapes them; the one tears the web, the other slips through it.[20]

The big question is whether voters prompt democratically elected governments to take corrective policy actions so that levels of inequality remain in the "middle range" to which Rousseau referred.[21]

Evidence from top incomes and top wealth shares suggests that democracies do not, in fact, tax the rich more heavily when inequality is high. In chapters 3 and 4 we consider the relationship between inequality and top rates of income and inheritance taxation. Using data on top incomes and top wealth shares, we show, first, that there is only very weak evidence that governments, on average, respond to high prevailing levels of inequality by increasing taxes on the rich. Second, high taxes on the rich are indeed associated with lower subsequent levels of inequality. This means that high top tax rates can be a powerful tool to address inequality, but the mere presence of inequality is insufficient to prompt governments to pursue this strategy. This also implies that ability to pay arguments were insufficient to carry the day. Therefore we must think of why governments might respond to inequality in some cases but not others.

"DEMOCRATIC POLITICS CAN BE CAPTURED BY THE RICH"

The rich in a democracy have one vote just like everyone else. But it would of course be naïve to think that wealth would bring zero additional advantage. A modified version of the democracy hypothesis is to suggest that democracy only results in greater taxation of the rich when the rich are unable to use their wealth to capture the political process. As we noted previously, theorists of republican government have long feared that inequalities in wealth would lead to the wealthy imposing their policies. It is possible today to think of multiple channels through which this effect might take place. The rich will logically be in a better position to lobby and give campaign contributions. They may also be better informed about how specific policies will influence them. Maybe they are also simply more likely to travel in the same circles as those who make policy.

When considering this problem many observers are quick to refer to the example of the United States today. For decades American political campaigns have relied on very substantial campaign contributions, and this phenomenon has only increased since the U.S. Supreme Court's 2010 *Citizens United* decision. Perhaps this is why careful studies by survey researchers, such as Martin Gilens and Larry Bartels, show that members of the U.S. Congress tend to vote in a manner that is most consistent with the views of their high-income constituents, as opposed to the general electorate.[22] The fact that the American government taxes the rich less heavily than it did may simply be a result of this broader phenomenon of capture. Some authors have examined this issue extensively, finding clear support for a link between money contributed and policy choice.[23] Others have claimed that capture helps to explain developments with regard to specific taxes, such as the estate tax.[24]

The capture hypothesis seems ideally suited for explaining recent events in the United States; private campaign finance is abundant and private expenditures on lobbying are arguably even more significant.[25] But if reference to campaign finance and lobbying is to be a convincing explanation for the big picture, then this hypothesis should also hold true for other democracies that have reduced taxes on the rich. A number of countries have actually gone further than the United States by abolishing inheritance taxation entirely. Top rates of income taxation have also come down dramatically elsewhere. The problem for the capture hypothesis is that these developments have included countries where the role of private money in politics is much more limited. So, even though Canadian electoral campaigns have, until recently, been publicly financed, the Canadian government abolished its inheritance tax in 1971. Sweden took a similar step in 2004 despite the fact that there is far less money in Swedish politics than in the United States.

Now, just because we fail to find a relationship between how campaigns are financed and how heavily the rich are taxed does not mean that there is no truth to the capture hypothesis. Nor does it mean that campaign lobbying by the wealthy has had no effect on taxation of the rich in the United States in recent decades. As an example, lobbying by members of the financial sector is no doubt preserving the policy through which hedge fund managers are able to classify their income as carried interest so as to reduce taxes due. Overall, though, the capture hypothesis is inadequate for explaining the broad variation in tax rates across many countries over time. Convincing evidence for the capture hypothesis would have to show that in a broad set of cases where democracies failed to tax the rich heavily, this failure was attributable to the persistence of elite power in a manner that has been suggested by Daron Acemoglu and James Robinson.[26] Such an account would also have to show that it was variation in the extent of capture that explained variations in taxing the rich between countries over time.

"GOVERNMENTS AVOID TAXING THE RICH WHEN THEY THINK IT IS SELF-DEFEATING"

A major claim in many arguments against taxing the rich is that this policy is self-defeating. Levying high taxes on the rich, it is suggested, will prompt them to work less, invest less, and, in a world of mobile capital, to shift their wealth abroad. Therefore it is better to not do it in the first place. Our goal is not to assess the plausibility of these claims.[27] We instead ask how much force these arguments have had in the political arena and whether they can account for changes in top rates of taxation over time. It may be that knowledge about these incentive effects changes over time, perhaps because of new theories or new evidence about how the economy functions. For example, when an economy's growth rate slows, people may infer that taxes on the rich should be cut because incentive effects are having a negative impact. In chapter 8 we analyze this possibility and fail to find evidence that governments in recent decades have, on average, cut top tax rates as growth slows.[28]

Another possibility is that until recent decades, people simply didn't believe incentive effects could be a major drag on the economy. Even astute observers sometimes suggest this.[29] History shows that nothing could be further from the truth. It is indeed the case that as economic theory has advanced, scholars have been able for the first time to construct mathematical models in which incentive effects from taxation are directly incorporated. The most salient contribution here is that by James Mirrlees in the early 1970s. However, it is certainly not true that incentive arguments began with Mirrlees, and he made no attempt to claim this. As early as 1897, we can find a clear statement by Francis Edgeworth that what might seem an ideal policy based on equalization of incomes should be more nuanced because of incentive effects. As Edgeworth put it: "The *acme* of socialism is thus for a moment sighted; but it is immediately clouded over by doubts and reservations."[30] Chapter 2 will show that arguments about incentive effects actually extend back to the sixteenth century.

Since the first date at which modern progressive tax systems were proposed, opponents have argued that they would harm investment and employment. However, we find little evidence to suggest that changes in beliefs about the importance of these effects can account for the major changes in policy that we observe during the nineteenth and twentieth centuries.

TREATING CITIZENS AS EQUALS

A basic principle of democracy is that people ought to be treated as equals, but when it comes to taxation, people often disagree about what "as equals" means. We argue that the most politically powerful arguments for taxing the rich have been compensatory arguments; the rich should be taxed to compensate for the fact that they have been unfairly privileged by the state. Compensatory arguments have come in different guises, and we will discuss all these, but over the last two centuries the most powerful compensatory arguments have been those associated with mass mobilization for war.

The arrival of an era of mass warfare in 1914 created the possibility for powerful new arguments for taxing the rich. If labor was conscripted then fairness demanded that capital be conscripted as well. Having the rich pay higher taxes than the rest was one way to achieve this goal. Mass warfare has been the main force shaping the development of progressive tax policies during the last century. In emphasizing this, we are in keeping with other recent work that emphasizes the effect of war on domestic politics.[31] However, this doesn't just tell us something about war; it also tells us that the most politically powerful arguments for taxing the rich are those based on compensation to restore treatment as equals.

The two world wars of the twentieth century involved mobilization of manpower on an unprecedented scale by both great powers and smaller states. Armies had once been recruited from a small segment of the population as volunteers or through limited conscription. Suddenly they were selected by universal conscription from the broad population. When raising a very large army, a state may find it necessary to recruit in this manner because the tax burden for paying volunteers would be unbearable. There is also a fairness argument for universal conscription. As Margaret Levi has demonstrated, universal conscription itself emerged from prior systems of limited conscription as a result of demands for equal treatment.[32]

The problem with even a system of universal conscription is that it does not truly ensure equal treatment, even in an ex ante sense before a draft lottery is run. In virtually any universal conscription system there are reasons for exemption from service, and it is likely that the rich will be more apt to have access to these opportunities than the rest. Age presents yet another reason for exemption in any universal conscription system, and it is well known that age is highly correlated with wealth. Finally, universal conscription satisfies only a state's need for labor while saying nothing about how capital is to be raised for the war effort. If those with capital benefit from increased demand for the products of companies in which they have invested, then this too can violate widely shared commitments to equal treatment.

During the twentieth century, the inability of even a system of universal conscription to ensure citizens were being treated as equals gave proponents of progressive taxation a new and powerful compensatory argument for taxing the rich. If there was unequal sharing of the war burden, then the rich should be taxed more heavily than the rest. In other words, instead of having to rely only on arguments involving ability to pay, advocates of progressive taxation could now say that without heavily taxing the rich they would not be doing their fair share for the war effort. The clearest exposition of this argument was offered by the Labour Party in the UK in its call for a "conscription of wealth" to match the conscription of labor. During the two world wars this same argument was made in many other venues.

Mass mobilization for war presented new possibilities for making compensatory arguments for taxing the rich. Because such arguments could only be made for a limited time, the compensatory theory helps explain not only why taxes on the rich went up but also why they eventually came down. As we show, in the wake of World War II compensatory arguments emphasizing war sacrifice were ubiquitous in former belligerent countries. As had been the case after World

War I, compensatory arguments remained prominent in discussions of how to repay war debts and, to a much greater degree than after World War I, with the provision of veterans' benefits. But ultimately, after mass mobilization wars ended, such arguments faded from view. Instead, high taxes on the rich became a new status quo that had to be defended strictly by referring to "ability to pay" or by saying that taxing the rich was "fair" without explaining why. In this environment it was inevitable that taxes on the rich would eventually come down. This does not explain the exact moment when taxes on the rich came down, but it does show why this evolution was inevitable.

If mass warfare created a new compensatory argument for taxing the rich, we need to recognize that not all wars open up this possibility. Some commentators have found it odd that the Bush administration lowered taxes on the rich during the recent wars in Iraq and Afghanistan. Others have even wondered why there aren't calls for a new conscription of wealth.[33] Yet there is a fundamental problem with such an argument. Most of the U.S. population has not been asked to sacrifice during these recent wars, so why should the rich be singled out for sacrifice? Today the United States fights limited wars in which a small percentage of the population is mobilized and those in the armed forces are recruited voluntarily. Therefore, arguments about conscripting wealth no longer carry the same weight.

There is also a final critical element to our interpretation of the history of progressive taxation. The way that countries like the United States have fought wars is to a very great extent dependent on the state of military technology and on the type of enemies being fought. The emergence of the railroad first made it possible to mobilize armies on the scale that occurred during the two world wars. Over the last fifty years technological developments have pushed in the opposite direction. It is still possible to field a mass army, but the invention of weapons like the cruise missile, the laser guided bomb, and the drone mean that it is no longer necessary to do so.

Our finding about military technology and international rivalry is important for two reasons. First, it tells us more about the deeper reasons why steeply progressive taxation happened when it did, and why it is more difficult to achieve political support for it today. Compensatory arguments did not become credible by accident. They became credible because the pattern of international rivalry and military technology changed the type of wars that states fought. Second, our finding also sheds more light on the question of whether taxation of the rich during the twentieth century, and perhaps even trends in inequality, was accidental, as Thomas Piketty has prominently argued.[34] While agreeing with his emphasis on war, our conclusions suggest that rather than high taxation of the rich being a simple accident, it was ultimately driven by long-run trends involving international rivalries and the technologies available for fighting wars.

THE FUTURE FOR TAXING THE RICH

Mass warfare mattered because it gave birth to new ideas and new arguments for why taxing the rich was fair. The extent of war mobilization was itself dictated by prevailing war technologies of the time. What does all this suggest for today's debates about taxing the rich? First, as technological change has led to a more limited form of warfare, there is unlikely to be a simple repeat of the twentieth-century conditions in which powerful compensatory arguments led to very high top marginal rates of income and inheritance taxation.

What about the effect of rising inequality? Won't this fuel demands for taxing the rich? Today it is most common to hear arguments in favor of taxing the rich simply because inequality is high and getting higher. In essence this is an invocation of the ability to pay doctrine. Yet two centuries of evidence show that governments, on average, do not tax the rich just because inequality is high. The rich are taxed when people believe not just that inequality is high but also that it is fundamentally unfair because the deck is stacked in favor of the rich, and the government did the stacking. In other words, they believe in compensatory arguments.

Based on current trends, future debates about taxing the rich will likely follow the familiar cleavage between those who adhere to ability to pay and those who emphasize equal treatment and/ or economic efficiency. It is unlikely that such a debate will result in significant increases in taxes on those in the top 1.0 percent or the top 0.1 percent. Change would instead depend on whether proponents of taxing the rich are able to develop compensatory arguments for an era of peace. We consider several such possibilities in chapter 9, concluding that those who want to tax the rich might do better to look at the type of compensatory arguments made in the nineteenth century rather than the twentieth. This was an era where many argued that income taxes needed to be progressive to offset the regressive incidence of other state levies. Such old arguments in a new era could lead to moderately increased taxes on the rich, though not to a repeat of the twentieth century. Change may also ultimately depend on whether those who want to tax the rich are themselves able to appeal to the logic of equal treatment. In some cases today those who are at the very top are paying a lower effective rate of tax than those who are merely well off. There is no need to appeal to ability to pay or rising inequality to argue against this. Such outcomes go against the basic equal treatment principles of fairness that opponents of taxing the rich have themselves espoused.

CHAPTER TWO

TREATING CITIZENS AS EQUALS

A basic principle of democratic societies is that people ought to be treated as equals by their government. Political equality is seen as being what is fair or just. As part of this general norm, citizens should be treated as equals with respect to taxation. When John Stuart Mill wrote in 1848 that "equality of sacrifice" should be a principal goal of tax policy, he saw this as part of the more general maxim that governments ought to treat people as equals. Even in societies with great inequality of status, elites that are exempt from taxation have often felt the need to claim that all are being treated as equals in the area of taxation. So, for example, if the nobility in Old Regime France were exempted from most forms of taxation, the reason offered was that they had military service obligations. This was one way of claiming, somewhat dubiously, that the French state was treating citizens as equals.

The clear implication of the political equality norm is that institutional privileges ought to be removed in order to establish a fairer society. So, society should not be divided into different estates where some have greater prerogatives than others. Likewise, the vote should not only be enjoyed by those with sufficient education or property. Finally, the state should not provide sinecures, pensions, or monopolies to a privileged few. Throughout Europe, and elsewhere, from the eighteenth through the beginning of the twentieth century there was a struggle for the abolition of privilege. The flipside of this development was the effort to ensure that the state did not place particular obligations on one part of the community. An example of this had been the system of *corvée* labor that existed in France under the Old Regime.

What does treating citizens as equals imply for taxation? Simply invoking the idea doesn't tell us what kind of a tax system there ought to be. Equality could apply to a lump-sum tax where all pay the same amount. Today this would generally be viewed as a regressive and unequal tax since those with more money pay a smaller fraction of their income. But this assessment was not always accurate. Take the example from the Book of Exodus that we cited in the opening pages of this book. The idea here was that all were equal before God. "The rich shall not give more, and the poor shall not give less than half a shekel, when *they* give an offering unto the LORD, to make an atonement for your souls."

Treating citizens as equals can also describe a tax where all pay the same percentage rate. The early intellectual proponents of the "flat tax" movement thought precisely this. We refer to this vision as *equal treatment*. As Robert Hall and Alvin Rabushka suggested in 1981: "Remember, until recently, fairness meant equal treatment under the law. Equating fairness and making the rich pay more is a modern invention of those who believe the tax system should be used to redistribute income to make everyone equal."[1]

Finally, treating citizens as equals might also imply a progressive tax in which the rich pay a higher rate of tax than do other citizens. However, it would need to be shown why progressivity of a tax treated citizens as equals instead of simply fulfilling the objective of redistribution to which Hall and Rabushka refer.

In this chapter we consider two potential answers to this question. The first is the *ability to pay* doctrine; the second is the *compensatory* theory. We review the historical development of these two concepts, and the objections to them, because it shows the persistence of these ideas from the sixteenth century to the present. We then turn to more contemporary evidence from experimental games and from a survey that we conducted. The contemporary evidence mirrors what we see in historical debates; people care about fairness when it comes to taxation, but across individuals there are profound differences in how "treating people as equals" is interpreted. These differences in turn result in different policy preferences about taxing the rich and ultimately affect the tax policies that countries adopt.

THE ABILITY TO PAY DOCTRINE

At first blush, the notion that those with more should be able to pay a higher rate of tax sounds so obvious that there may not be much point in asking who first came up with the idea. The real question is how those who agree with this principle have tried to reconcile it with the norm of treating citizens as equals. The precise phrase "ability to pay" only became connected with taxation at the end of the nineteenth century. Yet the underlying idea has a much longer history. This story shows how there have been permanent features to the debate about taxing the rich. Proponents of the ability to pay doctrine (sometimes also called the faculty theory) have suggested that it does involve treating citizens as equals. Those opposed have said that the doctrine is difficult to implement, and they doubt whether it is the right criterion for judging fairness. They would say that the ability to pay doctrine needs to be supplemented, or even replaced, by a consideration of whether people earned their money fairly or unfairly in the first place. While these critiques are powerful, historically, ability to pay arguments have had a substantial impact on attitudes toward taxing the rich.

What may be the first modern reference to the ability to pay principle dates from Florence in the early sixteenth century. The first critiques also date from this era. In 1500, the city's governing council had introduced (or actually reintroduced) a progressive tax on land income known as the *decima scalata*. The tax was a subject of great controversy, and these debates attracted the attention of Francesco Guicciardini. He wrote a short text, which has become known simply as *La Decima Scalata*, in which he presented imagined discourses of two orators before the council, one opposed and one in favor. Guicciardini himself was opposed to the tax, but it is presumed by historians that his text reflects the positions taken by both Florentine proponents and opponents of taxing the rich.[2] The discourse in favor of the *decima* contains a passage that mirrors ability to pay positions taken centuries later: "However, the equality of a tax does not consist in this, that the rate each person must pay should be the same from one to another, but that the payment should be of a kind that one and the other are inconvenienced to the same degree."[3]

The opponent of progressive taxation in Guicciardini's discourse had several responses to this ability to pay claim. The first was that the rich needed to spend more than the poor to maintain their standing.[4] The second was that, in a republic, people ought to be treated as equals in the sense of having equal political rights without striving to use the tax system to obtain either equality of sacrifice or equality of outcomes:

> I admit that equality is a good thing in a republic, indeed a necessary one, because it is the foundation of liberty. But the equality that we are seeking is as follows: that no citizen may oppress another, that each is equal before the law and its magistrates, and that the vote of each man who is eligible to participate in this Council has the same weight as that of any other.[5]

Florentine critics of progressive taxation also made one further comment—maybe the rich deserved their money because they had earned it. In other words, ability to pay isn't the right criterion to judge fairness in taxation. This has been common in critiques of the ability to pay doctrine up to the present day. Writing a century before Guicciardini, Matteo Palmieri in his *Della Vita Civile* suggested that if the rich had more money it was because they were more virtuous and more industrious. Therefore progressive taxation was unjust. In Palmieri's words:

> Those praiseworthy persons, who practice their craft or profession honestly and well, increasing the common good, and earning more for themselves personally, advancing beyond others, should under no circumstances be the object of envy. On the contrary, their virtue should be protected and encouraged. And, should they take advantage of some opportunity before others,

this privilege should be justly preserved, as they are the best and most useful citizens, worthy above all others.[6]

To see a more recent use of the ability to pay doctrine, we need to consider the expansion of commercial society during the eighteenth century. The emergence of new forms of wealth helped revive a debate that had also existed in Florence about the desirability of what was now called "luxury" and its potentially corrupting influence. In the eyes of some observers, luxury was at worst something to be tolerated in order to further commercial development, or in other cases even something to be celebrated. For the opponents, luxury was an inevitable yet entirely undesirable element of commercial society. One element in this broad debate about luxury was the question whether luxury goods should be subject to specific taxes.[7] Jean-Jacques Rousseau was one of the most fervent opponents of luxury and a proponent of luxury taxes. Calling for taxes on objects such as liveries, carriages, mirrors, and chandeliers, he suggested that they should be taxed precisely because they were not items of necessity. Rousseau observed:

> When all these things are carefully put together, the conclusion will be that in order to distribute taxation in an equitable and truly proportional fashion it should be imposed not only in proportion to taxpayers' goods, but in a proportion that takes account of the difference in their stations as well as of how much of their goods is superfluous.[8]

Like Guicciardini's proponent of the *decima scalata*, Rousseau was making an explicit reference to ability to pay as a fairness criterion.

There were also eminent eighteenth century opponents of luxury taxation. For these opponents the vague term "luxury" had no real meaning and could not be easily applied in the area of taxation. This was also the view of Voltaire. This idea of inapplicability has been a constant critique of the ability to pay doctrine.

A second eighteenth-century criticism of Rousseau's ability to pay arguments for luxury taxes followed the previous statements by Matteo Palmieri; ability to pay was the wrong criterion to begin with because it said nothing about how money was earned. Rousseau's text initially appeared as the entry for "political economy" in Diderot's *Encyclopédie*. In 1765, Jean-François de Saint Lambert contributed the entry on "luxury" for the *Encyclopédie*.[9] He suggested that it should not be the objective to judge whether luxury was good or bad; what mattered instead was how it was generated. If luxury was generated because some had an unfair initial advantage provided by the state, then this should be addressed by removing the advantages that led to it. If not, then it should be allowed to flourish. Saint-Lambert was one of the first authors to provide a fairness-based theory of inequality, suggesting when it was just and when it was unjust.

In the evolution of tax doctrine, Adam Smith stands at a waypoint between the luxury debates of the eighteenth century and more modern efforts to elaborate principles governing taxation of the rich. Smith's first maxim of taxation states that equity demands taxes be allocated according to "abilities" of taxpayers, and he then states that this means "in proportion to the revenue which they respectively enjoy under the protection of the state."[10] It is difficult to see this as anything other than a defense of proportionate, as opposed to progressive, taxation. However, there seems little doubt that Smith was also influenced by the luxury debates of the eighteenth century.[11] Though a fervent partisan of commerce, Smith was in favor of taxes on luxury. In at least one case he also defended the idea that a tax on house rents would fall more than proportionately on the rich by distinguishing between expenses of the poor, which he saw principally as necessities, and the expenses of the rich, which he saw principally as luxuries.[12] It is hard not to see ability to pay reasoning at work here.

It was left to John Stuart Mill to provide further clarity for Smith's first maxim while simultaneously clarifying ability to pay doctrine. In his famous passage from Book V, Chapter II of his *Principles of Representative Government*, Mill stated that taxes should be levied in such a way that there was "equality of sacrifice."[13] By this he meant simply that people ought to be treated as equals. Mill then posed the following question: Does equality of sacrifice imply a proportional tax or a progressive one?[14]

Mill's answer came in two parts. First, he suggested that the ability to pay doctrine was justified to the extent that necessities and luxuries should be treated differently. In other words, he referred directly back to the key question raised in the luxury debate of the prior century. Mill argued in favor of a plan previously proposed by Jeremy Bentham, the founder of modern utilitarianism; there should be a subsistence minimum level of income that would not be taxed. Above that subsistence minimum, all income should be taxed at a proportional rate.[15]

The next question for Mill was whether the ability to pay doctrine might also be invoked to argue for a progressive rate of taxation on income above the subsistence minimum. His answer to this was that it could not:

> It may be said, indeed, that to take 100*l.* from 1000*l.* (even giving back five pounds) is a heavier impost than 1000*l.* taken from 10,000*l.* (giving back the same five pounds). But this doctrine seems to me too disputable altogether, and even if true at all, not true to a sufficient extent, to be made the foundation of any rule of taxation. Whether the person with 10,000*l.* a year cares less for 1000*l.* than the person with only 1000*l.* a year cares for 100*l.*, and if so, how much less, does not appear to me capable of being decided with the degree of certainty on which a legislator or a financier ought to act.[16]

What we have here is a statement mirroring the position taken by previous opponents of luxury taxation. Following Mill's reasoning, we have no idea if the assumptions underlying the ability to pay doctrine are correct. Even if they are, it is beyond the capability of a legislator to implement them. Therefore, equality of sacrifice should take ability to pay into account, but only to a limited extent. This is not to say that Mill opposed taxing the rich. He denounced the ways in which certain taxes in place in the United Kingdom had a regressive incidence.[17] Mill was also an advocate of progressive taxes on those sources of wealth for which individuals had not themselves worked.[18] In other words, like Saint-Lambert and Smith before him, Mill also took into account how the money was made in the first place.

For John Stuart Mill, equality of sacrifice could be maintained while taking only limited account of ability to pay. In the second half of the nineteenth century equality of sacrifice would instead become synonymous with applying the ability to pay doctrine to the full extent. The intellectual development that led to this change was the marginal revolution in economics. The marginal revolution led to a more complete theory of utility than had existed during Mill's time, together with the mathematical tools to analyze it. Its cornerstone was the law of diminishing marginal utility. The work of Francis Edgeworth in his "Pure Theory of Taxation" published in 1897 provides a key example of this movement applied to progressive taxation. Instead of only exempting a minimum subsistence level from taxation, the question now became how to apply a progressive tax on income above the subsistence level.

Another important shift that took place with Edgeworth, as well as other authors to follow, and most notably Arthur Pigou, the father of modern welfare economics, was the move away from interpreting equal sacrifice as a fairness criterion.[19] Instead of pursuing an objective in which each individual would suffer the same loss of utility from taxation "equal absolute sacrifice," or the same proportion of utility lost "equal proportional sacrifice," the objective now became one of minimizing the total loss to society from taxation. According to Edgeworth, the solution to this was to set tax rates so that the utility loss from the last dollar of taxation for each individual was identical. This solution came to be called "equal marginal sacrifice" which can be simply understood as a situation where the final dollar of taxes for each member of societies represents the same sacrifice. This was the point at which discussions of taxation by economists shifted away from a fairness criterion, treating everyone as equals, and toward a welfarist one, maximizing aggregate social welfare.[20]

The final crucial development following the marginal revolution was that the debate between economists about taxing the rich became a highly technical one where scholars rarely referred to the basic question of whether wealth had been fairly or unfairly generated in the first place. This was quite distinct from what Smith and Mill had originally envisaged.

The work of Edgeworth and Pigou represented the apogee of the ability to pay doctrine. However, these arguments would subsequently be subject to two trenchant critiques. The first was emphasized by Lionel Robbins of the London School of Economics in 1932. It involved the impossibility of interpersonal comparisons of utility. Robbins made the case for the impossibility of a government knowing the utility functions of all citizens and thus the impossibility of applying any equal sacrifice standard for taxation. The implications that Robbins drew were stark. The Law of Diminishing Marginal Utility does not justify the inference that transferences from the rich to the poor will increase total satisfaction. It does not tell us that a graduated income tax is less injurious to the social dividend than a non-graduated poll tax.[21]

While the language was different, Robbins's argument was essentially the same as those of eighteenth-century opponents of luxury taxation. Two decades later, his arguments were used in a famous critique by Walter Blum and Harry Kalven published in 1952 and entitled "The Uneasy Case for Progressive Taxation." They emphasized the fundamental difficulty in gauging ability to pay. Blum and Kalven suggested that the most convincing arguments in favor of progressive taxation depended on showing that the initial distribution of income and wealth was unfair. This was a position they adopted from the early Chicago school economist, Henry Simons.[22] Now, neither Blum nor Kalven suggested that the pretax distribution of income at the time was in fact unjust. Yet in making this point they identified a fundamental problem with the ability to pay doctrine. Without some reference to whether income or wealth was justly or unjustly earned, arguments for progressive taxation were intellectually weak.

Blum and Kalven published their piece in 1952. It may seem absurd to suggest that arguments in favor of progressive taxation were weak at a time when the top marginal income tax rate in the United States stood at 92 percent. In the chapters to follow we provide an answer for this apparent contradiction; ability to pay arguments alone did not suffice to convince the public that the rich should be taxed. High top tax rates were instead adopted because those in the political arena also made compensatory arguments that questioned whether the initial distribution of income was fair. Before encountering these debates we need to first see their intellectual origin. To do so we consider the compensatory theory of progressive taxation.

THE COMPENSATORY THEORY

The compensatory theory suggests that if taxes on the rich compensate for some other privilege granted by the state, then in this case progressive taxation is fair. Though he gave the compensatory theory its name, Edwin Seligman was distinctly not in favor of this idea. He found it inapplicable and suggested that at best it could simply reestablish proportionality. In what follows we borrow Seligman's terminology while disagreeing with his conclusion. Compensatory arguments have proved to be the most politically powerful claims in favor of progressive taxation. Our goal in this section is to lay out the assumptions behind the compensatory theory while also tracing its historical origins. Demonstrating the relevance of compensatory arguments empirically will be a goal for subsequent chapters.

Before we proceed with the foundations of the compensatory theory, we should note that it bears some similarity to another proposed rule of taxation known as the benefit principle. According to this idea, those who benefit from a government-provided good should be the ones to pay for it and in proportion to their benefit. However, the benefit doctrine refers only to allocating taxes in response to publicly provided goods. It does not refer to using one tax to compensate another. Nor does it refer to using taxes to compensate for the effect of other government interventions, as we also do below.

Some authors believe that fairness in taxation depends on whether money is earned by effort or simply by being fortunate. This criterion is often referred to as "luck egalitarianism." So, Guicciardini's proponent of progressive taxation believed that Florence's landed elite ought to pay the *decima scalata* because they earned their money through idleness and inheritance, whereas the merchants of the city should be exempted because they had earned their wealth by being industrious. Fast forward three centuries and we see a similar attitude expressed by John Stuart Mill. He believed in proportionate taxation once a subsistence minimum was exempted, but he also argued that those who benefitted from appreciating land values should pay extra tax because their earnings came through no effort of their own. His case for heavy and progressive taxation of inheritance followed the same logic. In the twentieth century, Arthur Pigou argued for taxation of windfall profits, by which he meant "accretions to the real value of people's property that are not foreseen by them and are not in any degree due to efforts made, intelligence exercised, risks borne, or capital invested by them."[23] More recently, Thomas Piketty, as well as Roland Bénabou and Jean Tirole, have suggested that attitudes toward redistributive taxation depend on whether individuals believe that income has been earned through effort or luck.[24] Each of the preceding examples involves an argument where someone advocated taxing top earners because they owed their position simply to being in the right place at the right time.

In what follows we suggest that arguments of the type described will be strongest when the rich owe their good fortune not just to being lucky but to being made lucky by state action. In such cases the norm of the state treating citizens as equals has been violated, and so there is a compensatory argument for taxation of the rich to restore it. This can be the case if the rich have benefitted from a special state granted privilege. It can also be the case if average citizens have been obliged to bear an extra burden.

The argument we make here is related to a more general point made by Liam Murphy and Thomas Nagel.[25] When designing a fair tax system, they say, one should not simply start with the market income that each person earns and then decide how much each person should pay. One should instead consider all the ways in which government action influences each person's market income and allocate tax responsibilities in light of this fact. Taxation ought to be designed such that it compensates for other privileges or responsibilities determined by the state.[26] Murphy and Nagel make a normative case in their book; this is what they believe governments should do. To fully implement their idea, one would need to know all the ways in which government action influences pretax income, and one would need to even consider what income would be earned if the state was totally absent. One can draw on their reasoning in a more restricted way to make a positive prediction about what governments will do in practice. If people are motivated by the norm of treating citizens as equals, then when obvious examples of privilege emerge they will want the state to use the tax system to correct or compensate.

A first way to think of the compensatory argument is to consider whether one tax should compensate for another. Historically, many governments raised most of their revenue from indirect taxes, often levied on common consumption goods. Such taxes often required less bureaucratic capacity to collect than did a direct tax levied on the individual or household. Indirect taxes have a regressive incidence to the extent that poor and average people spend a greater fraction of their income on common consumption goods than do the wealthy. Under such conditions it is possible to argue that any form of direct tax, such as an income tax, should take a progressive form in order to compensate for the regressive incidence of indirect taxes.

The argument that the rich should be taxed because others were bearing the burden of indirect taxation was widespread in the nineteenth century, and we show this in greater detail in chapter 6. However, this argument actually appeared at a much earlier date. Between AD 1287 and 1355, the independent commune of Siena was ruled by a merchant oligarchy known as the regime of The Nine. The communal government funded itself in part through indirect taxes, known as *gabella*, as well as through direct taxes and forced loans levied on two different books of assessments, the Table of Possessions and the *lira*. While the city's poor would have been subject primarily to the *gabella*, the direct taxes were targeted at the city's rich. According to William Bowsky, the foremost historian of Siena during this period, the leaders of Siena thought it was a fair system that they apply a mix of taxes so that the incidence of one might help compensate the other. To support his claim Bowsky cites the following question posed by a legislative commission to the Sienese city council on May 9, 1323:

Whether the commune of Siena ought to live and accomplish its business by means of the Table [of Possessions] ... or indeed whether it should live and accomplish [its affairs] by making a lira or through the lira, or by means of the gabella ... ; or if it rather please the same council that all of the aforesaid three methods be reduced to one and the same, and then the exaction of some money that will be made in the future for the commune of Siena be exacted of the citizens in this way, namely, a third part by means of the table, a third part, indeed, by means of the lira, and a third part by means of the gabella ... *And this because a greater equality will be maintained among the citizens in this way, because if anyone is burdened in the table he can be relieved in the lira and in the gabella and so on.*[27]

The idea that fairness dictates taxing the rich to compensate for other taxes borne by the poor clearly has a very old heritage. Observers have also considered compensatory arguments in more recent times. The clearest formulation of this argument came from none other than John Stuart Mill. He argued that because the incidence of indirect taxation fell especially on the poor and middle classes, the system of income taxation then in place, exempting income below one hundred and fifty pounds, was fair. Mill's opinion on this question came in parliamentary testimony on the income tax that he gave in 1852:

> Joseph Hume: We understand you to say that in order to call for an equal sacrifice from all parties, not the income tax only, but the other items of taxation bearing on the different classes of the community ought to be taken into consideration before a judgment can be pronounced as to what would be a fair and equal rate of taxation upon all classes.

> John Stuart Mill: Certainly.[28]

Mill's statement makes clear that equality of sacrifice ought to be based on a consideration of all taxes to which individuals were subject, and not just the income tax. If the great majority of households in the UK at the time were exempted from the income tax, then this made sense because they bore the majority of the weight from indirect taxation. Mill thought that an income tax in which the first one hundred and fifty pounds of income were exempted was fair, but he did not use this compensatory argument to support an income tax with graduated rates. Subsequent observers would soon take this step.[29]

The above examples refer to a narrow yet clear type of compensation. If one believes in treating people as equals, then it is difficult to dispute the idea that indirect taxes on common consumption goods violate this principle; the further one goes down the income scale, the greater the fraction of income one pays. Therefore, a progressive tax on income is needed to compensate. But might it be possible to use progressive income (or inheritance) taxation to compensate for other ways in which the state fails to treat citizens as equals? When Liam Murphy and Thomas Nagel wrote that a fair tax system ought to take into account all the ways in which government actions influence market income, they certainly did not only have in mind compensating for the incidence of indirect taxation. We could say the same for John Rawls when he suggested that "even steeply progressive income taxes" might be necessary if other existing policies treat people inequitably. In his words, "Two wrongs can make a right in the sense that the best available arrangement may contain a balance of imperfections, an adjustment of compensating injustices."[30]

To follow on the insights of Murphy and Nagel, and of Rawls, we need to think beyond the case of taxes to consider other privileges that the state might grant or other burdens that it might impose. A primary objective of states throughout history has been to provide for external defense. In many cases defense is funded through taxation, but historically many states have also provided for their defense through various forms of military obligation or appeals to patriotism. Earlier we referred to one example where it is thought that if one segment of society is subject to a military obligation, then they ought to receive more favorable tax treatment. This was the justification often offered for exempting members of the French nobility from taxation under the Old Regime. By being willing to bear arms they were in effect paying a tax levied only on them, and so they ought to be exempt from other levies. There are also examples in history where it has been considered fair that the poor and middle classes be compensated for military obligations that they have borne.

In any society, if some individuals have been obligated to serve the common defense while others have not, this creates a particularly strong rationale for taxing those who stay home. In the modern era the military context of the French Revolution gave birth to this argument. By the early months of 1793, there were calls from many quarters in France to establish a system of progressive taxation so as to fund war expenditures. In many cases partisans of this policy used ability to pay arguments to justify it. However, others made a compensatory claim. The municipality of Paris had been recruiting young men from the city's popular classes to fight against the different armies that had invaded France. On March 9, 1793, when speaking to the French National Convention, the procureur general of the commune of Paris, Pierre-Gaspard Chaumette, made the following speech:

> Citizens, for too long a time the poor man alone has made the greatest sacrifice. He has withheld nothing, giving even his blood and that of his children. He has provided everything for to save the State. It is time that the rich egoist that isolates himself and hides behind his treasures have these torn away from him and that he be forced to give a portion of these for the needs of the Republic and his own happiness. We ask you to impose on this class of men, up to now useless, and even harmful to the Revolution, a war tax of which a part should be allocated to relieving the burdens of wives, fathers, mothers, and children of the defenders of the country.[31]

In response to Chaumette's speech the National Convention immediately adopted the principle of imposing a war tax on the rich. The speech itself provides an ideal illustration of how a compensatory argument can be used to expand political support for progressive taxation. All the evidence suggests that, like many of his Jacobin contemporaries, Chaumette was favorable toward progressive taxation based on ability to pay grounds alone. However, he must have known that this was not the case with all of the Convention's members.

So far we have suggested how compensatory arguments can be used to expand the basis of support for progressive taxation, but we have not considered criticisms of this idea. One criticism was made by Edwin Seligman, echoing early observations by Francis Walker, the first president of the American Economic Association.[32] Taken to its logical extent, the compensatory theory could apply to any government action that influenced an individual's market income. Yet clearly it would be hopeless to try to make such a complete assessment.

We need to ask what compensatory arguments could resist the criticism levied by Seligman and Walker. To prove convincing in the political arena, a compensatory argument must certainly be one that seeks to correct a clear and obvious inequality generated by state action. We should admit though that we do not pretend in this book to offer an ex ante prediction about the point at which a prior inequality becomes sufficiently large or sufficiently clear that a compensatory claim becomes credible. One thing we can say is that, historically, effective compensatory arguments have hinged on prior inequalities that were recently created. During the nineteenth century some authors suggested that progressive taxation could be justified, at least for a time, based on a whole history of failures by the state to treat people as equals.[33] We have not seen arguments of this type in major political debates about taxation.

The second criticism of the compensatory theory is the same one that Saint-Lambert levied against proponents of luxury taxation during the eighteenth century. If the state had created an unjust inequality by giving someone a position of privilege, then the logical response should be to remove the initial source of this inequality rather than to tax it. As with the first criticism of the compensatory theory, we need to consider how this second criticism affects the political influence of compensatory arguments. If a government creates an unnecessary privilege for some that brings no general benefit, then the stronger political argument will probably be that this privilege should simply be removed rather than taxed. However, there will be other cases where a privilege cannot be so easily removed. Indirect taxation is necessary, but it tends to have a regressive incidence.[34] Conscription is necessary in some cases, but it isn't feasible to have people of all ages serve. It is in cases such as these that compensatory arguments in favor of progressive taxation will have the greatest impact.

DO PEOPLE BELIEVE IN TREATMENT AS EQUALS?

There is tremendous discussion about fairness in taxation as a normative standard. In other words, fairness is seen as something that governments should try to attain. The discussion in this chapter has focused on normative claims of this sort. But there is much less scholarly effort to consider whether beliefs about fairness might motivate what people prefer and what tax policies governments choose. When they try to explain the tax policies that governments pursue, most scholars instead conceive of people as only trying to maximize their own income, without reference to any fairness constraint. Does fairness have a role to play in predicting or explaining what governments do? We do not need to assume *either* that people are only concerned about maximizing their income *or* that they are singularly devoted to adhering to some fairness norm. It is perfectly possible that individuals give some weight to each of these goals. These weights may also vary from person to person. Some individuals will be more motivated by such fairness norms than others. In order for our interpretation of the history of progressive taxation to be accurate, we only need to assume that some individuals are partially responsive to fairness norms.

Over the last several decades an overwhelming amount of evidence has accumulated suggesting that in a laboratory setting humans (and maybe other primates) engage in what is often termed "prosocial" behavior. Prosocial here means that individuals do not make choices that maximize their own income because they leave money on the table for others. The bulk of this evidence has been accumulated in very basic experimental games that are much simpler than the taxation context we consider in this book. Even so, these results can be instructive. They suggest two important things: first, that some people believe in equal treatment; and second, that some people subscribe either to the ability to pay doctrine or to compensatory ideas.

Consider first the evidence from "ultimatum" and "dictator" experimental games. These have been conducted extensively in laboratory settings as well as "lab in the field" games in a very wide range of different contexts. In the ultimatum game a proposer makes an offer to a responder on how to divide a sum. If the responder accepts, then the sum is divided according to that rule. If the responder refuses then both players receive a payoff of zero. Narrow self-interest in this game would dictate that the responder should accept any positive offer because something is better than nothing. Anticipating this, the proposer should know that they would be able to leave almost everything for themselves. In practice, however, proposers offer substantially more than this, and in a significant number of cases they offer a fifty-fifty split. [35]

Analogous results about treating people as equals have been obtained in the "dictator game." In this game the recipient simply has to take what he or she is offered. [36] This removes the question of whether the proposer who makes a positive offer is anticipating that the recipient will refuse a low offer. Evidence shows that when "dictators" give a positive sum, there is clearly a very strong resonance with a fifty-fifty split. A meta-analysis of dictator games shows that offers clustered around a fifty-fifty split are far more frequent than offers further above or below this criterion. [37] This speaks very directly to treatment as equals. In a further study of this phenomenon, scholars have used a panel of one thousand American subjects to implement a modified version of the dictator game in which there is a price of "redistribution" from the dictator to the recipient. This richer setting allows for distinguishing between self-interest and fairness while also taking into account efficiency concerns. In keeping with the results from simpler dictator games, these authors find that a substantial fraction of their respondents were motivated strongly or at least partially by fairness. [38]

There is substantial debate about the precise reasons why proposers make positive offers in dictator and ultimatum games. There is also substantial cross-cultural variation in behavior, with individuals in more market-integrated societies typically proposing more.[39]

Now consider a simple extension of either the dictator or the ultimatum game that is relevant to the compensatory theory of taxation. In this extension either the proposer or the recipient has to first earn the sum that is to be distributed, say by taking a math test. How does this affect behavior? Consistent with the compensatory theory, proposers who have earned their own money tend to propose less. When the responder is instead the one who earned the money, proposers tend to offer more.[40] These results suggest that the compensatory theory of taxation might predict how people behave. However, in these experiments there is no difference between luck as an act of nature and as a result of government action, so the fit with what we have called compensatory arguments is not perfect.

We can also examine whether people adhere to the ability to pay doctrine by reviewing results from another experiment where individuals must decide how much they will contribute to a public good.[41] If individuals begin the game with varying endowments, a norm emerges where those with high endowments pay more. However, and this is a crucial point for our study, they also show that within these games with heterogeneous endowments, different fairness norms can emerge. It may be the case that all contribute but contribute equally. It may also be the case that those with greater endowments contribute more.

The public opinion literature on economic policy preferences also provides substantial evidence that individual policy opinions are informed by fairness concerns in addition to self-interest.[42] To investigate more specifically whether the different fairness norms that we discuss in this chapter influence tax policy preferences, we, together with Xiaobo Lü, designed and implemented a survey in which we asked a representative sample of five hundred individuals from the United States in 2014 to express a preference for a proportional or progressive tax scheme.[43] We then gave respondents an opportunity to explain their choice. We used their open-ended responses to draw inferences about fairness norms. We do not intend the results of this survey to be a comprehensive test of the argument about taxation that we have laid out in this chapter. That will instead come with the historical evidence to follow. We offer these results simply as a suggestion that people may be motivated by fairness concerns, yet these fairness concerns differ. The exact question we asked in the survey was:

> Many observers in the United States have suggested that the Federal Government's budget deficit should be addressed with a combination of spending cuts and income tax increases. Suppose that federal income taxes are going to be increased in order to raise revenue to help decrease the deficit. We are interested in what you think about different plans for increasing income taxes.
>
> We will now provide you with several proposals for increasing income taxes all of which raise about the same amount of revenue. We will always show you two possible proposals in comparison. For each comparison we would like to know which of the two tax codes you prefer. You may like both or not like either one. In any case, choose the one you prefer the most. In total, we will show you four comparisons.
>
> People have different opinions about this issue and there are no right or wrong answers. Please take your time when reading the potential changes.

For each choice, we showed respondents two plans. Plan A was a proportional plan that proposed to increase individual income taxes by 1 percentage point for all individuals. Plan B was a progressive plan that proposed no increase for individuals making less than $25,000, a randomly assigned larger increase for those making between $25,000 and $200,000, and a randomly assigned even larger increase for those making more than $200,000.[44] Overall, respondents chose Plan A 39 percent of the time. The experimental variation in the exact rates for Plan B is not our main concern. The point is simply that Plan A is a proportional increase and Plan B is a progressive increase. What reasons did individuals give for supporting these alternatives?

In asking individuals to explain their choices, we instructed them to think specifically about the last of the four pairs of tax plans that they considered. Using a prespecified protocol, we then coded their responses according to a number of commonly observed arguments, including several alternative fairness considerations.[45] The categories were:

- Equal Treatment [fairness]—Preference for the government treating citizens the same through a proportional or flat tax.[46]
- Ability to pay [fairness]—Specifies that the rich are better able to afford or will be less harmed by a tax increase than the poor.
- Compensatory [fairness]—Suggests a higher tax on the rich is justified because of other inequalities or advantages.
- General Fairness [fairness]—Refers to fairness but not specifically to "Equal Treatment," "Ability to Pay," or "Compensatory" conceptions of fairness. These responses are often of the form "because it's fair" and were employed to justify choices for both Plan A (proportional) and Plan B (progressive).
- Progressive Treatment—Argues for a plan that taxes the rich more or poor less but does not give any reason why.[47]
- Economic Efficiency—Argues that the preferred plan is good for the economy in some way.
- Self-interest—Chooses the plan that makes the respondent better off economically.
- Other—All other arguments.[48]

A striking feature in the pattern of these responses is that a majority of individuals appeal to fairness norms to justify their policy opinions. Fifty-three percent of respondents gave arguments classified in the "Equal Treatment" (15 percent), "Ability to Pay" (19 percent), "Compensatory" (4 percent), and "General Fairness" (16 percent) categories. For those who might be concerned about the subjective nature of our coding, we can also replicate some of these results using objective indicators. Not surprisingly, the use of the word "fair" is an excellent predictor of being in one of the four fairness categories. Likewise, use of the word "afford" is an excellent predictor of being in the ability to pay category. A final question one might ask about our survey results is why so few people employed compensatory arguments given the importance we place on this theory. This is completely consistent with the core argument of this book. Compensatory arguments are powerful, but the current context affords less of an opportunity to make them than was once the case. Today the United States is involved in wars of limited mobilization where the wartime compensatory arguments used in the twentieth century no longer apply. There remain peacetime compensatory arguments that can be made, but in recent public debate these have been less salient.

We make no claim that the above results show definitively that some individuals are motivated by fairness norms. It is of course possible that appeals to fairness simply provide a cloak for naked self-interest. The well off may simply prefer a proportional scheme because they pay less, but say that it is the best way of treating people as equals. The less fortunate may prefer a progressive tax for exactly the same reason while saying that the real reason is that they believe in ability to pay.

One way to examine this question is to consider how responses differed depending on income levels. Two hundred and fourteen of the respondents made less than $25,000 a year; two hundred and eighty-one made between $25,000 and $200,000, and three made more than $200,000 (two further individuals did not reveal their income). If strict self-interest dominated choices, then we would expect those making less than $25,000 to favor a progressive tax scheme and those making more to favor a proportional one. We will refer to individuals fitting this pattern as making a "congruent" choice. Overall, about 53 percent of individuals made a congruent choice while the remainder expressed a preference for what we will call a non-congruent choice. Now, in practice there could be several reasons for individuals to make a non-congruent choice. They might be motivated by fairness, but they might also believe that a non-congruent choice was best because of some other self-interested reason. For example, those in the low-income category might prefer a proportionate tax scheme if they feared that higher taxes on the rich would hurt economic growth.

In order to get at this issue, we can consider the distribution of justifications for individuals who made congruent and non-congruent choices. Justifications are divided between those who subscribed to any of the four types of fairness arguments (simply called "fairness") and those who made "other" justifications. Overall, 49 percent of individuals who made congruent choices—that is, opting for their apparent self-interest—provided a fairness justification. For these individuals we have no way of separating between fairness and self-interest. Now consider the case of non-congruent individuals, those who chose a tax scheme that went against their apparent economic self-interest. Roughly 58 percent of non-congruent individuals provided a fairness justification for their choice. What counts here is not that the fraction is higher than the 49 percent in the congruent case; it is simply interesting to note that a large fraction of non-congruent individuals made fairness arguments. We still don't know with certainty whether fairness was what truly motivated these individuals, but we have a clearer indication that this may have been the case. When we separate out these responses between different income groups we see similar results. Among those earning less than $25,000 who were non-congruent, just below 58 percent of individuals provided a fairness justification. Among those earning more than $25,000 who made a non-congruent choice, just above 58 percent provided a fairness justification.

We do not know for sure whether the results indicate that individuals were truly motivated by fairness, but they do provide a good indication that this was indeed the case. Equally importantly, they provide support for another theme: when it comes to taxation there are different plausible standards for what is fair.

SUMMARY

Throughout history when people try to justify their preferred tax system, they have said it involves the state treating citizens as equals. We saw this in Medieval and Renaissance Italy, in eighteenth-century debates on luxury, and in nineteenth- and twentieth-century discussions about taxing the rich. Finally, we saw this also in evidence from our survey of citizens in the United States today.

One way to treat people as equals is to invoke the ability to pay doctrine. It has remained the most common fairness argument for a progressive tax, but many see its potential weaknesses. Many people might find the doctrine plausible but also difficult to implement, and therefore an imprudent basis for policy. For others, ability to pay is simply the wrong criterion to use in the first place. If people have earned their money through talent and effort, then they should not suffer from a higher rate of tax just because they have more.

The compensatory theory of progressive taxation provides an alternative to the ability to pay doctrine. In its broadest form it suggests that people ought to be taxed more heavily when it is clear that effort and talent have played less of a role than luck in the accumulation of their earnings. We have argued that compensatory arguments in favor of taxation will be most powerful in cases where it is clear not just that the rich have been lucky, but that their luck has involved privileged treatment by the state. The simplest way to deal with this problem would seem to be to do away with the initial injustice, but there are prominent cases where this is neither feasible nor desirable.

In the end, the greatest support for taxing the rich will exist when it is possible to refer not only to ability to pay, but also to a compensatory argument for making taxes progressive. Countries tax the rich heavily when political and economic conditions allow compensatory claims to be made. It is critical to understand that such arguments need to involve the correction of initial inequalities that are clear and manifest. Inequality in war participation provides a particularly stark example here, but it is not the only one. Finally, we need to recognize that convincing compensatory arguments cannot simply be invented out of thin air. They emerge in response to concrete political and economic conditions that make such arguments credible and convincing.

USING HISTORY TO EVALUATE THE ARGUMENTS

In the remainder of this book we present a wealth of information on taxation of the rich over time, and we use this evidence to help discriminate between the different theories that we have laid out in these first two chapters.

In the introduction we discussed what might be called the conventional view of the political economy of taxation—high taxation of the rich is normal in a democracy because that is what the majority wants, but there can sometimes be obstacles that prevent this from happening. As part of this story, we also suggested that we should expect democracies to tax the rich more heavily when inequality is high. These are theories that lend themselves to being tested with broad historical evidence that considers when governments taxed the rich. We can analyze whether transitions to democracy have been associated with increased taxation of the rich relative to the rest. We can also investigate whether governments tend to increase taxes on the rich in response to increased inequality. In chapters 3, 4, and 5 we present our main evidence on the evolution of progressive taxation, and we suggest that it provides little support for the conventional view. Democracy on its own, or democracy in conjunction with inequality, appears to have had a surprisingly small impact on taxation of the rich. The big conclusion of chapters 3, 4, and 5 will instead be that governments mainly moved to tax the rich in response to the conditions of mass warfare. But why was this the case?

One possibility is that the war effect simply reflected the ability to pay doctrine in operation. Arthur Pigou wrote in his *Political Economy of War* that if a government needs exceptional resources during wartime, then it should logically take more from the rich than from the rest because the rich are better able to pay. Perhaps governments were simply following this maxim. One obvious problem with this prediction is that if governments were not following the ability to pay doctrine during peacetime—otherwise taxes on the rich should have risen in response to high inequality—then it is not clear why they should have suddenly decided to apply the doctrine in wartime. We present further evidence on this question in chapter 6, where we show that there was a curious disappearance of "ability to pay" arguments during World War I.

The second possibility we consider is that the war effect on taxes reflected an attempt to compensate others for the sacrifices they had made; if existing state policies put the rich in a privileged position, then progressive taxes should be levied to correct this. Interestingly enough, as we will discuss in chapter 5, it was also Arthur Pigou who suggested this when supporting a levy on capital following the UK's participation in World War I. To investigate the compensatory argument, we make use of evidence on tax debates in chapters 6 and 8. But in chapter 3 we first consider the long-run evolution of income taxation.

PART TWO

WHEN HAVE GOVERNMENTS TAXED THE RICH?

CHAPTER THREE

THE INCOME TAX OVER TWO CENTURIES

The income tax is among the most important policy tools that modern governments use to raise revenue. The choice to have an income tax at all, and at what rates to tax different incomes, is also among the most important policy decisions affecting inequality. The income tax is often the policy instrument that dominates conflict about redistribution and the role of government more generally. Studying it is the natural place for us to begin the empirical investigation. In this chapter we ask when governments have used the income tax to tax the rich heavily. In so doing it will become apparent that this doesn't happen just because universal suffrage has been achieved or because income inequality is high. Governments have primarily used the income tax for this purpose during and in the wake of mass mobilization for war. The interpretation of this war effect will then be considered in later chapters.

Prior to the nineteenth century, states had little experience with an income tax. Modern income taxes are marked by the assessment of individual or household income and comprehensive taxation of most, if not all, forms of income. For centuries, the assessment of income was considered either impractical or an unnecessary violation of individual privacy. When states wanted to tax income and wealth, they typically taxed property or the income that was assumed to have been produced by property. Some of these taxes had features that resonate with an income tax. The idea was to tax earnings, but there was usually no attempt to assess actual income, and the taxes were aimed at specific sources of income.

Edwin Seligman notes two important exceptions to this pattern: Renaissance Florence and eighteenth-century France. In each case, an attempt was made to assess and tax many forms of income. In both settings, norms about treating citizens as equals played a role in the adoption of the tax. It was evident in each polity that there were new sources of income and wealth that were not tied to land. Part of the motivation for an income tax was to ensure that these new sources of income and wealth were also taxed. In practice, the assessment and general application of these early income taxes proved difficult. It turned out that sources of revenue that were easier to assess were more likely to be taxed. This led both taxes to becoming more like property taxes than actual income taxes. These problems of assessment were magnified by widespread and arbitrary exemptions. Neither set of income taxes survived into the nineteenth century.[1] Consequently, the story of the modern income tax is primarily one that begins with the adoption of an income tax in the United Kingdom in 1799. The remainder of this chapter will focus on determining from this date when states adopted income taxes and in particular income taxes with high top rates.

TOP MARGINAL RATES 1800–2013

To make this assessment systematically, we, along with Federica Genovese, constructed a new dataset that records yearly data on the top marginal income tax rate levied by the national government for an individual in twenty countries from 1800 (or independence) to 2013.[2] The top marginal rate is the rate applying on the highest income category. A country is considered to have adopted a modern income tax system if an independent national government levies taxes annually on comprehensive and directly assessed forms of personal income.

We wish to provide a picture of the burden of income taxation on wealthy citizens across time and countries. The top statutory marginal rate is an indicator of this burden that can be collected for a large set of comparable countries over a very long time period. Moreover, these top statutory rates are often the focus of political debate. These data improve on many previous analyses by measuring not just when a country adopted an income tax, but also the rates of taxation on high incomes. It allows us to see how factors such as expansion of the franchise, democratization, the rise of labor and socialist parties, and war influenced the taxation of high incomes. This is not possible with datasets focused on only the last several decades.

Figure 3.1 presents the average top marginal income tax rate for the twenty countries in the sample from 1800 to 2013. This view of the data reveals several interesting patterns. For one, there is tremendous variation across time. The average top income tax rate ranges from 0 in the two and a half decades after the end of the Napoleonic Wars to 65.2 percent in 1952. In addition, although the income tax had been implemented by the United Kingdom in 1799 and proven to be a good source of revenue, elsewhere the tax was either not adopted or adopted with very low rates throughout the nineteenth century. The highest rate adopted during the nineteenth century was 10 percent in the United Kingdom during the Napoleonic Wars, the United States during the Civil War, and Italy during the last five years of the century. Finally, the average top rate during the twentieth century exhibits an inverted u-shape, with rates increasing from single digits to more than 60 percent in mid-century, holding steady until the early 1970s, and then declining thereafter to 38 percent in 2013. It will be essential for us to explain both the rise and fall of top income tax rates over the course of the twentieth century.

From the late nineteenth century onward, the average top rates in Figure 3.1 mask significant differences between individual countries. Figure 3.2 presents the top marginal income tax rate for each country in the sample for selected years between 1900 and 2000. The first thing to notice is that although there is significant cross-country variation, most countries exhibit the inverted-u-shaped pattern of rising rates for most of the first half of the twentieth century, followed by declining rates after the middle of century. Switzerland is one departure from this pattern.[3] A second important pattern in this figure is

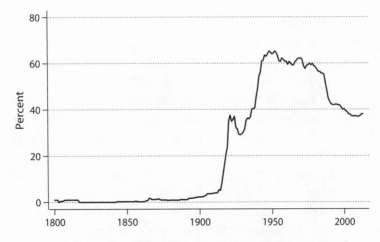

Figure 3.1. Average Top Rates of Income Taxation, 1800-2013. This figure reports the average top marginal income tax rate for the twenty countries in our sample (each country entering the sample in 1800 or first year of independence).

that not only do the rates change significantly over time, the ordering of the rates between countries changes as well. In 1900, only seven of the fifteen countries in the sample for that year had an income tax, and Italy led with a rate of 10 percent, with Austria, Japan, and New Zealand next with rates around 5 percent. By 1925, eighteen of the nineteen countries in the sample had a national income tax and the country leaders had completely changed identity, with France at 60 percent and Canada, Norway, and the United Kingdom at 50 percent.

What political and economic factors drove this variation?

Before addressing this question, we should ask whether our focus on national-level statutory rates paints an informative picture. Many countries in the sample adopted local income taxes levied by municipalities or other subnational governments. To address this issue, we also collected data on local income taxes for each country. These data can highlight any important differences that arise from also considering these taxes, but it turns out that there are relatively few.[4]

A second potential concern is that the top rate may measure income tax burdens on the wealthy, but it may not be a good indicator of overall progressivity. However, since countries often do not tax

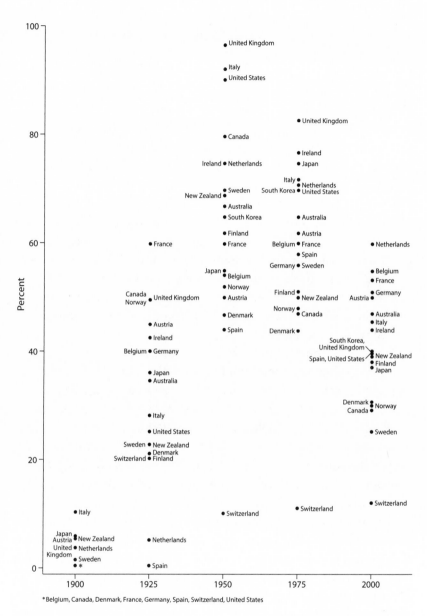

Figure 3.2. Top Rate of Income Taxation, Selected Years. This figure reports the top marginal income tax rate for the twenty countries in our sample (each country entering the sample in 1800 or first year of independence) for selected years. Germany is missing for 1950 because taxes were set separately in each occupation zone.

individuals with low incomes, the top marginal rate is a good linear approximation of progressivity. To check this claim more closely, we collected statutory rates across the income distribution for selected countries. Although there is interesting variation in rates by income, the top rate is a reliable indicator of the overall progressivity of the income tax.

Figure 3.3 presents the full schedule of statutory income tax rates for France, Germany, New Zealand, Sweden, the United Kingdom, and the United States for selected years from 1875 to the present.[5] We report not the raw schedules but the schedules in terms of multiples of gross domestic product per capita. This allows us to compare across time and across countries what the marginal tax rate would have been for individuals with incomes at various places in the income distribution. We use multiples of GDP per capita rather than percentiles in the income distribution because we do not have reliable information on income percentiles for all countries in all years. The multiples we select are based on the income thresholds in France reported in Piketty (2001).[6]

Figure 3.3 reports a rich array of information about the evolution of marginal rates across the income distribution over time. For purposes of validating our focus on top marginal rates, two patterns stand out. First, statutory rates are non-decreasing with income in all country years except New Zealand in 1925.[7] Keeping this minor exception in mind, figure 3.3 clearly indicates that countries enact higher statutory rates on higher incomes. Second, one simple measure of the progressivity of these tax systems is the difference between the top marginal rates—in figure 3.3, these are the rates on incomes for the 100 times GDP per capita multiple—and the marginal rates for low-income individuals—in figure 3.3, the rates on incomes for the 0.5 times GDP per capita multiple. Top marginal rates are highly correlated with this difference. The overall correlation across all country-years in the figure is 0.93. Four of the six cases have individual country correlations over 0.9. This suggests that top rates can be studied not only as an indicator of income taxation on the wealthy, but also as an intuitive, simple measure of the overall progressivity of the income tax system.[8]

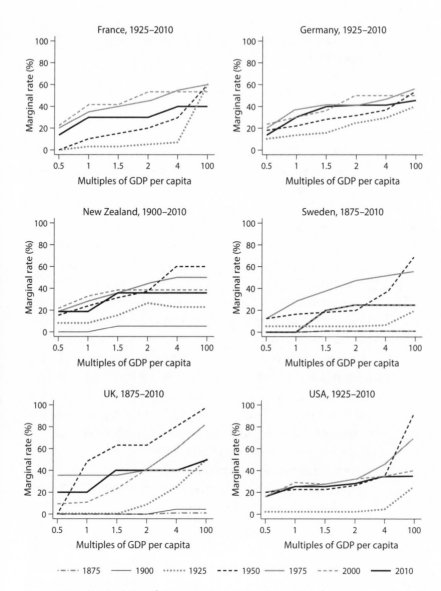

Figure 3.3. Full Schedules of Statutory Income Tax Rates. This figure reports the full income tax schedules for six countries for the years 1875, 1900, 1925, 1950, 1975, 2000, and 2010 if a modern income tax had been adopted. See text and endnotes for sources and methodology.

A third potential weakness of using top statutory rates is that modern tax codes are multidimensional. They contain a myriad of tax deductions that influence the effective tax rate paid by citizens. Some countries tax income from capital gains at lower rates than other sources of income. Other countries link wealth taxes with the income tax by limiting the total percentage of income from the combination of these taxes. This effectively lowers the top marginal rate of income taxation. Wealthy citizens are often the biggest beneficiaries of these policies. Certain types of tax compliance can also influence the effective rate. The potential difference between effective and statutory marginal rates varies across the income distribution and can be substantively quite important. Fortunately, for selected countries, we are able to evaluate the correlation between the statutory top marginal rate and effective rates paid by high earners over very long time periods.

Figure 3.4 presents the statutory top marginal income tax rate and the effective income tax rate on incomes in the top 0.01 percent of the income distribution for Canada, France, Sweden, and the United States and the top 0.05 percent for the Netherlands and the United Kingdom for most of the twentieth century. The bulk of the data on effective rates derives from authors who have produced papers for the top incomes project.[9] The six panels in figure 3.4 provide several important lessons. Consider first the panel for the Netherlands. The solid line plots the top statutory rate and the dashed line indicates the average effective rate for individuals in the top 0.05 percent of income earners. The first thing to notice about the plot is that the two series move closely together over time with a correlation of 0.91. This indicates that the top statutory rate is an extremely good proxy for the effective income taxes paid by very high earners in the Netherlands if the primary goal is to understand how these taxes varied over time. Another important insight from figure 3.4 is that there is a clear wedge between statutory and effective rates, and the magnitude of this wedge varies over time. For example, it was relatively small in the 1940s but expanded in the 1950s and '60s. Further, the effective rate is below the statutory rate, indicating that other aspects of the tax code work to reduce the taxes citizens pay. The statutory rates also change less frequently than the effective rates. These patterns

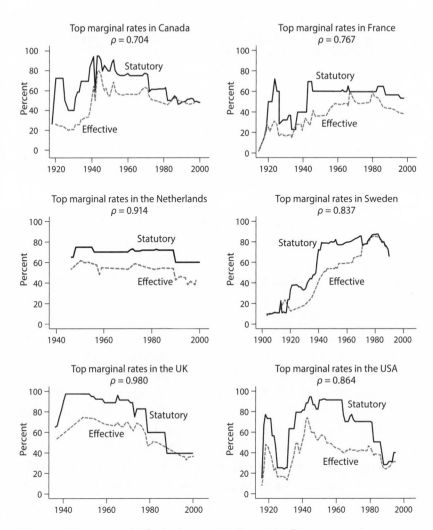

Figure 3.4. Statutory and Effective Income Tax Rates. This figure reports the statutory top marginal income tax rate and the effective income tax rate on incomes in the top 0.01 percent (0.05 percent for the Netherlands and UK). ρ is the correlation coefficient for the two series by country. See text and endnotes for sources and methodology.

show that legislation and behavior combine to produce changes in the effective rate even without a change in the statutory rate.

An obvious question to ask is whether the statutory top rate is a good proxy for the effective taxes paid for individuals further down in the income distribution. The answer to this is almost surely no if one considers much smaller incomes. The effective tax rate on the poor and middle class departs substantially from top rates of income taxation. Not only is there a large wedge between the rates, but also they do not necessarily move together over time. Political and economic forces that push states to adopt lower top rates may very well push rates on lower incomes higher to generate a flatter overall tax schedule. That said, in some countries, like the Netherlands, the top statutory rate is correlated with effective rates on income in the top 10 percent of the income distribution despite the fact that the wedge between the statutory and effective rate is larger than for incomes in the top 0.05 percent.

Overall, the data presented in figure 3.4 suggest that the top statutory rates are highly correlated with effective rates on very high earners in the top 0.01 (or 0.05) percent of the income distribution. Since the objective of this book is to identify the factors that have driven the taxation of the rich over the last two centuries, this evidence provides considerable confidence in our use of statutory rates in a great deal, though certainly not all, of the analysis. That said, the figure also clearly highlights that the top rate is a better proxy in some countries, for example the UK, than others, say Canada. The same caution should be made with respect to different time periods. In the United States a very substantial gap between the top rate and the effective rate opened up after 1945 and did not close until 1980. Projecting ahead, this characteristic of U.S. rates means that there is clear evidence that both the statutory top marginal rate and the average effective rate for the top 0.01 percent increased significantly during World War II, but the statutory rate remained very high for much longer.

Because effective rates in five of the six countries tracked statutory rates closely, we feel confident in using statutory rates for the analysis in this chapter. However, the results for the United States do imply that we need to be very careful before assuming that a top statutory rate exceeding 90 percent, as was true for much of the postwar period, meant that the rich were being taxed extremely heavily. Thomas Piketty and Emmanuel Saez have considered this question in detail in an analysis beginning in 1960. They have suggested that by 1960 a very substantial gap had emerged between the top marginal rate of income taxation and the effective rate for the top 0.01 percent in the United States. This is consistent with our own findings, and they attribute this result primarily to the classification of much income for this group as capital gains.[10] However, they also suggest that when one considers the additional burden on the top 0.01 percent posed by corporate taxation and estate taxation, then the rich in the United States during this era were in fact very heavily taxed. They also conclude that by the end of the twentieth century the top 0.01 percent in the United States were taxed much less heavily than had been the case in 1960.

CHANGES IN TOP RATES: A ROLE FOR DEMOCRACY?

The dominant narrative of the politics of redistribution in political science and economics highlights the role of electoral democracy and political parties that mobilize working-class groups. As we discussed in chapter 1, this story can be applied to income tax policies in a straightforward way. When voting is limited or a country is nondemocratic, the poor and middle class lack influence, and the wealthy generally choose tax policies that favor their interests. This should imply no income taxes or income taxes with low rates. Governments under these conditions would instead depend more on indirect taxes, such as trade and excise taxes. When countries expand the franchise or democratize, it is the middle class and poor citizens who become voters, and they are more likely to support the adoption of income taxes and especially income taxes with higher rates on the rich. One version of this story emphasizes how the rise of electoral democracy influences the policies chosen by all political parties. With an expanded suffrage, parties of the right would face an incentive to shift left in order to remain electable. Other versions suggest a partisan account in which policy change takes place only once labor and socialist political parties gain power.

The logic of the preceding argument is clear. Voters have every reason to adopt public policies consistent with their economic interests. Poor and middle-class voters should plausibly have a greater interest in high income taxes on the wealthy. Carrying this logic to its extreme, however, quickly leads to an obvious empirical problem. In democracies around the world, the poor generally do not expropriate the rich. In the context of income tax policies, the data in figures 3.1 and 3.2 show that democracies do not often choose to tax high incomes at very high rates. By 1900, a number of countries in the sample had been democracies for many years and had near universal suffrage, but none of them had adopted income tax rates above 10 percent. By the end of the twentieth century, national top marginal rates ranged between 11.5 percent and 60 percent with an average of 40 percent. These rates, while clearly higher than at the beginning of the century, are well short of those adopted in the middle of the twentieth century. They are also well short of what would be expected if the poor and middle-class majority were voting to expropriate the rich.

Even if the more extreme predictions of the democracy hypothesis have not been borne out, democratization and the expansion of the franchise may still have had an effect on the income tax. There are a number of ways to look at the data to try to learn the impact of democracy on the top rate of income taxation. A natural place to start is to compare average top rates among countries with and without universal male suffrage in selected years. Focusing on suffrage as the measure of democracy makes sense. It captures the feature of democracy of most direct interest—the eligibility of poor voters to participate in elections.[11] In 1900, countries with universal male suffrage had an average top income tax rate of 1.4 percent (seven countries) while those countries without universal male suffrage had an average rate of 2.9 percent (eight countries). This difference is small in magnitude and in the opposite direction of that predicted by the democracy hypothesis. By 1925, nearly all the independent countries in the sample had adopted universal male suffrage, and so cross-country comparisons for later periods do not shed light on this hypothesized relationship. That said, it should come as no surprise that if one pools all the data in the sample, the average top income rate in country-years without universal male suffrage is substantially lower than in country-years with universal male suffrage (4.5 percent versus 40.7 percent).

This sort of cross-country evidence is generally not compelling in determining whether and to what extent democracy leads to heavy taxation of the rich. For cross-country comparisons within a given year, it is not clear whether the lack of evidence for the democracy hypothesis is because the hypothesis is wrong or because there were other factors that influenced income tax policies. There are many reasons why Italy might have higher income taxes than Canada. Moreover, democracy itself may be determined by other factors that also influence tax policies. In other words, correlation may not imply causation. Combining all the data across all years does not help much either. We would still be using these cross-country comparisons as well as introducing new sources of potential bias from common secular trends. By this we mean that all countries in 1950, for example, might have been different than all countries in 1900 for reasons specific to these two time periods and not specific to the presence or absence of democracy.

An alternative way to use the data is to look at the relationship over time within each country. For example, are the top rates of income taxation higher or lower in the ten years before and after a country reaches full universal male suffrage or before and after democratization? What is this difference, on average, for all the countries in the sample? This approach allows us to "control" for all the factors that do not change over time that make a country like Italy different from a country like Canada.[12]

Figure 3.5 plots the top marginal income tax rate for the fifteen countries in the sample that transitioned from less than universal male suffrage to universal male suffrage in the ten years before and after the transition. The light gray lines plot the top marginal tax rate for each country and the thick black line plots the average. Australia, Germany, Ireland, Norway, and South Korea are excluded from this analysis because universal male suffrage already existed at independence or very soon thereafter. The black line plotting the average tells a mixed story for the democracy hypothesis. Universal suffrage does not appear to lead to a significant increase in the top marginal rate. The average is just below 20 percent prior to the first year of universal male suffrage and remains at approximately 20 percent for

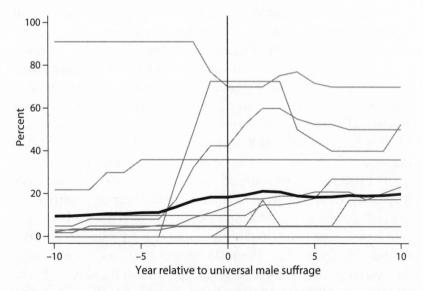

Figure 3.5. Universal Male Suffrage and Top Rates of Income Taxation. This figure reports the top marginal income tax rate for the fifteen countries in our sample that transitioned from less than universal male suffrage to universal male suffrage. The light grey lines plot the top marginal tax rate for each country and the thick black line plots the average. Australia, Germany, Ireland, Norway, and South Korea are excluded because universal male suffrage already existed at independence or very soon thereafter.

the ten years after this transition. Given that there are only fifteen countries in this analysis, it is worth considering whether these averages are being driven by extreme cases. However, if we consider the median top marginal rate, the picture looks very similar.

The light gray lines do raise questions about potentially important cases. The top light gray line is for the United States, which in practice did not have universal male suffrage until 1965.[13] The United States displays a pattern of decreasing rather than increasing rates around this date. There are also two light gray lines that appear to increase substantially in the years near the transition to universal male suffrage. Canada is one of these cases. The increase, however, is prior to the adoption of universal male suffrage. The top rate increases from 0 in year –4 to 25.9 in year –3 followed by increases to 48.9 in year –2 and 72.5 in year –1. As we discuss, these policy changes were made during Canada's mobilization for World War I. There was no additional increase in 1921 after universal male suffrage was adopted. The second case is the United Kingdom, and it seems consistent with the democracy hypothesis. Higher top marginal rates were adopted in 1919 and 1920 following the transition to universal male suffrage in 1918. This case highlights some of the limitations of single-country before and after comparisons. Top marginal rates were already beginning to increase in the United Kingdom before universal male suffrage was adopted. They rose from 8.3 percent in 1914, four years before universal male suffrage, to 42.5 percent in 1917, one year prior to the transition. Moreover, the before and after comparison suffers from the fact that it is implausible to assume that had universal male suffrage not been adopted, rates would have remained the same.[14] As we discuss in depth later in this chapter, the top rates of income tax in both these countries cannot be understood without considering the impact of mobilization for World War I.[15]

One potential objection to the evidence is that if countries are slowly expanding the suffrage over time, then the final achievement of full universal male suffrage may not impact tax policy. We considered this possibility by measuring partial expansions of the franchise, specifically estimating the years at which 25, 50, and 75 percent of men were eligible to vote. We failed to find evidence that these partial expansions of the franchise had an effect on the top rates of income taxation that countries adopted.[16] The United Kingdom provides a useful illustration of this result. It slowly expanded the franchise over the course of the nineteenth and early twentieth centuries.

Figure 3.6 plots the top marginal rate of income taxation for the United Kingdom between 1800 and 1925 along with key reforms that expanded voting rights. Generally, this graph shows mixed evidence at best for the argument that expansion of the franchise had an impact on income tax rates. The Reform Act of 1832 reduced and standardized income and property qualifications, leading to a small but important expansion of the franchise. The Reform Act of 1867 further reduced these requirements for England and Scotland. The Third Reform Act in 1884 introduced uniform franchise requirements in all of the United Kingdom and again reduced the income and property restrictions. At this point a majority of adult males, including the urban working class, were eligible to vote.

Income taxes in the UK were eliminated after the Napoleonic Wars. In 1842, Robert Peel's Conservative government introduced a new income tax law with a top rate of 2.9 percent. For the remainder of the nineteenth century, the income tax remained between 0.8 percent and 5 percent. The most important legislative change before World War I was the adoption of a "Super Tax." This was a graduated system with higher-income groups bearing a heavier burden than other tax-payers as part of the "People's Budget" in 1909/10. The super tax set a higher rate of 8.3 percent on high earners. In sum, the franchise expanded steadily over time reaching very high rates of eligibility, but there were only modest increases in the top rates of income taxation.

Even if rates moved little, it is still likely that granting voting rights to middle- and working-class citizens influenced the tax choices of UK governments. For example, Peel's 1842 budget reinstating the income tax also reduced a substantial number of customs duties. This made the overall tax system more progressive. This may have been part of an effort to court the growing number of middle-class voters following the Reform Act of 1832.[17] Peel's reinstatement of the income tax was also an example of compensatory fairness arguments at work. A salient argument in these debates was that trade and excise taxes had become too burdensome on the poor and that the income tax could compensate for these other taxes. In a similar fashion, the name of the 1909 "People's Budget" indicates that it was an effort to improve the Liberal government's standing with working-class voters and to respond to the electoral threat from the Labour Party. That said, the franchise was constantly expanding during the nineteenth century, but the top marginal rate of income tax hardly changed. This prior expansion of the franchise further undermines any association between the adoption of universal male suffrage in 1918 and the higher rates of income taxation thereafter. Universal male suffrage increased the fraction of males that had the vote, but the suffrage had already been significantly widened by prior reform acts.[18] If the extension of the franchise was driving the setting of income tax rates in the UK, we should have observed increases

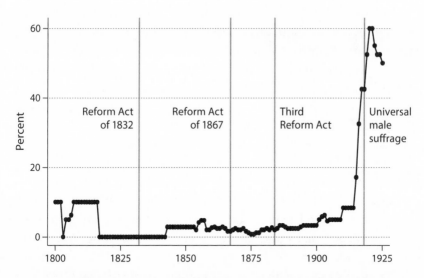

Figure 3.6. Suffrage Expansion and the UK Income Tax. This figure plots the top marginal income tax rate for the United Kingdom from 1800 to 1925 along with key reforms that expanded voting rights.

during many, if not all, of the significant expansions highlighted in figure 3.6, but we do not.

While suffrage is central to arguments about democracy and income taxation, other features of democratic government could also be influential. One possibility is that competitive elections, with or without a full expansion of the franchise, will lead to greater taxation of high incomes. We also evaluated the democracy hypothesis using a measure of competitive elections. We coded a country as having competitive elections if the legislature is elected in free multiparty elections, if the executive is directly or indirectly elected in popular elections and is responsible either directly to voters or to a legislature elected according to the first condition, and finally if at least 50 percent of adult males have the right to vote.[19] All the patterns, or lack thereof, that we have discussed for universal suffrage also hold when using this competitive elections measure.[20]

A closely related argument to the democracy hypothesis is that the impact of the inclusion of poor and middle-class voters is only fully realized when political parties of the left actually lead governments.

This partisan hypothesis predicts that left governments will lead to higher income taxes on the wealthy. But this argument is somewhat incomplete. Knowing that labor and socialist party governments tend to tax high incomes at higher rates does not really explain the underlying reasons why such governments are elected at some times and not others. Parties of the left have often pushed for higher top tax rates. It would not be surprising if they tended to implement them more frequently than do governments of the right. That said, it is still useful for us to know if left parties are associated with higher rates in practice. Given that these parties had no chance at leading governments before the franchise was expanded, observing a correlation between left parties and income tax policies would provide some evidence that political inclusion and democratic institutions do contribute to taxing the rich.

We can also use the data to learn about the relationship between partisanship and the top rate of income taxation. The cross-country evidence is rather mixed. In 1925, there were only two countries with left governments, and they had an average top rate of 21.8 percent, compared to an average top rate of 33.4 percent among the seventeen countries in the sample for that year that did not have left governments. If we move to 1950, there were more left governments, and rates were higher, but there was not a substantial difference between countries with left governments (68.3 percent) and without (66.5 percent). Nor is there evidence of higher rates in countries with left governments in 1975 or 2000.[21]

This cross-country evidence is again not particularly convincing in deciding whether governments of the left enact higher tax rates on top incomes. In any given year, there are many characteristics of these countries that might lead them to enact different tax policies. This could account for why there is little evidence for the partisan hypothesis in these comparisons even if such a relationship was prevalent. A more compelling use of the data is to once again look at what happens within a country before and after left parties take control of government.

Figure 3.7 reports the top marginal income tax rate for each time that a country transitioned from a non-left to a left party in control of

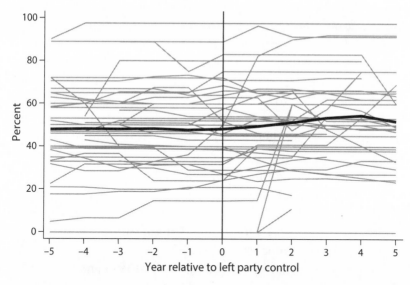

Figure 3.7. Left Partisanship and Top Rates of Income Taxation. This figure reports the top marginal income tax rate for each time that a country transitioned from a non-left to a left party in control of the government. We plot the rate up to five years before to five years after the transition with the exact duration depending on the term of the non-left and left governments before and after the transition. We include only transitions for which the period of non-left government before the transition is at least three years, and the period of left government is at least three years. The light grey lines plot the top marginal tax rate for each transition and the thick black line plots the average.

the government.[22] We plot the rate up to five years before to five years after the transition with the exact duration depending on the term of the non-left and left governments before and after the transition. We include only transitions for which the period of non-left government before the transition is at least three years and the period of left government is at least three years. The light gray lines plot the top marginal tax rate for each transition. The thick black line plots the average. The figure suggests that on average, left governments have been associated with a higher top rate of income taxation, but this increase takes a couple of years to occur and is small in magnitude. The average top rate in the five years preceding transitions to left governments is 48 percent and constant across all five years (years –5 to –1 in the figure). The average in the year of transition (year 0) is also 48 percent, but then the average top rate rises to 49 percent in year +1, 51 percent in year +2, 54 percent in year +3, and 55 percent in year +4 before dropping back to 52 percent. The median top rates in the years preceding transitions are 50 percent and then rise to 51 percent in year +2, 52 percent in year +3, and 53 percent in year +4 before returning to 50 percent in year +5. This suggests that left partisan governments were associated with a small increase in the top marginal tax rate, which is broadly consistent with the partisan hypothesis.

This partisanship result comes with several caveats. It should be remembered that this is an average pattern in the data. Inspection of each individual case reveals substantial heterogeneity. For some countries, there are clearly important partisan patterns. In the United Kingdom, left governments raised top rates in the 1930s and right governments significantly lowered top rates in 1979 and 1988. However, there are also important cases like Sweden that pose difficult questions for the partisanship hypothesis. The left was in power in Sweden for decades starting in 1932, and the top rate of income taxation rose from 24 percent to a high of 70 percent at mid-century. But the left was also in power as the top marginal rate was cut to 25 percent during the second half of the twentieth century. There are also many transitions for which there seem to be no changes in the top rate at all. Another problem, discussed earlier, is that the time series evidence requires us to believe that had a country not transitioned to a left party government, tax policy would not have changed and that left party governments came to power for reasons unrelated to other factors influencing the top rate of income taxation.[23] Finally, left partisanship raises the more general possibility that countries implemented higher income taxes when they feared the rise of Communist parties either through election or revolution. While in individual cases there may be something to this argument, like democracy, the threat of communism often preceded substantial increases in income tax rates by many years. Further, if one takes the view that the threat was commonly shared by most of the countries in our sample, it cannot explain the substantial variation in rates that we observe across countries within time periods.

INEQUALITY AND TOP MARGINAL INCOME TAX RATES

Inequality is another potential driver of income tax policy. As we discussed in chapter 1, this argument comes in several variants. Citizens may find it in their self-interest to tax the rich more heavily as inequality grows. Citizens may also feel that rising inequality is a sign of unequal opportunity, and therefore it is fair that the rich should be taxed. Finally, citizens may want heavy taxes on the rich when inequality is high because they fear for the democratic political order.

Evaluating the preceding arguments is difficult because we need to keep in mind that top rates of income taxation may influence the distribution of income, but inequality may also influence tax rates. In what follows we first consider static correlations; that is what the relationship is between today's level of inequality and today's top tax rate. We then consider a dynamic relationship, asking whether recent inequality affects subsequent tax choices and whether recent tax choices determine today's level of inequality. Examining how past values of one variable influence future values of another (and vice versa) helps move us one step toward saying which way the arrow of causality runs.

We measure inequality using the share of pre-tax income earned by individuals at various percentiles of the income distribution. Though the most obvious effect of top income tax rates on inequality would be via the difference between pre-tax and post-tax income, there are also reasons to believe that high top income tax rates can lower pre-tax inequality.[24] The top incomes shares data, based on income tax returns, is from *The World Top Incomes Database* and is the work of a wide number of scholars led by Tony Atkinson, Thomas Piketty, and Emmanuel Saez.[25]

We start by considering correlations between inequality and top rates across the twenty countries at different moments in time. In 1925, one of the first years for which at least a handful of countries have top income share data, the correlation between the top 0.01 percent share and the top rate was 0.22. By 1950, this correlation strengthened considerably to 0.65. Higher top rates prevailed in high-inequality countries. This relationship completely reversed itself later in the twentieth century. In 1975, the correlation for the top 0.01 percent share was -0.05 with a similar pattern holding in 2000. We also examined the cross-country correlations between the top 1 percent share and the top rate and found a similar pattern.[26] In short, there has been no stable static correlation between top shares of income and top rates of income taxation over the course of the twentieth century.

Our next step was to consider the static relationship between inequality and top rates in individual countries over time. Figure 3.8 reports the income share going to the top 0.01 percent of the income distribution and the top marginal income tax rate for Canada, France, the Netherlands, Sweden, the United Kingdom, and the United States for the years that we have comparable income share data. We selected these cases to match the data that we show in figure 3.4 for the relationship between statutory and effective rates, but the patterns are similar for the other countries for which we have data. The over-time correlation between the top 0.01 percent share and top marginal income tax rates is consistently negative. Figure 3.8 reports correlations between -0.13 for Canada and -0.90 for the United Kingdom. We also examined these same trends and correlations for the top 1 percent, and although the magnitude of the negative correlations was smaller, they were still negative for all but one country.

Our final step was to consider the dynamic relationship between inequality and top marginal rates of income taxation. To do this we performed what is known as a "Granger causality" test. The name of this test is misleading because in the test a "causal" relationship is one where past values of one variable influence current values of another. However, it may still be possible that some third factor determines both the variables being tested. To at least partially control for this latter possibility our test included controls for fixed characteristics of countries in addition to factors common to all countries in a time period.[27] In performing the Granger test we ask first whether past top tax rates are negatively correlated with today's level of inequality. This makes sense because behavioral responses to tax rate changes may take some time. We asked, second, whether past levels of income

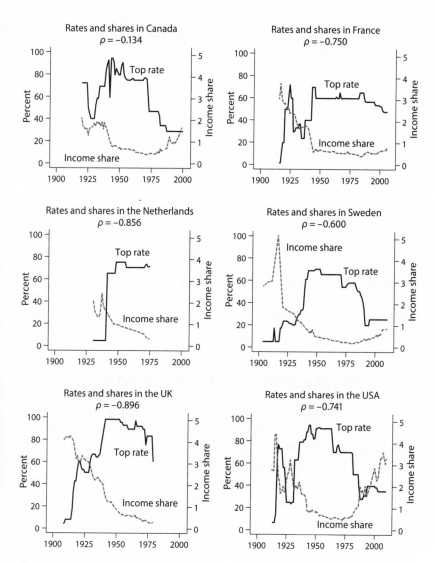

Figure 3.8. Inequality and Top Rates of Income Taxation. This figure reports income share going to the top 0.01 percent of the income distribution and the top marginal income tax rate for Canada, France, the Netherlands, Sweden, the United Kingdom, and the United States for the years that we have comparable income share data. ρ is the correlation coefficient for the two series by country.

inequality influence current tax rates. This too makes sense because levels of income inequality are only learned with some delay. When we pooled data for the twenty countries and performed these tests we found only very weak evidence that past levels of income inequality determine current tax rates. This was true irrespective of whether we used the top 1 percent or top 0.01 percent measures of income inequality. In contrast, we did find that current top tax rates influence future levels of inequality.[28]

Overall, there is very little evidence in the data consistent with the claim that increasing inequality leads countries to adopt higher taxes on top earners.[29] What we do see are clear indications that high top rates reduce income inequality. This fits with other recent research on this question.[30] This second finding also helps to suggest that the data are not so noisy that it is impossible to find any relationship at all. Given the difficulty of disentangling the effect of inequality on income tax rates and vice versa, we should treat this conclusion with caution. We will revisit it in the next chapter on the inheritance tax. There we find a similar pattern.

WAR MOBILIZATION AND TOP INCOME TAX RATES

Countries have gone the farthest in taxing the rich when there have been compensatory arguments for doing so. The most important context for this has been mass mobilization for war. We will now begin to evaluate this argument empirically by focusing on war mobilization and income taxation during the twentieth century. Our objective in this section is to establish that major increases in the taxation of high incomes coincided with mass mobilization for war. A full assessment of why war had this effect is left for later chapters.

Our discussion focuses on the period prior to and around the time of World War I. This conflict was the first war in which a significant proportion of the countries in the sample mobilized large armies that constituted a substantial share of their populations.[31] It is critical to note that the war effect that we hypothesize requires mass mobilization. Strategically important and expensive wars, such as recent U.S. conflicts in Afghanistan and Iraq, and many conflicts in the seventeenth and eighteenth centuries, are not expected to have the same impact on tax politics. World War I is also a natural place to begin because the descriptive statistics in figures 3.1 and 3.2 show that the first big increase in top income tax rates took place around this time.

To evaluate the impact of the war, we first need to set the context for income tax policy on the eve of the war. As we have already noted, the United Kingdom reestablished the income tax in 1842, but rates were kept extremely low by modern standards. Even with the introduction of the "super tax" in 1909, the top marginal rate in the UK was just 8.33 percent. During the nineteenth century, the possibility of establishing an income tax also became a subject of debate in numerous other European countries, in no small part because of the perceived success of the British innovation. During periods of significant unrest some individuals even proposed graduated tax systems with top rates that resembled modern rates.[32] By all accounts, however, the idea that up to half of an individual's income might be drawn away in taxes was seen by most observers at the time as what the *Economist* called a "preposterous system of finance."[33] In the decades leading up to World War I, a number of states joined the UK by creating an income tax, including Sweden in 1862 (with a more fully modern law in 1903), Italy in 1865, Japan in 1887, New Zealand in 1892, the Netherlands in 1893, Austria in 1897, and Denmark in 1903. The United States first adopted a federal income tax in 1862 in connection with the Civil War, but after 1872 Congress did not renew the tax. A federal income tax was not reinstated until 1913, though Congress passed income tax legislation in the 1890s that was struck down by the U.S. Supreme Court.

These developments seem to indicate that there was a general trend toward the adoption of an income tax. It was also the case that a graduated income tax became the norm. These developments were significant and may have been a consequence of an expanding franchise and of labor and socialist parties influencing political competition.[34] However, what is most striking is that even after the adoption of graduated income taxes, top earners prior to World War I paid only a small portion of their income in the form of tax. These low rates are consistent with the evidence that we have presented so far. Democracy, partisanship, and inequality generated a lively debate about taxing the rich, but this had relatively small effects on policy. One might wonder whether the failure to adopt higher rates of income taxation was attributable to limits on state administrative capacity. However, we show in chapter 4 that the same pattern of low rates also prevailed for inheritance taxes, and at the time these required far less administrative capacity to collect. The lesson then is that in the early months of 1914, it may have appeared that the income tax was the wave of the future, but it would have been considered unlikely that within a matter of a few years, some countries would adopt taxes that saw the richest members of society pay as much as half of their income in taxes.

World War I placed substantial financial demands on the countries participating in the conflict. Governments needed to respond to this demand by some combination of an immediate tax increase and increased issuance of debt, which implied future tax commitments. What was new about this conflict was that heavy burdens were placed on top-income groups. Debates about top marginal tax rates also took on a new political salience. Either during or soon after the end of the war, participant countries adopted steeply graduated rate schedules with top rates that the *Economist* had previously deemed "preposterous." In the UK a series of war budgets saw the top rate of income tax increase from 8.33 percent in 1914 to 60 percent by 1920. Observers at the time also suggested that in a country such as the UK, the changes in the tax system had an important effect on the distribution of both income and wealth.[35] In the United States the top marginal rate of income tax rose from 7 percent at the outset of the war to 77 percent by the end.[36] A similar pattern of events took place in Canada, which first established a federal income tax in 1917 with a top rate of 25.9 percent and which subsequently raised this rate to 72.5 percent by 1920.[37] In France, a national income tax was first implemented in 1915 with a top statutory rate of 2 percent. By 1920 the top rate had risen to 50 percent. Germany's policy choices differed from these cases in that it did not adopt a national income tax during the war. Also, the rates of income taxes at the local level, at least for Prussia (for which we have data), did not increase. That said, this departure was a temporary one. After the war, Germany created a federal income tax with a high top marginal rate of 60 percent in part to help pay for the war and war reparations. Moreover, as we discuss in greater detail in subsequent chapters, Germany, like other participants, adopted war profits taxes.

The top income tax rates that we refer to certainly applied to a small percentage of households, and more generally only a small fraction of households in these countries were liable for any income tax at this time. In the case of the UK the super tax was initially paid by something on the order of 0.1 percent of households.[38] In other countries, such as France and Canada, the fraction of households liable at the top rate of income tax was even smaller, on the order of 1,000 households and 500 households, respectively.[39] While the revenues generated by this top rate were certainly too small to solve France's postwar fiscal problems, the move to a high top marginal tax rate obviously had major implications for the large fortunes to which it applied.

One important aspect of the World War I period is that at the same time that we observe the evolution of tax systems in countries that mobilized heavily for the war, we can also observe what happened in those countries that remained neutral. The Swedish and Dutch cases are particularly interesting for our purposes, because Sweden and the Netherlands were subject to many of the same political developments that occurred in war participants such as France and the UK. In both Sweden and the Netherlands universal male suffrage was adopted around this time.[40] In addition, in both of these countries parties of the political left first gained a significant share of parliamentary seats at this time, and both countries experienced episodes of working-class unrest and a fear of Bolshevism similar to those in war mobilization countries.[41] However, despite these shared political conditions, outcomes with regard to top tax rates were very different from what happened with war mobilization countries. Dutch national top income rates remained in the single digits and although Swedish national rates increased, they remained around 20 percent until the 1930s.[42]

Figure 3.9 presents the available information on top tax rates between 1900 and 1930 for the ten sample countries that were heavily mobilized and participated in World War I and in the seven sample countries that were either neutral or that did not mobilize heavily. To code a country as mass mobilized for the war, it had to be a participant and had to mobilize at least 2 percent of the total population in the military. Japan was the only participant in the sample that did not reach this threshold at some point in the war. Finland, Ireland, and South Korea are excluded because they were not independent during most of the time period. It is apparent in figure 3.9 that in mobilized countries the war was accompanied by a huge shift toward taxing the rich. While there was also an increase in top rates in non-mobilization countries, it was much smaller. For purposes of estimating the effect of the war, it is useful to think about the nonmobilization countries as a counterfactual. Absent the war, we would expect the differences between the mobilization and nonmobilization countries to have remained approximately the same. Since prior to World War I the mobilization cases had slightly lower top rates, we would expect this difference to continue even if other factors led rates to increase in all countries. The fact that this difference was relatively constant in the years leading up to the war strengthens the plausibility of this assumption. The "difference in differences" before and after the war between the mobilization countries and nonmobilization countries is our best estimate of the effect of the war on top income tax rates. Figure 3.9 shows that in 1920 this difference was about 34 percentage points. The magnitude of the difference attenuated over time but remained large many years after the end of the war.

A potential concern about this approach to determining the impact of World War I is that countries may have selected into the war based on their ability to raise income taxes once the war had begun. A few considerations suggest this was unlikely. First, a large literature on entry into World War I suggests that few initial participants expected the long costly war that ensued. They instead anticipated a short and decisive conflict. Second, with the partial exception of the United States, the war mobilization countries in the sample did not select into the war at all. It was forced upon them. The event

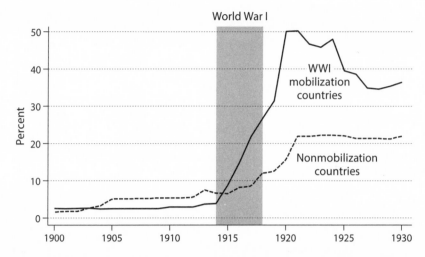

Figure 3.9. World War I and Top Rates of Income Taxation. This figure reports the average top marginal income tax rate for the ten WWI mobilization countries and the seven nonmobilization countries in our sample. Finland, Ireland, and South Korea are excluded because they were not independent during most of the time period.

that precipitated the war was of course a political assassination. The participation of France, the UK, and Canada was not certain until Germany decided to follow the Schlieffen Plan for a general European war that started with a Western offensive.[43]

The evidence in figure 3.9 supports our argument that states began to tax high incomes heavily when they mobilized for World War I. The question of why the war had this effect will preoccupy much of our discussion in the remainder of the book. While most of the analysis on this question will appear in subsequent chapters, here we want to consider two important questions for interpreting the impact of the war: Did income tax rates become more progressive, or did they simply increase across the board? Was the impact of World War I on top rates the same across all countries or did it vary by political regime?

To address the first question we examined changes in progressivity within the top 10 percent of income earners for a subset of four mobilization and four nonmobilization countries in the sample.[44]

Table 3.1. World War I and Progressive Income Taxation

	Prewar	Postwar	Difference
90th percentile			
Mobilization countries	0.0	4.3	4.3
Nonmobilization countries	2.8	3.3	0.5
Difference-in-differences			3.8
99th Percentile			
Mobilization countries	1.4	12.1	10.7
Nonmobilization countries	3.7	5.0	1.3
Difference-in-differences			9.4
99.9th Percentile			
Mobilization countries	2.6	25.0	22.4
Nonmobilization countries	5.7	7.6	1.9
Difference-in-differences			20.6
Top rate			
Mobilization countries	4.3	63.0	58.7
Nonmobilization countries	9.7	16.5	6.8
Difference-in-differences			51.8

Note: The table reports pre (1913) and postwar (1920) average marginal income tax rates for the 90th, 99th, and 99.9th percentiles in mobilization and nonmobilization countries. See Scheve and Stasavage (2010) for sources.

Table 3.1 reports the changes in mobilization and nonmobilization countries in average marginal income tax rates for individuals at the 90th, 99th, and 99.9th percentiles and in top rates before and after World War I.[45] The table shows that the war was associated with increased taxes in mobilization countries compared to non-mobilization countries at all of these high income levels but that these differences increased as incomes increased. For example, marginal taxes at the 90th percentile increase by 3.8 percentage points more in mobilization than nonmobilization countries compared to a difference of 20.6 percentage points at the 99.9th percentile (51.8 percentage points for top rates). The tax rates reported here show that the increases in income tax rates adopted as a result of World War I involved the rich being asked to pay a much larger fraction of their incomes than was the case with individuals who merely had incomes within the top decile. This increase in progressivity is anticipated by our argument about the effect of war mobilization on beliefs about tax fairness but not with a pure revenue maximizing account.

To address the second question, we compare the average top marginal income tax rate in democracies that mobilized for World War I with non-democracies that also mobilized. The seven countries in the first category are Australia, Belgium, Canada, France, New Zealand, the United Kingdom, and the United States, and the three countries in the second category are Austria, Germany, and Italy. Figure 3.10 reports these averages on an annual basis from 1913 to 1919. Here we look at a small window immediately before, during, and after war because both Germany and Austria democratized after the war. In both sets of countries, top rates of income taxation increased on average during the conflict. However, the rates rose much more dramatically in the democratic war mobilization countries than in the nondemocratic ones. In the democracies, the average top rate was

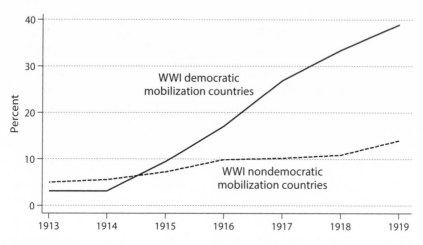

Figure 3.10. World War I and Top Rates by Political Regime Type. This figure reports the average top marginal income tax rate for the seven WWI mobilization countries that were democracies and the three WWI mobilization countries that were not democracies in our sample.

3 percent in 1913 and grew to about 39 percent by 1919 (and would continue to increase after the war) while in the nondemocratic countries, the average rate grew from about 5 percent to 14 percent over the same period. Importantly, after democratizing, both Austria and Germany subsequently adopted high top rates that looked very much like those in the democratic mobilizing countries.

What should we conclude from this difference between democratic and nondemocratic countries? Leaders in both types of countries have an incentive to maintain public support for their governments and commitment to the war effort. One way to do this is to adopt compensatory tax policies that enhance a sense of equal sacrifice in the war effort. That said, the incentives to do this are clearly stronger in democracies where treatment of citizens as equals is part of the bedrock of the political system. The pattern of data in figure 3.10 is therefore consistent with our proposed mechanism for the war effect.[46]

Did mass mobilization for World War II also lead to higher top income tax rates? The simple answer to this question is yes. In 1938, the average top income tax rate among the eleven countries in the sample that mass mobilized for World War II was 47.9 percent. Note that this relatively high rate reflected two facts. First, most of the countries that mobilized for World War II had previously mobilized for World War I, and the positive impact of that conflict persisted. Second, there is some evidence that in responding to the budget deficits created by the economic crises of the interwar period, countries that had participated in World War I were more likely to increase top income tax rates to try to balance their budgets than countries that did not mobilize for World War I. Interestingly, tax debates during the Great Depression returned to some of the language of equal sacrifice that was so prevalent during World War I to meet the new national emergencies of the early 1930s. Despite this somewhat high starting point, the World War II mobilization countries increased their income tax rates during the war and had an average top marginal rate of 75 percent in 1946.

While this "before and after" evidence is striking and consistent with our core arguments, it assumes that rates would have remained the same absent the war. This assumption is somewhat difficult to justify. In the eight countries in the sample that did not mass mobilize for World War II, average top rates increased from 30.5 percent in 1938 to 49.4 percent in 1946. This means that the difference-in-differences estimate of the effect of World War II participation is 8.2 percentage points. This is a substantial effect and is consistent with our argument, but it is smaller in magnitude than the effect of World War I.

The smaller estimated effect of World War II needs to be understood in context. First, most of the countries had already mass mobilized for a war. With rates still high from the previous war, it is logical that another mobilization would have a smaller absolute effect on rates. Second, the quality of the difference-in-differences estimate for World War II is not nearly as strong as that for World War I. The sample of nonmobilization countries includes four countries—Belgium, Denmark, the Netherlands, and Norway—that were occupied during the war and were substantially affected by it. Among the four remaining countries in the nonmobilization sample, Sweden and Switzerland—though not combatants—mobilized a substantial proportion of their population (more than 6 percent in Sweden and more than 12 percent in Switzerland). Further, the timing, scope, and expense of the conflict did not provide the surprise that World War I did. At least some of the already high rates in 1938 were in part due to efforts to rearm in anticipation of future conflict. All of these factors would contribute to attenuating our estimates of the effect of World War II on top income tax rates. It bears repeating that despite these issues, we still see evidence of a large effect of the war on the taxation of high incomes.

Given the evidence that we have presented for the early and mid-twentieth-century mass mobilized conflicts, it is useful to briefly consider what the data have to say about the overall impact of mass mobilization on top rates of income taxation. We have data recording whether a country fought in an international conflict and the extent it mobilized its population from 1816 to the present. This evidence, combined with the inverted-u shape of average top rates presented in figure 3.1, is broadly consistent with our argument that mass war mobilization played a central role in the trajectory of taxation of high incomes. Prior to 1900, rates were low and there was only a single conflict—the Franco-Prussian War—for which at least 2 percent of the population was mobilized to fight.[47] After 1970, no countries had any conflicts with mobilization above the 2 percent threshold. As we have already noted, top income tax rates slowly but surely decreased from this point to the present. In chapter 8 we turn to a more detailed examination of the decline in top income tax rates in the second half of the twentieth century. In regression analyses employing a wide variety of econometric specifications and reported in the online appendix, we find clear evidence that mass mobilization wars are associated with an increase in top rates of income taxation and that it is plausible to give this relationship a causal interpretation.

There is a final feature of the effect of war mobilization; it may have eventually also led to higher taxes in nonmobilizers. We have emphasized that attitudes toward taxing the rich depend on self-interest, fairness considerations, and finally judgments about economic efficiency. When belligerents during and after World War I raised top marginal rates to levels that had previously seemed unimaginable, this showed that it could be done without causing an economic catastrophe. This could have led governments in nonmobilizing countries to alter their calculations about how much to tax the rich. To the extent this was true, it might mean that our difference-in-differences comparisons are underestimating the effect of war on top tax rates.[48]

INITIAL EVIDENCE ON WAR AND INDIVIDUAL ATTITUDES

The preceding evidence about mass warfare is all macro in form; it tells us what countries did, but it says nothing about whether war mobilization led to a shift in individual attitudes and in the type of fairness arguments used to debate taxing the rich. Much of the rest of this book will be devoted to this issue. Tracking individual attitudes is a difficult task given the absence of surveys or opinion polls for the World War I era and their extremely limited availability for World

War II. The United States is the one country for which World War II era surveys can be plausibly used to gauge the effect of mass mobilization on tax attitudes. Two early Gallup surveys provide us with prima facie evidence that entry into war did in fact prompt individuals to favor increased taxation of the rich, though it does not say whether individuals were responding to specific fairness arguments. We present these surveys as suggestive evidence of shifting attitudes before delving into this subject in greater detail in the chapters to follow.

In July 1941, with U.S. participation in World War II still an open question, the Gallup organization asked the following question to a sample of the national adult population: "In order to help pay for defense, the government will be forced to increase income taxes. If you were the one to decide, how much income tax, if any, would you ask a typical family of four with an income of $X to pay?"

Using a split-ballot questionnaire, the survey elicited preferred tax rates for eight different income categories ranging from $1,000 per year to $100,000 per year. In March 1942, after the attack on Pearl Harbor, Gallup asked the identical question, substituting the word "war" for "defense." The timing of the surveys and the corresponding difference in question wording allow for a before and after test of whether war mobilization shifts attitudes in favor of taxing the rich. Figure 3.11 presents the observed opinion changes. The three panels report data for respondents in different socioeconomic status (SES) groups as determined by the interviewer's coding of the respondent on a subjective class scale. The scale ranged from "poor" to "average" to "wealthy." In each panel, the preferred effective tax rate of the median respondent is plotted against the income of the hypothetical family of four referred to in the question. Across all three SES groups, the war had virtually no impact on the tax rate that respondents thought relatively low- and middle-income families should pay. In stark contrast, across all three categories we see a preference for increased taxation of the highest income groups.

The two Gallup polls from the 1940s provide strong preliminary evidence that mass mobilization for war can prompt all income groups to prefer increased taxation of the rich. They do not of course say why individuals preferred to tax the rich. It might have been

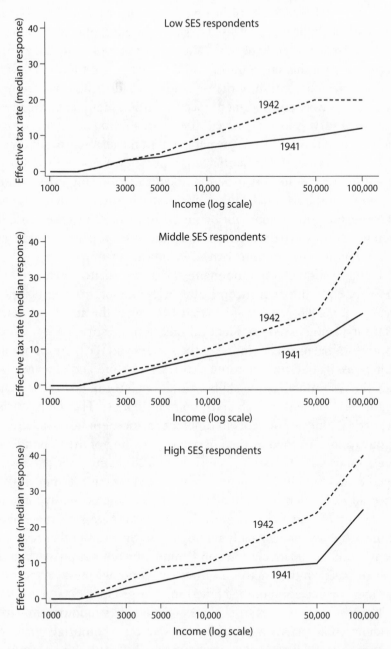

Figure 3.11. World War II and U.S. Opinion on Tax Progressivity. The figure reports median responses to Gallup questions eliciting effective tax preferences in the U.S. public before and after the onset of World War II for a family of four with various levels of income. Preferred tax schedules are reported separately for low, middle, and high SES respondents as determined by the interviewer's coding of the respondent on a subjective class scale. Sources: Gallup Poll #1941-0242 and Gallup Poll #1942-0263.

because of the power of compensatory arguments, as we suggest, or it might have been for other reasons. In the rest of this book we use more detailed evidence on what people said in public debate to try to get at this question.

THE DETERMINANTS OF TOP INCOME TAX RATES

With this chapter we have begun our empirical investigation of when and why countries tax the rich. The data on top marginal income tax rates show a number of important trends for which any "why" explanation will need to account. The idea of the modern income tax and its effectiveness were established from the early nineteenth century. Despite this fact, most countries did not adopt an income tax until the late nineteenth or early twentieth century. Even when they did do so, they set top rates at very low levels—typically in the single digits. Income taxes with high top rates simply did not exist prior to the second decade of the twentieth century. High income tax rates were first adopted in countries mobilized to fight in World War I. After this conflict, sustained differences remained between those countries that fought in the war and those that did not. That said, the war seemed to make the idea of adopting higher rates more plausible in all countries, and in all countries political conflict over the income tax became a central feature of political competition. The Great Depression and the fiscal shortfalls associated with it led countries, especially those that had participated in the war, to raise their top rates to levels similar to those adopted during the war. World War II pushed rates even higher, with top rates in some countries surpassing 90 percent. Although rates fell a bit after the war, they remained quite high during the 1950s and 1960s and then substantially declined in most countries from the late 1970s to the present.[49]

The question we consider in the remainder of this book is how we can best understand the effect of war on taxation of the rich.[50] Can it be explained by the fact that mass mobilization allowed for new compensatory arguments for taxing the rich? The initial evidence we have provided on mass opinion is consistent with this interpretation, but it could also be consistent with others. Chapter 6 provides a broader view of how World War I shifted the types of fairness-based arguments used for taxing the rich. Before we do that, however, it is important to consider several alternative explanations for the war effect that have nothing to do with fairness. Four of these fail to convince and can be quickly dismissed.[51] Two further alternative explanations will require greater discussion in chapters 4 and 5.

A first possibility involves nationalism. Were the rich more willing to be taxed simply because they were filled with patriotic fervor? The problem with this argument is that nationalism could just as well inspire the rest of the population to sacrifice on the battlefield without demanding that the rich also be taxed.[52] We therefore need to consider fairness arguments in order to understand why the rich were asked to perform a fiscal sacrifice.

A second possibility is related to the idea we considered in chapter 1—perhaps top rates increased as the size of government increased. This could account for the war effect if rates on the rich increased because of higher levels of spending due to the war effort. But this argument would logically imply that rates across the income distribution should increase to a similar degree. As we have seen in table 3.1, and as we document further in chapter 5, this was not the case. During the war, governments raised rates more on the rich. Further, figure 3.12 plots the average top income tax rate and the size of government as measured by average tax revenue as a percentage of gross domestic product. The figure strongly suggests that the size of government has not generally driven rates as revenue continued to grow during the twentieth century but top rates of income taxation declined.

A third possibility is that support for taxation increased because governments were spending the money on fighting wars rather than providing peacetime defense or basic public goods. The idea here would be that the taxes the public supports depend on how the money is spent. We find some evidence consistent with this view. At various points during the Second World War, the Gallup polling organization asked respondents whether they thought that the amount of federal income tax they were currently paying was fair.[53] During the war itself, a strikingly high fraction of respondents said that the amount of taxes they paid was fair, an average of 86 percent across four polls conducted between 1943 and 1945. But by February

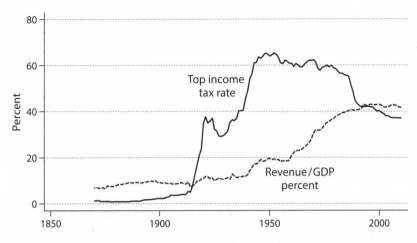

Figure 3.12. Average Top Income Tax Rates and Government Size, 1870–2010.

1946, the first time Gallup asked the same question after the war had ended, the overall percentage of respondents who said they paid a fair amount of income tax dropped to 65 percent. A similar result was obtained when the same question was asked in November 1946.[54] These results are consistent with public opinion about taxation changing depending on how revenue is spent. However, the evidence shows changes in support for taxes on the part of all income groups. Therefore it does not account for why the largest wartime increases in taxes were on the rich.

A fourth possibility is that the political position of the rich was somehow weakened relative to the masses by the war, perhaps because of wartime destruction of their assets or because the poor and middle class gained valuable skills through mobilization, including how to fight. This argument also fails to fit the evidence. Governments in countries where wartime destruction of assets did not take place, such as the United States and Canada, did just as much or more to tax the rich as did governments in countries, such as France, that were devastated by World War I. Similarly, the poor and middle class presumably gained skills across both democratic and nondemocratic countries, but the effect of mobilization on taxation of the rich was more pronounced in democracies.

If these explanations fail to convince, there are two further alternatives that will require more discussion in the chapters to follow. These involve the role of state administrative capacity and simple fiscal necessity, or the fact that governments taxed the rich because that's where the money was.[55] State capacity may have mattered if democratic governments would have preferred to tax the rich, but they lacked the administrative capacity to do so. This would cause us to revisit our conclusions about democracy relative to mass mobilization. Moreover, wars may have increased state capacity and made countries better able to collect income taxes with high rates. To investigate this possibility, in chapter 4 we consider the history of the inheritance tax, a tax that requires less administrative capacity for collection and enforcement when compared with the income tax. Chapter 5 will then have a more complete discussion of the role of fiscal necessity in prompting governments to tax the rich.

CHAPTER FOUR
TAXING INHERITANCE

In the many ways that governments might tax the rich, the taxation of inheritance has throughout history been one of the most controversial. By taking a fraction of the estates of the deceased, governments can limit the concentration of wealth. To the extent that wealth concentration is bad for democracy, this can be a desirable goal. Taxing inheritance can also help reduce inequality of opportunity for future generations. Some will still have the good fortune to begin life with more money than others, but this inequality will be less extreme if a tax first reduces the disparity. Others argue that the taxation of inheritance has major downsides. If saving is seen as good behavior, then inheritance taxation penalizes the virtuous. It also interferes with the ability to provide for one's children; something else that is certainly desirable. In this chapter we consider what history can tell us about when and why governments have taxed inheritance.

The taxation of inheritance is an ancient practice, much older than comprehensive income taxation. In one very frequently cited example, in AD 6, Caesar Augustus established a tax of 5 percent on inheritances with the objective of funding soldiers' salaries. The original version of this story can be found in Cassius Dio's history of Rome.[1] Over the centuries governments have taxed inheritance in different forms. When we turn to the modern period, we see that governments at first often levied flat fees, commonly called stamp taxes. These were associated with an inheritor obtaining legal right (or probate) to the deceased's estate. England established a probate duty in 1694 in imitation of a similar tax that had been levied for some time in Holland. The United States first established a probate duty with the Stamp Tax Act of 1797 in the context of an undeclared war with France. This tax was soon repealed. France was the first country to establish something resembling a modern inheritance tax. This was a tax first approved by the National Assembly in 1791 that was to be levied on the person (or persons) inheriting an estate. In other modern cases, governments have adopted the practice of levying a tax directly on the estate itself, as is the case with the U.S. estate tax that has been in place since 1916. Though stamp taxes, inheritance taxes, and estate taxes certainly differ in their technical details, in the end they are all taxes that impact the ability of those with wealth to pass it on to the next generation. For simplicity's sake, in the remainder of this chapter we therefore use the generic term "inheritance tax" to refer to all three types of taxes.

As we have pointed out previously, one of the key features of inheritance taxes is that in many countries these are very old taxes, predating the income tax by a century or more. There is good reason to believe that the arrival of modern income taxation depended in part on the emergence of an industrial economy with a modern banking system where it was possible to track incomes. Even in an industrial economy, considerable bureaucratic capacity is required to collect an income tax on an annual basis. One can imagine that these problems of capacity are exacerbated when governments seek to levy high rates of income taxation because of the greater incentives for evasion. Historically, inheritance taxes have required much less bureaucratic capacity to collect. They are levied only once per individual, as opposed to annually. Also, those who inherit wealth of the deceased have a strong incentive to disclose this to state authorities in order to obtain title to the wealth. Historically this has made the job of tax authorities considerably less complicated. It is for this reason that a former director of the UK's Inland Revenue observed, "The estate duty is thus to a large extent a self-collecting tax and requires no elaborate machinery for enforcement."[2]

The fact that inheritance taxes require less bureaucracy to collect than do income taxes gives us important leverage on a question we raised in the previous chapter. We observed that the small effect of suffrage extensions on top income tax rates could be attributable to weak state capacity. Perhaps governments elected by universal suffrage would have preferred to levy high top tax rates, but they lacked the ability to implement this. A look at inheritance taxation can help solve this problem. Precisely because inheritance taxes require less bureaucratic machinery to collect, if we see that a democratically elected government fails to tax the rich heavily through this channel, then the explanation must lie elsewhere.

DEBATING INHERITANCE TAXATION

In chapter 2 we offered a general overview of debates about taxing the rich. That discussion was focused above all on taxes on income. Several additional issues arise in debates over inheritance taxation, and so it is worth discussing them before we proceed with our analysis.

Much of the discussion about fairness in inheritance taxation has focused on two key ideas expressed by its advocates. The first notion is that when someone inherits wealth, those who inherit more are in a better position to pay a larger tax. This is the direct analogue of ability to pay arguments for progressive income taxation. Reflecting on the debates of the early twentieth century, in 1926 William Shultz observed, "By far the largest number of champions of progressive rates in inheritance taxes base themselves on the doctrine of 'ability' and its psychological successor 'equality of sacrifice.'" This same assumption continues to motivate today's analytical work.[3]

If the debate over inheritance taxation was limited to the positions taken above, then we might think that political conflict over this topic would simply mimic that found for income taxation. There is also another key difference, however. While income for most people derives from a mix of effort versus exogenous circumstances, in the case of inheritance the amount one receives very clearly has nothing to do with the individual merit of the beneficiary. It is precisely for this reason that, while John Stuart Mill was wary of progressive taxation of income, he was an ardent advocate of taxing inheritance. Ultimately, however, whether one accepts this prescription depends upon whether one sees people as individuals or as members of ongoing family dynasties. The beneficiary of an inheritance certainly did not work for it, but her parents may well have. In most, and maybe all, societies, saving—and in particular savings for one's children—is seen as a desirable trait. It is arguably the conflict between these two very strong and compelling norms—saving for one's children and preserving equal opportunity—that has made debates over inheritance taxation so vociferous.

As with the income tax, debates about inheritance taxation have also focused on economic efficiency. The presence of an inheritance tax may dissuade individuals from saving if they believe that this choice will simply result in their money winding up in state coffers. The more one believes this dissuasion will happen, and that its economic consequences will be negative, the stronger the case for limiting inheritance taxation even if one believes that maintaining it would be fair. In the case of income taxation, efficiency costs emerge when individuals choose to forego earnings because they might be taxed. In the case of inheritance taxation, efficiency costs emerge when individuals choose either to consume their wealth or to not exert effort to accumulate wealth in the first place.

Finally, revenue considerations have, of course, played a role in debates about the inheritance tax. Here we confront a curious reality. Despite the ease of collecting it, inheritance taxation has never composed more than about a tenth of any state's revenues, and in recent decades Federal Estate and Gift Tax Receipts in the United States have comprised only about 1 percent of federal revenues.[4]

A DATASET OF TOP INHERITANCE TAX RATES

We have compiled information on inheritance tax rates in nineteen countries over a period of nearly two centuries (1800–2013). This is the same group of countries for which we have compiled income tax data with the exception of Spain. Compilation of historical rates of inheritance taxation is often a painstaking process. Because rates are not reported in regular publications by national statistical offices or ministries of finance, it is often necessary to consult the original legislative act where a tax rate was set. The inheritance tax dataset was compiled based primarily on original legislation, in addition to other reliable sources.[5] It is important for us to be transparent about what exactly the data on statutory top inheritance tax rates can and cannot tell us. There are three main issues to consider.

First it might be that the threshold for the top rate is set so high that it only applies to a vanishingly small number of estates. As was the case with the income tax, we need to determine when and where the top rates were purely symbolic. We consider this at the end of the chapter by reviewing evidence from complete inheritance tax schedules.

Tax avoidance is a second factor to consider. Some suggest that heavy inheritance taxation becomes meaningless because the rich can engage in estate management by transferring money to their kin or others prior to death, or else by placing their wealth in trusts that are not taxable. This argument should not be overdone. Once they established substantial inheritance taxes, countries moved quickly to create "gift" taxes to guard against this possibility. Moreover, James Poterba demonstrated that in the United States "inter vivos" giving is far below the level one would expect if those with wealth were seeking to maximize dynastic utility by passing on as much as possible to their heirs.[6] In the popular imagination it is also suggested that the wealthy are able to avoid inheritance taxation by placing their funds in trusts. Though trusts may certainly have this effect, we should also consider data on how much trust wealth there is in practice. According to Wojciech Kopczuk and Emmanuel Saez, in 1997 the total value of all trusts in the United States represented only 1.5 percent of total private wealth.[7] This small percentage is evidence against the idea that it is a qualitatively important phenomenon.

A third issue involves valuing and excluding certain assets. Large family estates come in all shapes and sizes and are often composed of many different types of assets. Some of these assets may be difficult to value if they are not marketed frequently. In this case an inheritance tax law must specify how such assets are to be valued, and this can have a major impact on the amount of tax due. In other instances certain assets may be excluded entirely. While dealing with these issues in full for the nineteen countries would require a book-length treatment of its own, we focus on the rates that would apply to inheritances of cash to facilitate comparisons across countries and time.

In addition to the preceding three issues, we should remember that while taxation of inheritance is a primary means governments have used to tax wealth, it certainly has not been the only means at their disposal. Annual property taxes have historically been an important source of revenue for some governments. We therefore might think that wealth was taxed heavily during the nineteenth century, but this occurred via property taxation instead of inheritance taxes. The evidence suggests otherwise. After reviewing European experience with property taxation, Edwin Seligman suggested that during the nineteenth century this form of taxation became "an anachronism" largely because in practice it fell almost exclusively on real estate and not other forms of property.[8] Even in the case of real estate, there is little indication that rates were substantial. In the case of France, direct taxes on property were equivalent to only 2 percent of annual income.[9]

The United States during the nineteenth century was an exception to this European pattern, but even so it would be inaccurate to say that wealth was heavily taxed. Thanks to the work of the U.S. Bureau of the Census, we know total property taxes paid at the local, county, and state level in every U.S. state between 1860 and 1912. We also have the census estimate for total taxable wealth (mostly real estate) and non-taxable wealth (what was called "personal" property). As the country industrialized, personal property made up an increasing share of total national wealth. This was the principal reason why Seligman suggested that the property tax had become an anachronism. However, during this half-century period the sum of property taxes divided by total national wealth remained stable in the 0.6–0.7 percent range annually.[10] If we hypothesize that a wealth holder earned a 5 percent annual return on his property, then a tax on wealth of 0.6–0.7 percent would amount to a tax of between 12 and 14 percent on that income stream. The implication then is that wealth was more heavily taxed in the United States than in Europe, but it was still taxed at levels far below those that would be applied in the twentieth century.

Over the past hundred years several governments have also levied comprehensive annual net wealth taxes. A net wealth tax is a tax that is levied on an annual basis at a specified rate on a tax base representing an individual's or family's net wealth after allowing for deductions and exemptions. Net wealth taxation was most common in the Scandinavian countries, and the best-documented case is Sweden, as discussed in a recent paper by Gunnar Du Rietz and Magnus Henrekson.[11] Sweden's rates of net wealth taxation did not become significant until several decades after the establishment of universal suffrage. Therefore, if we ignore net wealth taxation in this chapter we are not running the risk of falsely concluding that there was no effect from the suffrage. Rates of wealth taxation did become significant in Sweden beginning in the 1940s, but a simple simulation suggests that ignoring them does not lead us to drastically underestimate the extent to which the rich were taxed in Sweden.[12]

It is also the case that at various points in time governments have levied one-off taxes on wealth, often referred to as capital levies. By ignoring these levies we are missing one substantial way in which governments have taxed the rich. However, as we show in chapter 5, capital levies in modern times have most frequently occurred in the immediate wake of wars of mass mobilization. Political parties in many countries debated the imposition of a capital levy following World War I, and among the study countries these taxes were attempted in Italy, Austria, and Germany. In the wake of World War II, Japan imposed a capital levy.[13] While the existence of huge debt overhangs provided an impetus for a one-off levy of this sort, it's also important to recognize that in political debates of the time, fairness in war participation was used as motivation. The material we present in chapters 5 and 6 will demonstrate precisely that.

As an addition to these three issues, we should also emphasize that when it comes to the effect of inheritance law in general, there is more to be considered than simply the level of taxation. Historically, the question of primogeniture has been one of the most hotly debated issues by those concerned about the effect of intergenerational wealth transmission on inequality.[14]

WHEN AND HOW INHERITANCE WAS TAXED

We can consider the data by breaking things up into three historical periods: the long nineteenth century, the period of the two world wars, and the contemporary era. Over these three periods top rates of inheritance taxation have followed a very similar pattern to that seen with the income tax. To aid in visualizing developments, we first show in figure 4.1 average rates of inheritance taxation across the nineteen countries.

During the long nineteenth century, inheritance tax rates invariably remained very low by modern standards. For much of this period inheritances were taxed either through a stamp tax or through a flat rate tax with a specified amount exempted. It's interesting to contrast this with what prominent writers at the time were advocating. John Stuart Mill advocated heavily taxing inheritance so as to minimize inequality of opportunity. This point of view had relatively little initial effect. As late as 1880, the highest marginal rate of inheritance taxation across the nineteen countries was only 3.25 percent. This was the rate that applied in the United Kingdom. Inheritance taxes at such low rates obviously had very little effect on the transmission of wealth from one generation to the next.

During the later decades of the nineteenth century there were renewed debates about inheritance taxation. Several countries that had previously implemented stamp duties now created inheritance taxes that were more comprehensive in scope. Many also called for inheritance taxation to be made progressive, so that those earning more would be taxed at a higher rate. Among the nineteen countries we consider, the United Kingdom was the first to levy a graduated inheritance tax beginning in 1894. Other countries soon followed the UK's lead.

In many quarters and by many scholars the arrival of graduated inheritance taxation was treated as a major victory for the political left.[15] It is important to consider the evidence though before judging the actual magnitude of this change and how far it really moved

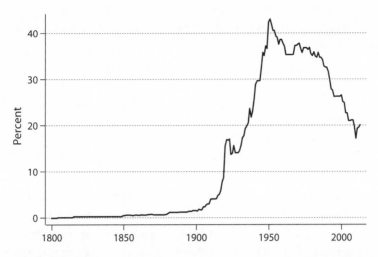

Figure 4.1. Average Top Rates of Inheritance Taxation, 1800–2013. This figure reports the average top marginal inheritance tax rate for the nineteen countries in our sample (each country entering the sample in 1800 or first year of independence).

societies toward taxing the rich. Even in those countries that had established comprehensive inheritance taxes with graduated rates, top rates remained very low. As late as 1913, the country applying the highest rate of inheritance taxation taxed the largest fortunes at a rate of only 17 percent. The average rate across all countries was only 4 percent.[16]

As was the case with the income tax, from 1914 or thereabouts the industrial countries entered into a new era where rates of inheritance tax applied that would have seemed like outright expropriation just a few years prior. Overall, across the nineteen countries the average top rate of inheritance taxation by 1920 stood at 15.5 percent. The highest maximum rate had jumped to an unheard of 75 percent (this was in Weimar Germany). Compared with where they stood prior to World War I, several countries had entered into a new era of progressive inheritance taxation. For the first time in modern history, governments were taxing inheritance sufficiently heavily to have a real impact on the transmission of wealth from one generation to the next.

While governments after 1914 moved, on average, to tax top estates, this average ignores a crucial distinction—governments that had participated in World War I moved to tax estates heavily, whereas non-belligerents did not. By 1920 Germany had raised its top rate of inheritance taxation to 75 percent, followed by 40 percent in the UK, 38 percent in France, and 25 percent in the United States. Now consider what happened in countries that did not mass mobilize for the war. Sweden had a relatively high rate in this group, but this was still only 8 percent, and the average rate in the nonmobilization group was only 5.4 percent.

While top rates of inheritance taxation rose in mobilization countries after 1914, we shouldn't automatically assume that this form of taxation became a major source of government revenue. In fact, just the opposite was the case. For most countries the share of their total revenues coming from inheritance taxation peaked sometime around 1900. Even in the UK, where the move to tax inheritance had been the strongest, inheritance taxes never represented more than 12.4 percent of total tax revenue.[17] From this point the aggregate importance of the inheritance tax grew steadily weaker. Why was this? The inheritance tax became less relevant because it was supplanted by the income tax.

What happened after the First World War? The gap in top rates between former mobilizers and nonmobilizers was largely maintained. In chapter 3 we saw that when the Great Depression arrived, it was above all governments that had previously participated in the First World War that raised their top income tax rates. This was less evident with inheritance taxation with the very notable exception of the United States. In 1936 the Roosevelt administration chose to increase the top rate of inheritance taxation to 70 percent. This built on an earlier increase by the Hoover administration.

If the effect of the Great Depression on top inheritance tax rates was small for most countries, World War II proved to be an entirely different story. At the time of the Munich crisis in 1938 the average top rate of inheritance taxation was 21.8 percent. By the time the United States dropped atomic bombs on Hiroshima and Nagasaki this average rate stood at 32.3 percent, a significant increase. For the reasons already presented in chapter 3, it is more difficult to conduct an effective difference-in-differences comparison for mobilizers and nonmobilizers in World War II. Among the nineteen countries for which we have inheritance tax rates, few did not mobilize for the war, and all were affected by the war in some way.

The first few decades after the Second World War were a period of relative stasis for inheritance taxation. Apart from France, which lowered its top rate from 30 percent to 15 percent in 1960, there were no significant changes in top rates, and in many cases there was no change at all. In the United States the top rate for the estate tax remained at 77 percent from 1940 all the way to 1976.

Observers of contemporary trends in the United States often paint a picture where the assault on inheritance taxation is explained by phenomena specific to the United States. These include the importance of lobbying groups, campaign contributions, and clever rhetorical devices, in particular the relabeling of "the estate tax" as "the death tax."[18] It is important to realize, though, that the movement away from inheritance taxation has been a general one, and it has occurred in countries with very different types of political systems. Many might be surprised to learn that the first of the countries to abolish its inheritance tax was America's neighbor to the north, and this despite Canada's reputation for having more social democratic policies. The Canadian government abolished its inheritance tax in 1971, and it was followed by Australia in 1979, New Zealand in 1993, Sweden in 2004, and Austria in 2009. So, if the United States ever abandons the estate tax, it would hardly be at the forefront of this movement.[19]

WEALTH INEQUALITY AND INHERITANCE TAXATION

Any satisfactory account of why inheritance has been taxed needs to show both why some governments moved to tax large fortunes heavily and why these same governments later reversed or at least substantially modified the policy. Much existing work on the subject tries to account for either the rise or the demise of inheritance taxation, but not both simultaneously. Here we examine these trends. Once we look at the timing of political changes and tax changes in different countries, we can hope to disentangle the causal role of inequality, democracy, and mass warfare.

In chapter 1 we offered three reasons why citizens may want to tax the rich more heavily when inequality is high. These involved self-interest, the fact that inequality of outcomes might signal inequality of opportunity, and finally fears for the stability of a democratic form of government. In chapter 3 we found very little support for the idea that these three motivations prompt governments, on average, to increase top rates of income taxation when income inequality is high. We now ask the same question for wealth inequality and arrive at the same conclusion.

Long-run data on wealth inequality are harder to come by than are data on income inequality. With this said, we do have high-quality wealth inequality data for nine of the study countries thanks to Jesper Roine and Daniel Waldenström, who have compiled the most comprehensive dataset available.[20] These data are expressed in terms of the percentage of total national wealth held by either the top 5 percent or the top 1 percent of individuals. We use the latter measure in our analysis to follow. In other words, these are exactly like the top income shares with which readers may be more familiar, but in this case concentration of wealth, rather than income, is the focus. The Roine and Waldenström study is a compilation of the results of individual national studies on wealth inequality, and in some cases there are multiple studies per country. Roine and Waldenström used multiple studies per country when no one individual study provided adequate time coverage. It should be evident that compiling data from so many different sources, often using different methodologies, is difficult, and so the results of any analysis of this data should be viewed as informative but treated with some caution.

To consider the effect of wealth inequality on inheritance tax rates, consider first the situation in 1914. At this date countries with greater wealth inequality did indeed tax inheritance at higher rates (see figure 4.2). So, in the UK, the top 1 percent held 69 percent of the country's wealth, and the UK government applied a top inheritance tax rate of 15 percent. In Norway, in contrast, the top 1 percent owned only 37 percent of the wealth, and the government applied a top inheritance tax rate of only 4 percent. The pattern is more general. Across the nine countries in 1914 there was a tight

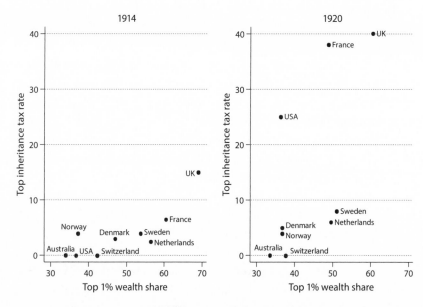

Figure 4.2. Wealth Inequality and Inheritance Taxes, 1914 and 1920. This figure plots the top inheritance tax rate against the top 1 percent wealth share for 1914 and 1920 for the nine countries for which we have data and that are independent countries in both years. See text and notes for sources.

correlation between the prevailing level of wealth inequality and the top marginal rate of inheritance taxation.[21] The correlation coefficient between these two variables was 0.82. This correlation may well have reflected a causal effect running from the former to the latter. In 1914 inheritance taxation above non-negligible levels was a recent occurrence while wealth inequality was not. This implies that if one of these two things caused the other, then the causal chain could only have gone from high inequality to high taxation.[22]

But there is an important twist to the story. Governments in 1914 chose higher tax rates when inequality was high, but they still didn't choose rates that were high enough to have an impact on wealth inequality. Take the UK example as an illustration. Those who died would still be passing on 85 percent of their estate to the next generation, a rate sufficiently high that the level of wealth inequality would diminish only very slowly. It was almost as if governments made a gesture toward reducing inequality where it was particularly high, but the measures they adopted were wholly insufficient for the task at hand.

Take next the situation in the nine countries in 1920, after the end of the First World War. This was a new context in which some governments levied inheritance taxes that were high enough to have a sizeable effect on the distribution of wealth. Among the nine countries we still see a phenomenon whereby more unequal countries taxed inheritance heavily, but this link was now weaker than before. The reason for this is that it was only the war participants that raised rates substantially. By 1920 the UK had increased its top rate to 40 percent, but the Netherlands, which had a top 1 percent wealth share of 50 percent, still had a top inheritance tax rate of only 6 percent. Likewise, among low inequality countries some maintained low rates of inheritance taxation, but in the United States a top rate of 25 percent was now applied. The conclusion from this exercise is clear. Even if wealth inequality may have prompted states to tax inheritance more heavily, it had a much smaller effect than did war mobilization.

The next step is to consider the long-run relationship between inheritance taxation and wealth inequality. To investigate this we use the same two strategies as in chapter 3. We first examine static correlations of today's level of wealth inequality and today's top tax rate. We then examine the dynamic relationship, performing a Granger causality test.

To look at static correlations, in figure 4.3 we have plotted the average top 1 percent wealth share for six selected countries for each year between 1911 and 2007.[23] In the same figure we also plot the top marginal rate of inheritance taxation. What does the graph suggest about the relationship between the two series? If we restrict our attention to the first half of the twentieth century, then casual observation might suggest that governments were indeed raising inheritance tax rates in order to produce a lower level of wealth inequality. Shift forward to the second half of the twentieth century, and we see a much different picture. Top inheritance tax rates have declined quite markedly.

The next step in our analysis is to conduct a Granger test of the dynamic relationship between wealth inequality and inheritance

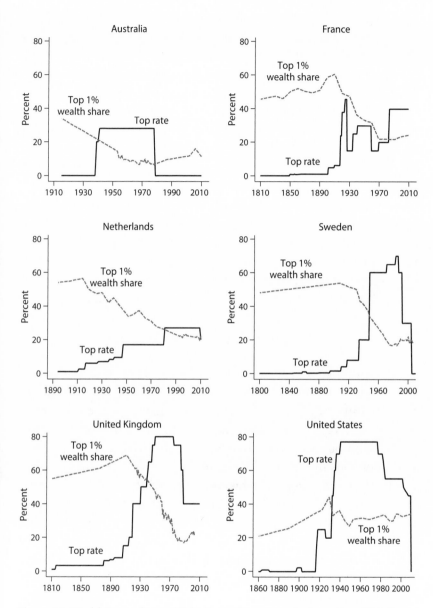

Figure 4.3. Wealth Inequality and Inheritance Taxes over the Long Run. This figure plots the top 1 percent wealth share and the top inheritance tax rate from the first year of available wealth inequality data to 2010 for six selected countries. See text and notes for sources.

taxation. The level of wealth inequality prevailing today is primarily determined by past rates of inheritance taxation and not current rates. Therefore, if inheritance taxation reduces wealth inequality, we should see that past tax rates are negatively correlated with current wealth inequality. Likewise, if current tax rates are chosen in response to levels of inequality, this will only be with a lag because wealth inequality data only become available with time. Therefore, we should expect to see that past levels of wealth inequality are positively correlated with today's top tax rates.[24]

Overall, when performing the Granger test we see some evidence that inheritance taxation has helped reduce the concentration of wealth across the countries for which we have sufficient data. However, we fail to see any evidence that governments have chosen higher inheritance tax rates just because wealth inequality is high. When they do appear to have done so, as in the first decade of the twentieth century, the magnitude of this effect has been minimal.[25]

DEMOCRACY AND INHERITANCE TAXATION

What about the effect of democracy on inheritance taxation? It may be the case that citizens would like to tax top fortunes heavily, but they can only do this when they have the right to vote and to freely elect their leaders. Many today might believe that democratic countries should be more likely to adopt progressive taxation of inheritance. Scholars in the first decades of the twentieth century thought exactly the same thing. So, in his work, *The Taxation of Capital*, Alfred Walter Soward observed that the adoption of graduated inheritance taxation in the United Kingdom

> had, indeed, become inevitable in the concluding years of the 19th century in response to public opinion which, due in no small degree to the ever increasing democratic influence on public finance, had for some time past been focusing itself upon a demand for equality of fiscal sacrifice by the machinery of some tax on property regulated by a scale of rates increasing in amount as the value of the taxable mass grew larger and larger.[26]

It is clear from this statement that Soward believed public opinion would have its greatest influence in a democratic context. Soward's comments join those of other authors mentioned in previous chapters who argue that democracy influences tax progression more generally.

The relationship between democracy and inheritance taxation is a subject that we have considered extensively elsewhere.[27] We found after using a battery of tests that there was very little evidence that the expansion of the suffrage was associated with an increase in top inheritance tax rates. One simple way to show the small effect of universal suffrage is to look at the average of top inheritance tax rates at the date suffrage became universal (14.1 percent) and the average of rates ten years after suffrage was passed (17.4 percent). There is some evidence of a suffrage effect here, but it is quite small.[28] Also, this simple method does not take account of any other factors that occurred concurrently with a suffrage expansion.

Even if the advent of universal suffrage sufficed to explain the arrival of heavy inheritance taxation, to sustain this interpretation about the effect of democracy we must also account for more recent trends. Top rates of estate taxation have dropped dramatically in many countries, and in other instances this form of taxation has been abolished outright. So how is this possible in a democracy? This is another important reason why the argument that universal suffrage on its own would deliver significant change is ultimately unconvincing.

Finally, what about the conjunction of inequality and democracy? Perhaps governments only taxed top fortunes heavily when inequality created a demand for this and when universal suffrage gave voice to these demands. The evidence doesn't support this explanation either. Think first of what happened at the beginning of the twentieth century. Each of the countries for which we have wealth inequality data adopted universal suffrage at roughly the same time, but only some moved to tax inheritance heavily. Also, each of the countries for which we conducted the estimations discussed previously was a democracy for the entire period, with the brief exception of France under German occupation during World War II. So, our test of the effect of inequality was already a test restricted to democracies.

THE IMPORTANCE OF WAR MOBILIZATION

As was the case for the income tax, the rise of inheritance taxation can best be understood by the arrival of an era of mass warfare. Its eventual demise can likewise be linked to the end of this era. We concentrate first on showing that mass mobilization for war mattered for inheritance taxation. In subsequent chapters we ask why it mattered.

The First World War ushered in a new era of inheritance taxation. But how do we know it was the war that drove this movement and not other factors occurring at the same time? This was a period where numerous countries were expanding political participation. The close of the First World War was also contemporaneous with the Bolshevik revolution in Russia, an act that spread fear among elites throughout Western Europe. This may have made elites more responsive to demands for taxing the rich as a way to avoid revolutionary upheaval.

As we saw with the income tax, the best way to judge the impact of World War I is to conduct a difference-in-differences comparison. Using a start date of 1914 and an end date of 1920 we can compare the change in top inheritance tax rates in war mobilization countries with the change in nonmobilization countries. This analysis will also help control for other plausible factors that may have driven top rates. All of the countries in our comparison group had adopted universal suffrage by the time this period ended. Likewise, the fear of Bolshevism was widespread throughout Western Europe. To the extent it had an effect, we should expect this effect to be fairly uniform.

The results of our difference-in-differences comparison are clear. Countries that did not mass mobilize for World War I increased their top rate of inheritance taxation on average by a little less than two percentage points between these two dates. So the rates were essentially unchanged. Governments in the mobilized countries increased their tax rates by eighteen percentage points on average—a far larger amount.[29] There was, however, a key difference between wartime developments with income taxation and those with inheritance taxation. Participant countries tended to increase their income tax rates during the war itself, whereas these same countries tended to wait until immediately after the war to raise their top marginal rates of inheritance taxation.

There is little doubt that the effect of war mobilization on the inheritance tax was intimately related to compensatory demands for the conscription of wealth. We build the case for this claim in chapters 5 and 6. At first blush, taxing inheritance might seem a less obvious way to achieve this goal than would something like a one-off levy on capital. What took place in practice was that compensatory demands created an environment in which there was political pressure for increasing all existing taxes on the rich, the inheritance tax among them.

OVERALL PROGRESSIVITY OF INHERITANCE TAXES

For reasons of feasibility we have focused on top marginal rates of inheritance taxation. As was the case with the income tax, by focusing on the top rate we have been able to collect information covering a broad number of countries and a very long time span. For a study of taxing the rich, the top rate is also particularly relevant. The risk, however, is that the threshold above which the top rate applies is so high that only a handful of estates are ever taxed at this level in a given year. There have indeed been cases like this within the nineteen study countries. So, for example, in France from 1902 to 1948 the top marginal rate of inheritance taxation applied for inheritances exceeding 50 million francs, but this involved fewer than ten cases annually.[30] To address this question, for a smaller set of countries we were able to collect not just the top marginal rates of inheritance taxation, but also the full rate schedule for the taxation of inheritance. To make best sense of this information, table 4.1 shows the marginal rate applying for inheritances expressed in different multiples of per capita GDP. The table distinguishes figures from countries that had recently mobilized for one of the two world wars by placing the number in boldface.

We can see from table 4.1 that the apparent effect of war is again very large. Take first the difference-in-differences comparison between

Table 4.1. Marginal Inheritance Tax Rates by Size of Inheritance

Country	Estate Size	1850	1900	1925	1950	1975	2000
United Kingdom	1	0.0	0.0	**0.0**	**0.0**	0.0	0.0
	10	2.5	1.0	**2.0**	**1.0**	5.0	0.0
	100	4.1	3.0	**4.0**	**15**	43.0	40.0
	1,000	3.4	4.5	**14**	**60**	70.0	40.0
	10,000	3.1	7.0	**28**	**80**	75.0	40.0
United States	1	0.0	0.0	**0.0**	**0.0**	0.0	0.0
	10	0.0	0.0	**0.0**	**0.0**	11.0	0.0
	100	0.0	0.8	**1.0**	**30**	35.0	55.0
	1,000	0.0	1.5	**9.0**	**45**	73.0	55.0
	10,000	0.0	2.3	**30**	**77**	77.0	55.0
France	1	1.2	1.3	**4.8**	**15**	5.0	0.0
	10	1.2	1.3	**9.6**	**25**	20.0	0.0
	100	1.2	1.3	**18**	**30**	20.0	40.0
	1,000	1.2	1.3	**34**	**30**	20.0	40.0
	10,000	1.2	1.3	**42**	**30**	20.0	40.0
Japan	1	0.0	0.0	0.0	**0.0**	0.0	0.0
	10	0.0	1.5	1.2	**0.0**	0.0	0.0
	100	0.0	1.5	2.0	**0.0**	50.0	50.0
	1,000	0.0	4.5	5.5	**0.0**	75.0	70.0
	10,000	0.0	7.0	9.5	**90**	75.0	70.0
Sweden	1	0.0	0.5	0.6	1.0	5.0	10.0
	10	0.1	0.7	1.8	11	44.0	30.0
	100	0.2	1.3	3.4	40	58.0	30.0
	1,000	0.3	1.5	8.0	52	65.0	30.0
	10,000	0.3	1.5	8.0	60	65.0	30.0
Netherlands	1	0.0	0.0	1.5	4.0	7.0	8.0
	10	0.0	1.0	3.0	7.0	13.0	23.0
	100	0.0	1.0	4.5	13.0	17.0	27.0
	1,000	0.0	1.0	6.0	17.0	17.0	27.0
	10,000	0.0	1.0	6.0	17.0	17.0	27.0

Note: Estate sizes are measured as a multiple of per capita GDP. In cases where a country had not yet established an inheritance tax, the marginal rate is listed as 0.0. For Japan, rates listed for 1900 are those enacted in 1905. Tax rates for periods immediately following mass mobilization for war are highlighted in bold. See Scheve and Stasavage (2012) for sources.

1900 and 1925. Using the case of an estate equal to either one thousand times per capita GDP or ten thousand times per capita GDP, we see a substantial increase in the marginal tax rate for each of the three countries that mobilized heavily for World War I. In the case of the three countries that did not do so, rates changed very little in Japan and increased only to moderate levels in Sweden and the Netherlands. When we next consider a difference-in-differences comparison between 1925 and 1950 the picture is somewhat more mixed, although still suggestive of a war effect. Among war mobilizers, the United States, the United Kingdom, and Japan all increased taxes on large estates, but France did not. Among countries that stayed out of World War II, rates remained more moderate, but Sweden was a notable exception.

CONCLUSION

There is good evidence that inheritance taxation has played a role in reducing wealth inequality. There is much less evidence that this has been the result of governments simply responding to wealth inequality. As was the case with the income tax, mass mobilization for war has been the most prominent and recurrent factor shaping the evolution of top rates of inheritance taxation. In chapter 6 we conduct a detailed investigation of why top income and inheritance tax rates went up during wartime. But first, in chapter 5 we consider the broader context for taxing the rich. We need to make sure that high wartime income and inheritance taxes reflected increased overall progressivity of the tax system.

CHAPTER FIVE

TAXES ON THE RICH IN CONTEXT

The historical evidence in the previous two chapters tells us that transitions to democracy tended not to result in large increases in top rates of income and inheritance taxation. But, such changes did take place during periods of mass mobilization for war. These conclusions seem clear, but three important questions remain unanswered.

Were there additional taxes on the rich that did not come in the form of standard inheritance or income taxation? Ignoring these other taxes might lead us to biased conclusions. For example, perhaps when governments expanded the suffrage they did not raise top rates of income and inheritance taxation, but they taxed the rich in other ways. A look at other ways in which governments have taxed the rich reinforces our general conclusion: compensatory arguments have had the greatest impact on taxation of the rich. We can see this in particular with the imposition of war profits taxes and capital levies.

Were increases in top rates a sign that tax systems were becoming more progressive? We have already established that when top income tax rates went up, the income tax system as a whole became more progressive. The same holds true for the inheritance tax. But how much did other taxes borne principally by the poor and middle classes increase at the same time? There is no doubt that when governments financed the two world wars they raised indirect taxes, in addition to direct taxes. The incidence of many of these indirect taxes fell on groups other than the rich. It needs to be established how our overall conclusions about taxation of the rich are altered once we take this into consideration. Looking at the overall tax burden on different income groups can help address this issue, taking into account both direct and indirect taxes. As part of this, we also briefly consider the allocation of government spending between different groups, as well as the role of government debt. The evidence shows that our overall conclusions still hold even after accounting for the incidence of indirect taxation, spending, and debt.

Was an increased tax burden on the rich during wartime dictated by simple necessity? Perhaps governments needed money, and they took it where it was easiest to find it. This would be a bit like the reason why Willie Sutton said that he robbed banks—because that's where the money was. In this chapter we show that this argument also fails to convince.

CAPITAL LEVIES AND WAR TAXES

In addition to taxing the rich through income and inheritance taxes, some governments during the twentieth century implemented one-off capital levies. A number of countries also established war profits taxes or excess profits taxes. Though these latter two terms were sometimes used interchangeably, the strict interpretation of the first is that it was a tax on all company profits earned during the war, whereas the second was a tax on the excess of company profits earned above a peacetime benchmark. To make matters even more complicated, some postwar capital levies were one-off impositions on all capital, whereas others were levies only on what was judged to be capital accumulated during the war. Readers interested in investigating the details further should consult the thorough 1941 study by Hicks, Hicks, and Rostas. In this section we confine ourselves to reporting instances where countries made use of one or more of these taxes. The arguments made in favor of capital levies, excess profits taxes, and war profits taxes inevitably took a compensatory form—given that many were sacrificing or had sacrificed, those who had done well out of the war should help pay for the war.

Capital levies are actually a very old idea, and they can have significant consequences for top fortunes. The question for us is when these levies have occurred and how it influences our broad conclusions about democracy, war, and wealth. Capital levies existed during the classical period in Athens, as well as in Rome. Some medieval rulers also imposed them. As an example, in AD 1188, wealth holders in England were obliged to pay a tax of one-tenth of the value of rent and movables in order to help finance the Second Crusade to expel Saladin from Jerusalem.[1] It would hardly be surprising if we concluded that most early capital levies were associated with war, because this is basically all that governments did with their money at this time.

Barry Eichengreen has charted the twentieth-century history of capital levies showing when they occurred and what the outcome was.[2] Based on this evidence, it seems clear that levies on capital have continued to occur for the same reason that they always did—because of war. However, in keeping with the new context of mass warfare, the rates imposed in twentieth-century levies were substantially higher than had been seen in prior centuries. In the wake of World War I the imposition of a capital levy was a very hotly debated topic in many countries across the European continent. In Czechoslovakia, Austria, and Hungary, governments implemented levies with marginal rates reaching up to 30 percent.[3] Postwar levies in Germany and Italy also had very high top marginal rates, although with a provision that they could be paid over a term of thirty or twenty years, respectively.[4]

In the United Kingdom the idea of a general levy on capital first found support both from those on the left of the political spectrum as well as from some economists, such as Arthur Pigou. He made an explicit compensatory argument in favor of a capital levy:

> From the statistics of estates passing at death it can be deduced that practically all the material capital of the country is held by persons over twenty years of age; that persons over forty-five, who constitute about one-third of these persons, own about three-fourths of the whole; so that the representative man over forty-five holds about six times as much material capital as the representative man between twenty and forty-five. But young

men, who excel older men in physical strength, have been forced to give their physical strength in the war, while older men have been exempted. The fact that old men excel young men so greatly in financial strength suggests that the balance might be partly adjusted, and something less unlike equality of sacrifice secured, by a special levy whose incidence would in the main fall upon persons exempted from military service.[5]

In the end the United Kingdom did not adopt a capital levy, but one of the main reasons for this was that it was recognized that very high top rates of income and inheritance taxation were already serving essentially the same purpose.

In addition to implementing one-off capital levies, during the twentieth century wartime governments also levied special taxes on excess profits or war profits. The story of war profits and of public dislike of them is an old one, extending in the United States back to the Civil War and even the American war of independence.[6] In 1937, the Gallup Poll asked Americans whether they thought the government should regulate profits during wartime. Fully 70 percent of those surveyed responded affirmatively.[7] In 1938, the British Institute of Public opinion asked whether profits of armaments manufacturers should be limited. Eighty-one percent of respondents supported restrictions.[8] Given these poll results, it is no surprise to see the following statement in the 1941 survey by Hicks, Hicks, and Rostas: "The sense of unfairness is particularly aroused when the high incomes are earned, not by those who are in the centre of the war effort, but by those who are on the edge of it." They then added:

> It is undoubtedly because of this feeling of unfairness that most of the schemes we are going to study have been imposed; even if it is recognized that the economic incentive to efficiency may be damaged by them, they are still considered to be justified as means of fostering national unity and maintaining morale.[9]

In the case of the two world wars, the unprecedented level of mobilization brought with it unprecedented opportunities for profit and unprecedented debate over what to do about the problem. Belligerent governments felt compelled to respond in some way with legislation designed to tax the windfall profits that many firms earned as a result of increased demand for their goods. The story of these war taxes tells us something about the extent to which the rich were taxed. It also tells us something about the terms of the debate.

Participants in World War I did not expect at first to be fighting a long war, and so there was a delay before debates began about the issue of war profits. The measures eventually adopted by governments were extensive but also sometimes only partially effective. This meant that political debates about taxing war profits would continue after war's end. The United Kingdom adopted an Excess Profits Duty in 1915 that remained in place through 1921.[10] The tax was a massive source of funds, bringing in one quarter of total tax revenue during the period. It was levied at variable rates that averaged out at 63 percent, but because of exemptions the average effective rate during this period was more like 34 percent. The United Kingdom was certainly not alone in imposing this type of tax. In the United States, in 1917 Congress passed legislation establishing an excess profits tax. The French government waited until two years after the war's outbreak, but it too eventually established an excess profits tax.[11] Meanwhile, Italy imposed a number of extra war-related duties on profits.

All the countries referred to in the previous section were democracies during the First World War. The autocratic countries that participated in the war also passed legislation to tax war profits. However, this legislation was less restrictive than in the case of the more democratic belligerents. Equally importantly, the autocratic countries were less effective at implementing this legislation. Germany still had a decentralized fiscal system with little revenue generated at the federal level. In the case of Austria-Hungary and Russia, fiscal institutions were simply less developed. These institutional differences make it difficult for us to know whether autocracies during World War I taxed war profits less because they were autocracies or because they had weaker institutions.

Debates about war profits took place not only in countries that were direct participants in the conflict. In neutral countries demands for war profits taxation also arose because of the windfalls that some industries enjoyed from increased demand for their products by belligerents. This was particularly the case in the Scandinavian countries, although marginal rates on these taxes were substantially lower than in belligerent countries.[12] This result is logical given the type of compensatory claims that could be made. Some citizens in Scandinavian countries were benefiting from a windfall, but this was not a windfall generated by other citizens sacrificing on the battlefield.

Now consider the case of war profits during World War II. On the Allied side the authorities generally adopted war profits taxes that were even more extensive than those adopted during the First World War. In the United Kingdom the excess profits tax provided in principle for a 100 percent marginal rate of taxation on those profits in excess of a prewar standard. In the United States the Roosevelt administration also adopted a very restrictive regime for taxing war profits, even if taxes in the United States did not reach the same marginal rates as in Great Britain. In France the government took measures to restrict war profits as early as 1939, but occupation soon rendered these impositions meaningless. As a result, debates about war profits would reemerge after the liberation of the country. We return to this question in chapter 8. Finally, war profits taxes were not unique to the Allied side. Germany passed a war profits tax in 1939, albeit with substantially lower rates than existed in the United States or UK. Japan also imposed an excess profits tax during World War II.

During the Second World War belligerent governments also addressed the issue of potential war profits in other ways. In some cases they intervened directly to limit incomes and redistribute wealth. In the United States, the government made a brief attempt to limit the pretax incomes of chief executives. In 1942, the Roosevelt administration placed a cap on after-tax salaries equivalent to $25,000 a year. However, Congress soon repealed this measure. A more long-lasting regulation involved a limitation on salary increases. The salary increase limit was left in place until 1946, and it had some effect on executive pay trends during the period.[13] Of more importance to the rich in some countries were the nationalizations of industries that took place immediately after 1945. In France a number of industries were nationalized, with their stockholders receiving either below market values for their shares or in some cases no compensation at all. The latter occurred in the case of Renault, which was judged to have collaborated with the enemy during the war. We return to this issue in chapter 8.

Overall, when we consider the broader context for taxation or levies imposed on the rich, our core conclusions are only reinforced. During the two world wars and in their immediate wake, the rich were taxed to an extent that previously would have seemed unimaginable. The story of war taxes and capital levies only reinforces our interpretation that compensatory arguments provide the most powerful political support for taxation of the rich. The question to which we now turn is whether other forms of taxation imposed equally heavy burdens on other segments of the population during wartime. To examine this we need to inquire especially about indirect taxation.

THE INCIDENCE OF INDIRECT TAXATION

In the previous section we concluded that, as with income and inheritance taxation, other taxes targeted at the rich have been closely associated with mass warfare. But so far we have said little about wartime levies that may have hit the poor and middle classes most heavily. This would have been principally a result of indirect taxes on common consumption goods. These are usually thought to be taxes with a regressive incidence because the poor and middle classes spend a larger fraction of their income on such items. There is no question that governments increased indirect taxes during the two world wars. We also noted in chapter 1 that prior to the nineteenth century, indirect taxes had been the primary means by which most European governments had financed their wars. The real question for us is whether the effect of indirect taxes during the nineteenth and twentieth centuries was large enough to outweigh the impact of increased income and inheritance taxes on the rich. In this section we present evidence to show that this was not the case. Even after the impact of indirect taxation is taken into account, wartime governments increased taxes on the rich more than the rest.

Calculating overall tax burdens is not a simple task. Ideally, we would like to know the percentage of an individual's income that winds up being paid in taxes of any form, be they direct or indirect. One option would be to assume that the burden of indirect taxation is borne mainly by the poor, that direct taxes impact mainly the rich, and so the relative share of indirect to direct taxes is a measure of the overall progressivity of the tax system. The problem with this is that some indirect taxes, such as those on luxury goods, are borne by the rich. Likewise, in the modern era direct taxes like the income tax have fallen not only on top incomes but also on the middle class. The issue is further complicated by the fact that with indirect taxation, an increase in the tax on a good may either be borne by the producer in the form of lower profits or passed on to the consumer in the form of higher prices. Finally, conclusions about the burden of indirect taxation depend upon assumptions about the goods each group consumes and how much it consumes.[14] Early tax burden studies of the sort that we consider in this section typically assumed for simplicity that either the entirety or a large part of indirect taxation was passed on to the consumer. The risk of this assumption is that the studies might overestimate the extent to which indirect taxation results in a decrease in progressivity. If we can show that war mobilization was associated with increased progressivity even under this assumption, our conclusions will be robust.

By far the best historical evidence on the overall tax burden comes from the United Kingdom. In 1919, Herbert Samuel published a study entitled "The Taxation of the Various Classes of the People" in which he attempted to calculate the overall tax burden on British households earning different incomes prior to and immediately following the First World War. One of Samuel's main conclusions was that tax changes adopted during the course of the war had made the British tax system substantially more progressive. This is important evidence that reinforces our main conclusions.[15]

Building on the study by Samuel, in 1943 G. Findlay Shirras and L. Rostas published a more extensive analysis of the burden of British taxation. They provide figures on how much tax a family of five would pay for specific fiscal years between 1903 and 1941. The calculation includes all income and surtaxes, in addition to most indirect taxes. The results are shown in table 5.1.

Table 5.1. Total Burden of Taxation in the United Kingdom, 1903–1941

£	1903	1913	1918	1923	1925	1930	1937	1941
100	5.6	5.4	9.9	14.1	11.9	11.0	10.4	19.1
150	4.5	4.4	9.0	13.5	11.6	10.9	9.5	16.7
200	4.8	4.0	7.9	11.8	10.2	9.6	8.4	14.8
500	5.3	4.4	10.2	8.0	6.2	4.5	5.6	18.4
1,000	6.1	5.2	16.9	14.1	11.0	9.7	11.8	32.2
2,000	5.7	4.9	24.0	17.9	15.2	15.7	18.0	40.5
5,000	5.5	6.7	36.6	28.5	23.2	26.3	29.2	56.1
10,000	5.0	8.0	42.5	37.1	31.2	35.8	39.1	68.3
20,000	4.9	8.3	47.6	42.3	37.5	43.5	47.9	80.7
50,000	4.8	8.4	50.6	48.0	44.4	51.4	56.7	90.7

Note: The estimate includes the burden measured as a percent of income from both indirect and direct taxes, including the incidence of death duties. Excluded taxes are non-exchequer taxes such as social insurance contributions, the petrol duty, and the purchase tax. All estimates are for the case of a married taxpayer with three children under the age of 16. Data are for fiscal years with the column title showing the beginning of the fiscal year. Data from Shirras and Rostas (1943), p. 24, p. 53. Samuel (1919) is the original source for the 1903, 1913, and 1918 estimates.

A first feature of the Shirras and Rostas results is what they have to say about taxation prior to World War I. In fiscal 1903 the overall tax schedule resembled that of a flat tax levied at around 5 percent of total income. This means that the burden of the income tax and of indirect taxes essentially canceled each other out. It was as if the compensatory arguments made in the nineteenth century about the need for a progressive income tax to offset regressive indirect taxes had resulted in the reestablishment of treatment as equals.

Now consider the figure for fiscal 1913/14. This figure would reflect the changes introduced during the People's Budget of 1909/10, but it would not yet reflect changes introduced during the First World War. The People's Budget is conventionally described as having made the British tax system substantially more progressive. To a certain point this was true, but the extent of the change needs to be put into perspective. Whereas the tax burden for the poor and middle classes remained largely unchanged, the tax burden for the rich now crept up from about 5 percent to around 8 percent of total income. This may have been an unprecedented change, but it was very small compared to what would soon follow.

If the People's Budget increased progressivity somewhat, the effect of World War I was on an entirely different level. By the end of the war, the tax burden on the lowest income groups had doubled, but the burden on the richest had increased more than fivefold. This is an extraordinary jump, and it shows that wartime increases in indirect taxation did not offset the massive increases in income and other taxes on the highest earners. It is also interesting to consider what happened after the end of World War I and during World War II. After the 1918/19 fiscal year, the overall tax burden on low- and middle-income groups remained essentially unchanged through the beginning of World War II. For higher income groups, the overall tax burden fell somewhat in the mid-1920s (between 6 and 13 percentage points), but was still dramatically higher than before the war. Between 1925 and 1937, rates on higher incomes returned to their end of World War I levels. This increase had two sources. First, Britain during the 1920s and 1930s was in a state of near permanent fiscal crisis. Second, by the mid-1930s, the international environment had become more dangerous, and the UK engaged in some rearmament (though not as much as Churchill and others advocated). An additional and more dramatic increase in progressivity occurred during World War II, as we can see based on the data for the 1941/42 fiscal year.

It is evident from the Shirras and Rostas data that mass warfare was associated with a drastic increase in the overall progressivity of the tax system in the United Kingdom. Ideally, we would have access to similarly detailed studies tracking tax burdens over time in the other countries. Unfortunately this is not the case. There are nonetheless some scattered studies for a few countries that provide useful information.

The most detailed study on French tax burdens during the First World War was conducted by Robert Murray Haig. Though his assessment was far less detailed than that of Shirras and Rostas, Haig did provide a comparison of the relative tax burden in 1913 and in 1919. To do so he took total revenues generated from different taxes and then made a judgment whether the incidence of the tax in question fell mostly on the poor or mostly on the rich. As Haig emphasized, this was preferable to a simple distinction between indirect and direct taxes, because many of the indirect tax increases that France had adopted during the war were on luxury items purchased primarily by the rich. Haig calculated that in 1913, 46.5 percent of France's taxes were weighted against the rich, 38.4 percent against the poor, and 15.2 percent had no definite weight. It is possible that this meant that the overall schedule in France at this time resembled a flat tax, just as was the case in the United Kingdom prior to the People's Budget. But of course this evidence is too approximate for us to make this judgment. Now turn to Haig's conclusions about the relative burden of taxation in 1919: 61.2 percent weighted against the rich, 31.2 weighted against the poor, and 7.4 percent with no definite weight. In other words, the burden of French taxation became more substantially progressive as a result of the First World War.

Unfortunately for our purposes, detailed studies of the overall tax burden in the United States did not begin until the 1930s. Given this, the best assessment of the effect of World War I on the tax burden was provided by none other than Edwin Seligman. In a study of U.S. war revenue acts, Seligman concluded that among the portion of war funds raised through taxation, fully 73 percent was raised through taxes on wealth, 13 percent through taxes on luxuries or "harmful" consumption (i.e., liquor), and the remaining 13 percent from other taxes that were more likely to impact groups other than the rich.[16] On this evidence alone it seems hard to deny that the First World War resulted in the overall U.S. tax system becoming substantially more progressive.

In 1937, Mabel Newcomer produced the first study that gives us a true picture of the overall burden of taxation in the United States. She based her study on tax figures from the Revenue Act of 1936. By this time the Roosevelt administration, as well as the Hoover administration in its last days, had raised taxes on the rich. This reversed a trend in which prior Republican administrations had lowered taxes on the rich relative to their World War I peak. In her calculations Newcomer included estimates of the effect of all direct taxes, including estate and gift taxes, as well as all indirect taxes. She then considered the tax burden for ten hypothetical families with annual income ranging from $500 to $1 million. The calculations also took account of the likely sources of income for people at these different levels (in particular capital versus labor income). Newcomer found that the very wealthiest households (those earning $1 million a year) would pay roughly 80 percent of their income in taxes, whereas at the next level down (those earning $100,000 a year) this figure dropped to roughly 40 percent. At the next level down (those earning $20,000 a year) the combined tax rate dropped to roughly 30 percent. The trend continued thereafter, with the lowest income groups paying between 10 and 15 percent of their income in taxes, depending on the assumptions. We can conclude from Newcomer's study that there was a high degree of progressivity in the U.S. tax system in the late 1930s.

Evidence for the World War II era suggests that the overall tax burden in the United States became even more progressive as a result of this conflict. It is known that during World War II the Roosevelt administration lowered the exemption limit for the income tax to make it a mass tax. We need to take this change into account along with any other tax increases to see the effect of World War II on overall progressivity. The best available evidence on this subject was compiled by John Adler in 1951, based on his estimates for the postwar tax burden and prewar estimates by Gerard Colm and Helen Tarasov. Adler's results suggest that the U.S. fiscal system became more progressive during World War II.[17]

In the end, it would be helpful to have more evidence, but the few studies that we have cited in this section all point in the same direction. Participation in mass warfare was associated with increased progressivity of the overall tax burden. In the next section we see if a look at spending and debt might alter our conclusions.

THE EFFECT OF SPENDING AND DEBT

In considering taxes on the rich, we are not directly interested in government spending, not with government borrowing, but since spending and debt have clear distributional implications, we still need to be concerned with these issues.

If taxes vary in their incidence on different social groups, the same is of course true with spending. One possibility is that the expansion of the suffrage did not lead to heavier taxation of the rich, but it did lead to greater welfare spending on the rest of the population. In other words, maybe governments didn't shift the tax burden toward the rich, but they did shift the benefit of spending more toward the poor and middle classes. The short answer to this question is yes, there was an increase in redistributive spending following suffrage expansions, but this increase was on such a low base that the end effect was minimal. It was not until World War II that governments created anything resembling modern welfare states, and this was well after the expansion of the suffrage.

One of the most frequently cited studies on this subject is Peter Lindert's book, *Growing Public*. Lindert compiled data on public spending in a set of industrial countries from 1890 to 1930. He looked in particular at public spending on welfare, pensions, health, and housing, the main categories of redistributive transfers at the time. Based on these data, Lindert argued that the suffrage played a significant role in the expansion of public spending on these categories. However, he also took pains to place this conclusion in context. By the 1930s, even in those countries where redistributive transfers were highest, they amounted to only about 3 percent of GDP. This is of course an extremely small figure by post-1945 standards.

We used Lindert's data to perform the same sort of differences in differences test that we have performed elsewhere in this book. This analysis suggested there was in fact no effect of extension of the suffrage on redistributive spending. However, when we substituted our competitive elections measure previously defined in chapter 3, we did see such an effect. Countries in which at least 50 percent of adult males could vote and where chief executives were elected in multiparty competition had overall redistributive spending that was one-half of one percentage point of GDP higher than those that didn't. This is a statistically significant effect, but it is small in terms of magnitude. In a related study using different data, Toke Aidt and Peter Jensen looked at the effect of suffrage extension on total public spending. Using a similar statistical procedure, they found that suffrage extensions were associated with an expansion of the public sector by about 1.5 percentage points of GDP.[18] This again is a statistically significant effect, but it is a small one.

Now, let's consider the effect of mass warfare on redistributive spending. The end of the Second World War is most often associated with an increase in welfare spending due either to programs explicitly targeted at veterans, such as the GI Bill in the United States, or programs targeted at the whole population, such as Great Britain's National Health Service.[19] Some observers have claimed such an effect for World War I as well.[20] However, if we return to the Lindert data we see that by 1930 overall redistributive spending was no higher in countries that had participated in World War I when compared with those who had not. Most of the distributional changes that occurred as a result of the First World War were due to changes in the tax system. This would not be the case with World War II, and we consider that issue further in chapter 8.

In addition to spending, we also need to consider the effect of government borrowing. During the two world wars, governments were forced to finance the bulk of their expenditures by borrowing. The alternative of financing the war only through current tax increases would have quickly asphyxiated their economies. At the time, and particularly during World War I, it was often argued that resorting to borrowing favored the rich. Allowing the rich to buy government bonds would allow their funds to be remunerated, which of course is not the case with taxes.

To what extent does a consideration of government debt alter our core conclusions about mass warfare and taxing the rich? We can first think about this problem in the abstract. Say that a society is divided into those who can supply labor and those who own capital. If capital owners invest in government bonds they earn a return on this asset, whereas if labor is conscripted then it runs great risks and is paid a below-market wage. The unfairness seems evident. One response to this is to say that a capital owner will be simply earning a return on government debt instead of on another asset.[21] While a true statement, in the early twentieth century this argument was often insufficient to quell the critics. It also ignores the possibility that if capital is in short supply, then government borrowing may push up interest rates, leading to a higher return for capital owners than they would enjoy in peacetime.

The first question we need to address then is whether investors in government debt during the two world wars earned higher returns than they would have had the wars not taken place. In an ex post sense the answer is no, this was certainly not the case. We know that investors suffered heavily from the inflation, and in other cases out-right default, following these wars. But what about in an ex ante sense; did investors earn higher expected returns on government debt than they would have otherwise? The short answer to this is that even if investors during World War I did earn higher nominal yields, it's not clear that they earned higher expected returns than would otherwise have been the case. For one, inflation crept up in most countries during the war, cutting into returns. Second, there must have certainly been a perceived increase in default risk for some countries. This too would have reduced expected returns.

The second question we need to address is whether governments did anything to address the perception that bondholders were unfairly profiting from the war effort. In fact, governments intervened quite heavily in capital markets during both wars to lower their effective cost of borrowing. There was an obvious financial incentive to do this, but this move also addressed perceptions about the unfairness of borrowing. In any case, these interventions certainly did not help investors. As an example, in the United States during World War II the Federal Reserve and Treasury pursued a policy of keeping the interest rate on long-term government debt below a ceiling of 2.5 percent.[22] Governments also used means other than explicit inter-est rate targets to intervene in capital markets. This was the case of the UK government in World War I, which controlled new capital issues from other sources and limited rates on deposit accounts in an attempt to steer more money into government bonds.[23] These were all forms of implicit taxation of capital owners.[24]

To summarize, a look at government spending and indebtedness does not alter the basic conclusions of this book. Compensatory claims associated with mass warfare led to heavy taxation of the rich, and a look at government actions in the area of spending and debt does not alter this conclusion. The final question we consider in this chapter is whether the design of wartime tax changes might be explained by pure fiscal necessity.

FISCAL NECESSITY—THE WILLIE SUTTON EFFECT

Willie Sutton said he robbed banks because that's where the money was. A key question for us is whether governments during the two world wars taxed the rich for exactly the same reason. Perhaps high top rates of income and inheritance taxation didn't have anything to do with fairness; they may have been a simple necessity for governments. This "Willie Sutton" argument has several different variants, and so we consider each here. According to the first variant, the rich were taxed because all other sources of finance had been used to their maximum, and therefore there was no alternative. According to the second variant, the rich were taxed because governments with finite fiscal capacity found it desirable to concentrate their energies where they would have the greatest yield in terms of revenue.

The first variant suggests that when other sources of revenue have been used up, then governments in desperation will be forced to tax the rich heavily. Perhaps this is what happened during the two world wars. More specifically, we might think that once a government had raised indirect taxes to a maximum that the economy could sustain, and once it had borrowed to the point where it no longer had access to credit, then taxation of the rich would remain the final option. In fact, in the case of World War I this is exactly the opposite of what happened. During the war itself the British and American governments went further than governments in Germany, France, Austria, or Russia in taxing the rich. It was also the case that in comparison with these other states, the British and American governments funded much more of their war effort out of current taxation, as opposed to borrowing. Under these circumstances it is difficult to argue that heavy taxes on the rich arose out of desperation. In fact, just the opposite seems to have been the case.

The other variant of the fiscal needs argument suggests that in a world where fiscal capacity is finite, it would make sense to focus attention on taxes on the rich because these would have the greatest yield. Once we consider this argument more closely we can see that there is little basis for believing that this is why governments taxed the rich heavily during the two world wars. If finite fiscal capacity were the problem, then governments would have chosen to tax the rich heavily centuries before the two world wars because bureaucratic capacity was certainly in shorter supply than in 1914. But this is not what they did.

There is also further evidence against this finite fiscal capacity idea. To see this, consider the structure of income tax schedules that were adopted during the First World War. In all countries with income taxes the vast majority of individuals or households were exempted. Now, it is plausible that this choice was influenced by considerations of administrative capacity—concentrated on the households that would yield substantial revenue. This might help us understand why only the top 10 percent of households were subject to the income tax instead of the top 50 percent. However, if this were all that was determining the choice of who to tax, the simplest strategy would be to raise taxes on the 10 percent by the same proportion by adopting a flat tax. After all, one of the key arguments for a flat tax is its administrative simplicity. As we already saw in chapter 3, this is precisely the opposite of what happened. During and after the First World War, governments raised income tax rates on the very richest households by considerably more than on those who were merely within the top 10 percent of households or even within the top 1 percent. This differential taxation within the top 10 percent also undermines the argument that wartime governments taxed the rich because of falling trade revenues. Chapter 3 also presented evidence that the effect of war on top rates of income taxation was greater in democracies than non-democracies. This difference again suggests that some factor other than finite fiscal capacity drove the war effect.

The history of the inheritance tax gives us a final reason to be skeptical about the finite state capacity argument. Recall from chapter 4 that historically, governments began taxing inheritance well before they began taxing income. They made this choice because it was easier to tax inheritance. This is a clear case where availability of administrative capacity influenced the choice of taxation. However, recall also another finding. Historically, governments have never relied on inheritance taxation as a principal source of revenue. Prior to the two world wars they also never levied inheritance taxes at very high rates. If governments had access to a tax that required little capacity to collect, yet they didn't tax the rich heavily, then it seems that state capacity alone cannot be the explanation. Once again, some other factor must have been operating.

We have shown that neither the first variant of the fiscal needs effect (desperation) nor the second variant (finite capacity) can explain why the rich were taxed so heavily during the two world wars. There's also a final fact to which we already referred in chapter 1. It is true that the two world wars were events that were more expensive than anything that had happened previously. However, it isn't the case that they were more expensive than what would happen subsequently. It's useful to remember that over the last half century many governments have steadily increased the amount of revenues they draw from their economies. They have done this to the point where, even in a normal year, governments are collecting as much revenue relative to the size of the economy as they were at the height of World War II. Has this resulted in a massive shift toward taxing the rich? In fact, exactly the opposite has taken place. Governments have reduced taxes on the rich. Therefore, just because a government needs a lot of revenue doesn't mean that it needs to tax the rich.[25]

To sum up, there's no doubt that when governments have taxed the rich, they have done so because they needed money. But that doesn't mean that this was the only way to achieve this objective. We have shown that the pattern of taxation of the rich does not support the Willie Sutton argument. The governments that have taxed the rich most heavily were not those that had the fewest alternatives for raising finance. Likewise, there were many cases where governments lacked fiscal capacity, yet they chose not to tax the rich heavily. All of this reinforces the idea that the story of taxing the rich has more to do with politics.

CONCLUSION

In this chapter we have asked if the patterns we saw with income taxation in chapter 3 and with inheritance taxation in chapter 4 tell us something meaningful about trends in the taxation of the rich relative to the rest of the population. A look at the broader picture confirms our prior conclusions. We have also argued that this trend cannot be explained by simple necessity. In the next three chapters we show how changing perceptions about a fair tax system helped to lead first to the rise and subsequently to the demise of taxing the rich.

PART THREE

WHY HAVE GOVERNMENTS TAXED THE RICH?

CHAPTER SIX

THE CONSCRIPTION
OF WEALTH

The reason wartime governments increased taxes on the rich more than the rest was because war mobilization changed beliefs about tax fairness. It created an opportunity for new and compelling compensatory arguments that increased support for taxing the rich. Comparing public tax debates before, during, and immediately after World War I in the United Kingdom, France, Canada, and the United States, we demonstrate that as a result of the war both elites and ordinary people changed the type of fairness arguments they employed when justifying their preferred tax system. Focusing on World War I has several advantages. No governments expected the long, expensive mass mobilized conflict that followed. The timing of the conflict was determined by the assassination of the Archduke Ferdinand of Austria in late June 1914. The war was an unexpected shock to the political environment that created new inequities in terms of what states asked of the mass of its citizens—manpower to fight the war—and how the state privileged the rich—increased war profits for many sectors of the economy. How did these new war-induced inequities change debates about taxation?

THE UNITED KINGDOM

The most important nineteenth-century reform shaping taxation in the United Kingdom was the reestablishment of the income tax in 1842 by a Conservative government led by Robert Peel.[1] The 1842 debate shows how compensatory arguments can influence tax debates even in a time of peace. The United Kingdom had successfully implemented an income tax during the Napoleonic Wars but then abandoned it after the wars ended. The tax system at this time relied substantially on trade and an extensive set of other indirect taxes. Since many of these taxes were unpopular, there was considerable debate, especially in the 1830s, about the possibility of reducing these taxes and substituting them with new property taxes or a general income tax. Even so, no significant policy changes were made.

Faced with both a persistent fiscal deficit and popular objections to existing indirect taxes, in 1842 Peel proposed reestablishing the income tax. Peel's budget speech had two main sets of arguments for this reform. The first was primarily an efficiency argument—the income tax was the best alternative for raising more revenue in order to balance the budget and revive the economy. The second was a compensatory argument. An income tax was necessary to equalize the tax burden because existing taxes were most burdensome for lower income citizens. As Seligman points out, Peel early in the speech noted the high prevailing level of indirect taxes and stated, "I cannot consent to any proposal for increasing taxation on the great articles of consumption by the labouring classes of society."[2] He then argued for the income tax, asserting:

> . . . for the purpose of not only supplying the deficiency in the revenue, but of enabling me with confidence and satisfaction to propose great commercial reforms, which will afford a hope of reviving commerce, and such an improvement in the manufacturing interests as will re-act on every other interest in the country; and, by diminishing the prices of the articles of consumption, and the cost of living, will, in a pecuniary point of view, compensate you for your present sacrifices.[3]

The subsequent debate was also noteworthy, highlighting the importance of arguments about the impact of the income tax on economic growth, expected administrative problems, the need to save the income tax for times of war, and the supposed inquisitorial nature of the tax. Importantly, fairness-based arguments featured in these debates across many issues related to the tax, and they were employed by both those in favor of and those opposed to the tax. Some made appeals to equal treatment because the government had proposed to treat different types of income differently by including an exemption for individuals with lower incomes. It was also suggested that the tax was unequal because it favored landowners over merchants.[4] Other speakers made ability to pay or compensatory arguments in favor of adopting the tax.

The 1842 debate also illustrates another dynamic that would be repeated later in the nineteenth century in the UK and elsewhere; supporters of trade liberalization sometimes accepted the need for an income tax to replace lost revenue from reduced custom duties. There are at least three important points common to nineteenth-century tax debates. First, there was an explicit compensatory argument that taxing the rich was justified because of other taxes that fell on the poor and working classes. Second, this phenomenon was also an efficiency argument made by free traders who thought that substituting modest income taxation for trade taxation would improve economic performance. Third, these compensatory arguments did not result in heavy taxation of the rich. They should instead be viewed as contributing in some cases to the adoption of income tax systems with relatively low rates.

Although Peel did not succeed in passing all of his proposed reforms, the income tax was reinstated in 1842 with a single rate of almost 3 percent. For the remainder of the nineteenth century the income tax remained in place, with the rate varying between just below 1 percent to just below 5 percent. The next significant innovation in income taxation was the adoption of the "Super Tax" in Lloyd George's People's Budget of 1909/1910, making the income tax progressive with a top rate of 8.3 percent.[5]

This reform coupled with the 1907 increase in the top rate of inheritance taxation to 15 percent are probably best understood in terms of the democracy hypothesis and the impact of partisan electoral competition. The franchise in the UK had steadily grown to near universal male suffrage, and the Labour Party was emerging as an electoral threat. The Liberals adopted a new fiscal system to respond to the interests of newly enfranchised voters and evolving accounts of what equality demanded of the tax system.

The Labour Party provided a revealing statement of its views of tax fairness in January 1909 in a memorandum of its party conference executive committee and an accompanying report. While Labour was naturally advocating policies in the economic interests of its members, the memorandum also illustrates the fairness considerations that the party thought to be the most persuasive in advancing those interests. Labour suggested that four principles should guide tax policy:

1. Taxation should be in proportion to ability to pay and to the protection and benefit conferred on the individual by the State.
2. No taxation should be imposed which encroaches on the individual's means to satisfy his physical and primary needs.
3. Taxation should aim at securing for the communal benefit, all unearned increment of wealth.
4. Therefore taxation should be levied on unearned income and should aim deliberately at preventing the retention of great fortunes in private hands.[6]

The report goes on to recommend the adoption of a graduated income tax, higher taxes on monopolies, and increased estate duties. The discussion included in the Report of the Conference echoes both the ability to pay and compensatory arguments. A key issue at this time was that even the government took it as given that more revenue was needed to pay for social reforms, but the question was what kind of taxes would be used to pay for them. The Labour Party argued that further trade taxes, or proposals to otherwise broaden the tax base, would be self-defeating. Therefore increases in taxes on the rich were necessary so that the tax system was more "in accordance with capacity to pay."[7] In addition to ability to pay arguments, the party also focused on high taxation of unearned income and monopoly profits in order to compensate for the advantages that allowed these sorts of income that it viewed as in part injurious to the mass of working people and in part unmerited by hard work and service. As Ramsay MacDonald put it in the Report's discussion, Labour "wanted to divide the non-producing parasite dependent upon society from the producer and the service giver."[8] Note that these compensatory arguments differ from those that we emphasize in the book. The state's role in generating inequities from unearned income and monopoly profits was indirect and highly contested compared to the direct and transparent role that the state would play in the inequities that we discuss related to World War I.

In the prewar political environment, shaped by growing competition from the Labour Party and the need to expand the early welfare state and strengthen the navy, Lloyd George introduced the People's Budget in 1909. In terms of income taxation, the adoption of a graduated rate was an important innovation, but the fact that the rate was just 8.3 percent is consistent with our contention that even under the conditions of an expanding franchise, fairness arguments were typically insufficient to persuade governments to tax high incomes and wealth heavily. While Labour may have been convinced that equality demanded high taxes on income and wealth, the Liberal party and the mass of voters were not yet ready to go so far.[9]

The People's Budget is essentially where the tax system stood in the years leading up to World War I. By 1914 the Liberals had been returned to power, and the government was led by Prime Minister Herbert Asquith. However, by May 1915, Asquith was forced to form a new coalition government with the Conservatives, and further setbacks in the war led in 1916 to yet another coalition government with Lloyd George as the new prime minister. Prior to the outbreak of hostilities, the government's 1914 budget proposal would have slightly reduced the income tax rate, and it proposed a combination of increased customs and excise taxes and reduced spending to balance the accounts.[10] It is clear that at least for 1914, the UK was not going to have a more progressive tax system absent the war. With the war, however, the first and second war budgets in 1914 and 1915 increased income tax rates significantly with a top rate in 1915 of 17.2 percent, while the top rate of inheritance taxation rose to 20 percent. These two changes made the system substantially more progressive.

The UK began the war with an effective and massive volunteer mobilization effort. Nonetheless, in January 1916, the government's Military Service Bill, which adopted conscription, passed quickly into law and was expanded several times throughout the remainder of the war. Once conscription was adopted, it became central to political debates about how the war was to be financed. It certainly appeared to lead to policy changes that made taxation even more progressive. For example, George Wardle argued in parliament:

> We have passed through this House a Bill compulsorily making men go into the Army to fight for their country. I know that you also have compulsory taxation. You take a certain proportion of the wealth and the income of the people of the country for the financing of this War, but the relation between the two does not strike the imagination. The sacrifice which the soldier is called upon to make is far greater than that asked of the man who has to part with part of his income, even though it be 5s. in the £, and there is a growing feeling, intensified again and again by the passing of this compulsory measure, demanding that a bigger proportion of the wealth of the country should be mobilised for the service of the nation in order to win this War, and mobilised at once.... If it be necessary to mobilise the men, the munitions, the factories and the businesses of the country in order to win it, it is equally necessary to mobilise the wealth of the country, and the Chancellor of the Exchequer, bold as he may think he has been and bold as some people certainly think he has been, might have gone even further than he has, and if he had gone further he would have done a great deal more to bring the end of the War nearer, to bring that sense of equality and sacrifice closer, and to have made a feeling in this country which would have enabled us all to be more united even than we are at present in securing a final victory.[11]

Calls for progressive taxation to equalize war sacrifices came in two forms. The first was simply more progressive income taxation, the "conscription of income," while the second was a capital levy or literally the "conscription of wealth." These demands came in part from the expected places, such as the Trades Union Congress, which held "that, as the manhood of the nation has been conscripted to resist foreign aggression ... this Congress demands that such a proportion of the accumulated wealth of the country shall be immediately conscripted."[12] However, the arguments were also reflected in publications like the *Economist*, which had previously opposed high levels of income taxation. The *Economist* opposed a capital levy, but it did support "direct taxation heavy enough to amount to rationing of citizens' incomes." It also explicitly endorsed an article in the *Economic Journal* by Harvard economist Oliver Sprague entitled "The Conscription of Income."[13] In the article Sprague argued: "Conscription of men should logically and equitably be accompanied by something in the nature of conscription of current income above that which is absolutely necessary."[14] The conscription of income was a clear compensatory policy. The state was asking the young with lower incomes and less wealth to fight in the war. Fairness demanded that this sacrifice be compensated with higher taxes on income and wealth.

United Kingdom policy responded to demands for greater progressivity in income taxation. The third war budget, introduced in April 1916, just after the conscription bill was passed, increased the income tax, with revenues from higher income taxes expected to generate more than twice as much additional revenue as increases in indirect taxes.[15] The capital levy debate also intensified following the introduction of conscription, though the levy was never adopted.[16] These remained the principles that informed tax policy to the end of the war and in the years immediately after as the country struggled to repay its war debts and meet the increased expectations of its citizens who had sacrificed so much to win the war. Top income tax rates peaked at 60 percent in 1920 and 1921. The top inheritance tax rate reached 40 percent.

War mobilization created a new context in which compensatory arguments were credible, and so the type of fairness claims proponents of progressive taxation made shifted. One might be concerned, however, that our take on how war mobilization changed fairness arguments is selective and fails to represent the systematic effect of the war. To address this possibility, we examined all parliamentary debates about the income tax for 1909, the period during which the People's Budget was debated, and the war period (1914–1918).

For each year, we searched digitized editions of the House of Commons and Lords Hansard, which is the official report of debates in Parliament.[17] We searched on the key words "income tax" and read all debates in which the phrase appeared for each year. We then included any speech that makes an argument for or against an income tax, for or against a higher or lower rate of income tax, or which considers another significant structural change in the tax, such as how it is collected. This process identified 428 unique parliamentary speeches about income tax policy over the six years. For each speech, we measured whether the main orientation of the argument was for or against the income tax or higher rates on the income tax and whether the speaker made an equal treatment, ability to pay, or compensatory fairness argument.[18]

Figure 6.1 plots the distribution of the different types of speeches made about the income tax over the six years in the dataset before and after the start of the war. Before World War I, about half of all speeches included one of these three fairness arguments. Among these fairness arguments, 44 percent were equal treatment, 51 percent were ability to pay, and just less than 6 percent were compensatory. The distribution of the three types of fairness arguments is broadly consistent with our view of fairness debates prior to the war's outbreak. Supporters of progressive tax policies used ability to pay arguments, while opponents made equal treatment and economic efficiency arguments. Given the importance of equal treatment arguments during most of the nineteenth century, it is somewhat surprising that the equal treatment argument was not even more prevalent. That said, the picture is consistent with our expectations that fairness arguments were salient in most tax debates and that equal treatment and ability to pay were the primary competing accounts of fairness.

In interpreting these data, we have to keep in mind several possibilities. One is that people have different beliefs about fairness and/or about the impact of taxes on economic performance, and

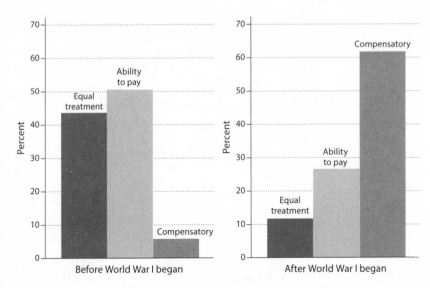

Figure 6.1. Debating the Income Tax in the United Kingdom. This figure reports the distribution of types of arguments about the income tax in the UK Parliament before and during World War I. The years coded are 1909, 1914, 1915, 1916, 1917, and 1918, with July 28, 1914 indicating the beginning of World War I.

that they employ arguments consistent with these beliefs to support their favored policy. Another possibility is that individuals, both members of parliament and their constituents, have interests in different policy alternatives based on how the policy affects them. They may only select the fairness or efficiency arguments that they think best make the case for their preferred policy. This potential selection problem is of some concern if we want to understand the factors that determine policy outcomes. It is a problem that we referred to in chapter 2 with our survey evidence. However, even if these speeches are just post hoc rationalizations of interests, they still inform us about what sort of arguments were viewed as likely to be persuasive to individuals whose policy positions were less clearly determined by their interests alone.

The data in figure 6.1 suggest that the war dramatically increased the use of compensatory arguments. The percentage of fairness arguments that were compensatory increased by a factor of ten, to 62 percent. The number of total speeches that did not make any of these three fairness arguments stayed about the same once the war began. This means that the increase in the presence of compensatory arguments reflects a real increase in their incidence across all speeches as well among those making fairness appeals.

The patterns for equal treatment and ability to pay are also interesting. The frequency of ability to pay arguments decreased significantly during the war. This suggests that the increased wartime use of compensatory arguments had two sources. It was in part due to the fact that existing supporters of progressive taxation switched from ability to pay arguments to compensatory arguments. This was evident in the behavior of trade unions and the Labour party. The equally dramatic decrease in equal treatment arguments is suggestive that another source of compensatory arguments was previous opponents of progressive taxation. Perhaps the most notable of these was the *Economist*, which switched positions and adopted compensatory arguments to justify increased progressivity.[19]

Any discussion of the impact of World War I on perceptions of tax fairness in the UK would be incomplete without returning to the Munitions Levy and Excess Profits Duty or "war profits taxes" discussed in chapter 5. These taxes were a central feature of the United Kingdom's war finance. They involved quite high rates, and they raised substantial amounts of revenue. The fundamental logic of these taxes was that firms and individuals who profited from the war were required to compensate the nation by paying higher taxes. The compensatory reasoning played out on at least four levels. First, the higher profits from war were due to state involvement in the war but were unmerited. Therefore they should be taxed to restore treatment as equals. Second, war profits were being earned at the same time that soldiers were being asked to make the ultimate sacrifice. Again, war profit taxes were justified as compensation. Third, these profits were being made while labor was being asked to make sacrifices. This included foregoing strikes and working long hours to simultaneously meet wartime needs and help prevent further inflation. High taxes on profits were necessary to establish equality in the war effort between capital and labor. Finally, higher profits stood in contrast to the rapidly rising prices and shortages of necessities faced by working people. War profits taxes were justified to help correct this inequality.

To be sure, there was some debate about war profits taxes. A number of firms complained that the Excess Profits Duty had an unequal incidence across industries because of arbitrary differences in their prewar standards of profits. Opponents also made various types of economic efficiency arguments, sometimes adapted for the wartime setting. Some emphasized that the tax prevented companies from investing in needed expansion to meet wartime needs. But overall, support for war profits taxes resonated across the political spectrum. This support existed because the tax was justified by a compensatory logic.

CANADA

The issue of trade tariffs dominated national tax debates in Canada in the late nineteenth and early twentieth centuries. After the British North America Act established the Dominion of Canada in 1867, the new national government at first struggled to establish a reliable revenue source and manage political conflict over trade protection. After a decade of attempts at freer trade on a reciprocal basis with the United States, in 1879 the Conservative Party enacted a new protectionist tariff policy known as the National Policy. This policy reshaped the existing tariff and solidified its central importance as a source of revenue for the national government. Average tariff rates rose from 20.2 percent in 1868 to a peak of 31.9 percent in 1889.[20] Although Canada adopted a preferential tariff with Britain in 1898, and the Liberal Party was in power for more than a decade, tariffs remained protectionist and the main source of national revenue. In the years leading up to World War I, customs duties typically accounted for more than 70 percent of tax revenue and almost two-thirds of all revenue.[21]

During this period municipal and some provincial governments adopted direct taxes, including the income tax, but these direct taxes were not a significant part of national tax debates. The Conservative Party strongly advocated a protectionist policy, along with excise taxes and various non-tax revenue sources. Prior to 1879 the

Canadian Liberals did consider an income tax and other direct taxes in order to reduce dependence on the tariff. They viewed the tariff as undesirable both because of their preference for freer trade and because of their dissatisfaction with its volatile and procyclical revenues. However, ultimately the Liberals chose to favor a less radical policy of relying on the tariff for revenue purposes only, but not for protection.[22] After 1879, the Liberals for the most part kept this "revenue only" approach to trade taxation and did not seriously advance proposals for an income tax or other direct taxes.

The Canadian election of 1891 nicely illustrates the lack of interest in the adoption of a national income tax at this time. The election was fought primarily over trade liberalization, and specifically over whether Canada should try to secure unrestricted reciprocity with the United States. The Liberals advocated this position, and the Conservatives argued for a continuation of the protectionist National Policy. Both parties raised the issue of direct taxation in their platforms, but neither advocated the adoption of something like an income tax. The Conservatives argued that unrestricted reciprocity with the United States would lead to such a large decrease in tax revenue that the national government would inevitably have to adopt direct taxes:

> There is, however, one obvious consequence of this scheme which nobody has the hardihood to dispute, and that is that Unrestricted Reciprocity would necessitate the imposition of direct taxation amounting to not less than fourteen millions of dollars annually upon the people of this country.[23]

The Liberals addressed this issue explicitly in their platform, but only to argue that it was not the case:

> Then it is stated that Unrestricted Reciprocity would be followed by such a loss of revenue as to necessitate the imposition of direct taxation ... The equilibrium between revenue and expenditure could be naturally reestablished by retrenchment in expenditure and by re-distributing taxation under the same methods than now obtain, and without inflicting any greater burden than is now borne by the people.[24]

The Conservatives won the election decidedly. Even when the Liberals gained power in 1896 and remained in office until 1911, the income tax still was restricted to serving as a tool of municipal and provincial governments without significant support by the major parties.

The Canadian election of 1911 echoed many of the themes that had been heard in 1891. The United States had finally agreed to a reciprocal trade agreement with Canada that Conservatives had blocked in Parliament. This forced the Liberal government to call an election to decide the issue. To the extent that income and direct taxes were discussed, they were once again seen as a potential negative consequence of freer trade with the United States, rather than as a policy that either of the major parties was strongly advocating.[25]

When war arrived, Canada had a Conservative government led by Prime Minister Robert Borden. The government was firmly committed to a protectionist policy and to continued reliance on trade, excise, and non-tax revenues. To finance the war, the government relied at first on tariffs, increased consumption taxes, and debt. In other words, the Conservative Party followed its usual preferences with regard to taxation. The first war budget in 1914 did not show a significant shift toward taxing the rich. This policy response was no doubt due to a number of considerations.[26] For our purposes, it suffices to note that the Conservative government shied away from implementing new direct taxes of any kind, including those on high incomes and wealth. Given their initial expectations about the duration of the conflict, they did not think it was necessary. To some extent this characterization applies to the 1915 war budget as well. It was still not clear how long and expensive the war would be, nor was it evident what manpower commitment was necessary. With this said, the 1915 budget did levy new corporate taxes and new taxes on luxury goods. To defend his budget Sir Thomas White, the finance minister, made use of both equal treatment and ability to pay arguments. He argued for the continued reliance on the tariff by appealing to equal treatment:

Taxation imposed by increased customs bears upon all classes because all are consumers and in paying additional taxation each member of the community will feel that he is to that extent contributing to the cost of the war and the defense of his country.[27]

But White also used ability to pay reasoning when he referred to other taxes, "the burden of which will fall more particularly upon those members of the community who are best able to sustain it."[28] As noted by Perry, the push toward income taxes was already part of the public debate in 1915.[29] White's budget speech included an extensive defense of the government's decision not to implement an income tax. Mass mobilization for the war initially raised questions about greater direct taxation, and specifically the adoption of a national level income tax, but the government made only modest policy changes.

This outcome began to change significantly in 1916 when the government adopted a war profits tax.[30] Arguments in favor of this tax followed those in the United Kingdom. The key issue again was that the state's entry into the war had generated unmerited benefits in terms of war profits for some but not all citizens. Moreover, the government's recruitment of a large number of volunteers, who were urged to sacrifice, only exacerbated the inequity. White's budget speech put these compensatory fairness considerations at the heart of his defense of the new tax:

[T]here are in time of war many businesses and industries which for one reason or another are able to maintain profits above the average return to capital in time of peace. . . . It has appeared to the government that persons, firms and corporations whose profits have been such might well be called upon to contribute a share to the carrying on of the war. Their position being advantageous as compared with less fortunate fellow citizens, it is just that a portion of their advantage should be appropriated to the benefit of the state.[31]

The 1916 war profits tax turned out to be just the beginning of what was to come.

Canada had initially been quite successful in recruiting volunteers with many of them being recent immigrants from the UK. However, by late 1916 and early 1917, the government needed more soldiers, and volunteers became harder to find. Conscription was an obvious alternative, but it was an alternative the government was reluctant to embrace. The government, in fact, spent much of the early years of the war assuring the public that it would not resort to conscription. The Postmaster General supported this view while also saying that those who fought would receive compensation:

> The question of conscription has not been brought before the Government either directly or indirectly. The Government is of opinion that recruiting is wholly satisfactory. We force no one to go, but we will make a privileged class of those devoting themselves to the salvation of the country.[32]

Nonetheless, as the war progressed, military and political leaders in the United Kingdom pressed harder and harder on Canada to enact conscription in order to meet the needs of the war effort. In May 1917, Prime Minister Borden proposed that conscription be adopted in the Military Service Act. For our purposes, the essential features of this act were that it increased mass mobilization for the war, and it changed the character of that mobilization, introducing a tax-in-kind in the form of conscription. In doing so, the act fundamentally changed the politics of taxation in Canada.

To understand the impact of conscription on taxes, it is instructive to note that despite the growing costs of the war, as late as 1917 the government still had no intention of implementing an income tax. In April of that year the Minister of Finance noted the use of the income tax in the United Kingdom and the United States in his annual budget remarks, but citing administrative expense and fairness in a time of rising prices, he concluded that in Canada "it would appear to me that income tax should not be resorted to."[33] It was not the case that the war was simply becoming too expensive to avoid establishing an income tax.[34] However, in July 1917, White yielded to increasing pressure to tax the wealthy more heavily. He introduced legislation for a general income tax on individuals and business.

Two characteristics of this policy change are significant. First, it immediately followed the government's announcement in May 1917 that it sought to introduce conscription.[35] Second, it was adopted in a political environment demanding greater sacrifices on the part of the wealthy in response to war sacrifice. Canadian Trade and Labor Congress leaders met with Borden in December 1916 seeking a commitment to not implement conscription and to equalize war burdens. Borden refused to tie his hands on conscription, but he did say that "the government accepted and acted on the principle that the accumulated wealth of the country should bear its due proportion of contributions and sacrifices in the war."[36] Once the government enacted conscription, organized labor pushed even harder for various versions of the "conscription of wealth."[37] Though the more radical proposals, such as a capital levy, did not receive mainstream acceptance, arguments for greater sacrifices on the part of the wealthy certainly did. In introducing the Income War Tax Act, White made the link between conscription and the income tax explicit:

Apart from this necessity from a financial standpoint, there has arisen, in connection with the Military Service Bill, both in this house and in the country, a very natural and, in my view a very just, sentiment that those who are in the enjoyment of substantial incomes should substantially and directly contribute to the growing war expenditures of the Dominion.[38]

Of course, even with the implementation of the income tax, conscription proved highly controversial, and in the fall of 1917 it became the focal point of a national election. The Conservatives had invited the Liberals to form a national union government in order to solidify support for the war effort, including support for the Military Service Act. Many Liberals did join the government, but their leader, Wilfrid Laurier, did not. Thus, the election was between the Union Party composed of the Conservatives and many Liberals pitted against the Laurier Liberals.[39] Laurier, though supportive of the war, was opposed to conscription on both personal and political grounds. Although the campaign was bitterly contested, the debate about how to finance the war clearly reflected a shared acceptance of compensatory arguments in setting wartime tax policy, though with different interpretations of how those considerations might be acted upon. The Liberal Platform argued, even after the government had introduced the income tax and war profits tax, that "A fundamental objection to the government's policy of conscription is that it conscripts human life only, and that it does not attempt to conscript wealth."[40] The government's Unionist Platform, however, clearly also recognized the importance of the principle. It promised this: "In order to meet the ever-increasing expenditure for war purposes and also to ensure that all share in common service and sacrifice, wealth will be conscripted by adequate taxation of war profits and increased taxation of income."[41] In Canada, with greater mobilization from conscription, support for taxing the rich on compensatory grounds increased in all quarters.[42]

THE UNITED STATES

The political context in the United States prior to World War I more closely resembles that of the United Kingdom than Canada. The income tax had been an important dimension of political conflict in American politics for the previous two decades. It had also been an important part of the North's financing of the Civil War. To understand the impact of World War I on fairness debates, we need to first consider this background.[43]

Before the Civil War, the U.S. federal government had not seriously considered significant taxes on high incomes and wealth. It instead relied primarily on trade and excise taxes. During the Civil War, the United States implemented an income tax with a top rate that was initially set at 5 percent, then briefly raised to 10 percent, and then finally returned to 5 percent. The United States also adopted an inheritance tax at a rate first set at 0.75 percent and then 1 percent.[44] Both taxes were eliminated in the early 1870s. Although the U.S. Civil War is not in the war data, because it is a civil war, it clearly was a war of mass mobilization. As such, it is an early example of mass mobilization leading a country to implement significant taxes on high incomes and wealth. One might object that the rates were lower than what would come in the future, and it is true the effect did not last. However, it is important to keep in mind that the 10 percent top income tax rate equaled the highest rate levied by any government anywhere during the nineteenth century. Also, given that the income tax was considered by some to be unconstitutional, it was a remarkable innovation.[45] The fact that it did not last was largely determined by Republican enthusiasm for protectionist tariffs after the war. It in many ways simply highlights the power of war mobilization to push policy in a direction that the ruling party did not want to go.

The administration did not initially propose an income tax to help finance the Civil War.[46] It instead proposed a combination of loans, increased custom duties, and excise taxes, as well as various direct taxes that were apportioned according to population. When Congress took up the bill, however, there was not much support. A major source of objection was that the proposed direct taxes did not satisfy the needs of ability to pay because they did not correspond to the distribution of wealth.[47] Responding to these arguments as well as the Union's defeat at Bull Run, Congress revised the bill. It reduced the originally proposed direct taxes and replaced them with an income tax.

In the debates about income taxation that followed throughout the Civil War, a number of different ability to pay and compensatory arguments were made in favor of the tax. As an example of ability to pay reasoning, one representative argued that "never was so just a tax levied as the income tax . . . an assessment upon every man according to his ability to pay—according to his annual gains . . . the only tax which makes any distinction between John Jacob Astor and the poorest drayman in the streets."[48] The compensatory issue often noted was that the burden of existing indirect taxes fell mostly on the masses rather than the wealthy. In the words of Senator John Sherman, "If you leave your system of taxation to rest solely upon consumption, without any tax upon property or income, you do make an unequal and unjust system."[49] Another set of compensatory arguments focused on whether alternative forms of direct taxation would tax important classes, such as government workers and bondholders. It was argued that the income tax was the most effective means of ensuring everyone contributed fairly to the war effort.

Because the Civil War involved mass mobilization, it also saw early versions of some of the equal sacrifice arguments that feature so prominently in our discussion of World War I finance in the UK. As Bank, Stark, and Thorndike note, the most progressive version of the Civil War income tax was passed after conscription was implemented in 1863.[50] The need to tax the rich to compensate for the sacrifices of the masses was made explicit. Senator Garrett Davis of Kentucky argued:

> The idea that millionaires and men whose incomes exceed $25,000 as a general rule go into the camp is not supposable. There may be some exceptional cases; but if they go into the camp at all it is not by shouldering the musket, unless in very rare cases. They do not send their sons there as a general rule unless the sons go with epaulets upon their shoulders.[51]

Finally, even in the context of the war, equal treatment arguments retained some influence. As Representative Justin Smith Morrill of Vermont put it, in arguing for a reduction in the top rate, "In a republican form of government, the true theory is to make no distinctions as to persons in the rate of taxation."[52] These equal treatment arguments also took an interesting geographic turn. Critics of the income tax emphasized its unequal distribution across districts and states. That said, the overall effect of the war was to substantially change the distribution of fairness arguments, with a focus on compensatory arguments that supported greater taxation of the rich.

In the years following the Civil War, the United States returned to reliance on protective tariffs and excise taxes under successive Republican administrations. In the two decades leading up to World War I, American politics was marked by intense debates about economic inequality and class conflict. Democrats, and especially Populists representing the West and South, argued for lower tariffs and other policies to advance the interests of farmers and workers. Fearful of political competition from Populists, who had long supported an income tax, the Democrats also began to advocate its adoption. An income tax was enacted by the Democrats in the Revenue Act of 1894 in response to the Panic of 1893, but the

Supreme Court struck down the law as unconstitutional in *Pollock v. Farmers' Loan & Trust Company*.

The decision by the Supreme Court was not the end of the push for taxing the rich. There were almost continuous efforts to find a way to implement a new income tax, or to find similar alternatives such as excise taxes on corporate revenue. However, despite high prevailing inequality there was very little initial change at the federal level.[53] In fact, Republicans won a massive electoral victory in 1896 and implemented record high tariffs in the following year. They successfully argued that not only were high tariffs good for economic stability and growth; they also protected jobs for the working class. Even so, Progressivism was becoming a growing force in politics, and it influenced policies advocated by both Democrats and Republicans. Among those Republicans affected by these ideas was President Theodore Roosevelt. Included in the ideas that he endorsed were progressive inheritance and income taxation. Finally, in 1909, Congress debated a lowering of the tariff favored not only by Democrats but also progressives in the Republican Party. As part of this debate, both an income tax and a constitutional amendment for an income tax were considered. The intention of the amendment was for it to fail but to gain support for compromise legislation favored by conservative Republicans. This would have kept tariffs relatively high while avoiding an income tax.[54] In the end the amendment was passed. It helped lead to the passage of the Payne-Aldrich Tariff, a much more modest reduction in tariffs than initially envisioned by the Taft administration and progressive Republicans in Congress.

The subsequent ratification process for a constitutional amendment initially followed expectations, with southern and western states being the first to ratify. Then, unexpectedly, many northeastern states also approved the measure. With Wyoming's ratification in February 1913, the amendment crossed the threshold to become the Sixteenth Amendment to the U.S. Constitution. The ratification debate featured all the arguments that we have discussed in this book. In an era of high inequality, ability to pay arguments featured prominently, as did compensatory arguments referring to high tariffs and excise taxes. Steven A. Bank has provided numerous examples of this latter phenomenon.[55] Expectations about what sort of policies the amendment would engender varied wildly. Some feared and some hoped that it would allow for adoption of high taxes on income and wealth that would have a significant impact on inequality. Others expected that it would simply allow for real tariff reform and lead to greater equality in taxation.

It would turn out that, at least initially, the latter of the above two expectations was more accurate. Soon after ratification, with Woodrow Wilson new in office, Congress passed the Underwood-Simmons Tariff bill. This significantly lowered tariffs and implemented an income tax with a top rate of 7 percent. Although the debate over this legislation again featured many of the arguments that were employed in the ratification process, what is remarkable is how modest the political conflict was over finally adopting an income tax. The most important observation for our purposes is that, after two decades of conflict, amid highly politicized inequality, the end result was an income tax with a top rate of only 7 percent.

The outcome of a top rate of 7 percent, and the arguments employed in the debate, are consistent with our claim that inequality and democratization did not lead to the adoption of high top rates of income taxation. Even with democratic institutions and with individuals making ability to pay arguments, as well as compensatory arguments about the need to counterbalance indirect taxation, on the eve of World War I the wealthy in the United States were still very lightly taxed.

Taxation debates during World War I should be analyzed in two parts. In the first part, prior to 1917, the war had engulfed Europe, but the United States was not a direct participant. When the United States mobilized for the war in 1917, the debate shifted.

For the first period, it is natural to ask, why would World War I matter for fairness debates if the United States had not yet entered the war? There were no soldiers in battle. There was no conscription of labor that needed to be compensated by a conscription of wealth. While true, the war reduced tariff revenues for the U.S. government. The environment also suggested that the country needed to spend significantly more money on defense in case it was unable to avoid the conflict. New sources of revenue were required. The simple need for revenue did not dictate how the funds would be obtained. Whether the new revenues would be raised in a more or less progressive fashion was the central question before the Wilson administration and congressional leaders. The key legislation that reflects this choice was the Revenue Act of 1916. It took taxes in a decidedly progressive direction.[56] It expanded the income tax by lowering the threshold of incomes required to pay. It also raised the top rate of income taxation to 15 percent, reintroduced an inheritance tax,[57] doubled the tax on corporate incomes, and introduced a war munitions tax. These policies were expanded early in 1917—still before the United States entered the war—with the adoption of a more general war profits tax and increased inheritance taxes.

During this initial period, prior to the entry of the United States into the conflict, war profits were the most important factor influencing the tax debate. As in the case of other non-participant countries, such as Norway and Sweden, the U.S. experience prior to entry into the war was that it created substantial profits for some. These earnings created an inequity that did not derive from the efforts and merit of those who benefited. But the profits were not clearly dependent on action by the U.S. government either, making compensatory arguments less forceful. Soon, however, some began to profit directly from the war preparations of the U.S. government. To the extent that the government was going to expand its war preparedness, a widely held view was that the wealthy were the ones likely to benefit the most from these measures. Another argument that would foreshadow the debate after the United States entered the war was that high incomes and wealth should be taxed, instead of laying a burden on those who would actually fight if the United States entered the war.[58] All of these claims had a compensatory logic. Some of these arguments came from Democrats, Populists, and Progressives that already wanted a more progressive tax system. The war changed the reasons they offered for adopting such policies. There was a clear reason for this shift. The war environment and these new fairness considerations made the case for progressive taxes more convincing to more people.[59] The frequency of compensatory arguments in this prewar period increased, focusing on why taxes on income, wealth, and profits were justified to pay for a war preparation effort that brought great profits for a few.

When the United States entered World War I in April 1917, the Wilson administration decided quickly that a large army and conscription were required. The impact on fairness arguments about taxation was almost immediate and was evident across the country. Leading academics, such as Oliver Sprague, Edwin Seligman, and Irving Fisher, argued in the press and in congressional testimony that conscription was a tax-in-kind on the masses. Therefore it was necessary to tax high incomes and wealth so as to better approximate equality of sacrifice in the war effort.[60] In a message sent to Congress after war was declared, a committee of economists argued for funding the war primarily with taxes, especially taxes on war profits and high incomes, rather than debt. They argued:

> The citizen who contributes even his entire income, beyond what is necessary to subsistence itself, does less than the citizen who contributes himself to the nation ... If conscription of men is just and right, conscription of income is the more so; conscription of both is just and right when the nation's life and honor are at stake.[61]

The economists ended their statement with four general policy recommendations: "a tax which will take substantially all of special war profits; a material lowering of the present income tax exemption; a drastic increase in the rates of the income tax, with a sharper progression in rates as incomes become larger; and high consumption taxes on luxuries."[62] These same arguments were repeated by many different interest groups, political parties, and politicians across the country.[63] Other compensatory arguments from the prewar period, especially those based on inequalities in the benefits of the war, also continued to be used to justify higher taxes on income, wealth, and profits. Ability to pay arguments were still made, but less frequently than before the war.

To be sure, not everyone agreed with the compensatory theory, and the excess profits tax especially met considerable resistance from business interests. Opponents primarily focused on efficiency arguments, yet as in the UK, there also was an appeal to equal treatment. These considerations were used to support further lowering of the income tax exemption level in lieu of higher rates and to object generally to excessive reliance on taxes targeted at the rich. Finally, some, such as Otto Kahn, claimed that the idea of a "Rich Man's War" was simply a myth.[64]

Arguments about the "conscription of income" or the "conscription of wealth" were not confined to elite and academic circles within the United States. They also resonated with the broader American public. As this period pre-dates the arrival of opinion polls and surveys gauging mass opinion, one of the best ways to demonstrate this is with evidence from small-town newspapers. One can find thousands of references to the phrase "conscription of wealth" deriving from local newspapers spread very widely across the American continent. Many of these references involve discussions of parliamentary debates either in the United Kingdom or in the U.S. Congress, so we cannot really use them as an independent indicator of mass opinion. However, many others do seem to reflect the policy opinions of citizens across the country. These come in several categories.

Within the set of newspapers, there are many reports of local groups adopting resolutions in favor of the conscription of wealth. As just one example, on July 1, 1918, the *Commoner*, published in Lincoln, Nebraska, reported that the Nebraska Non Partisan League (a successor to the populists) had adopted a resolution in favor of the war effort and in favor of the conscription of wealth.[65]

In addition to resolutions, many newspapers also published pieces in which individuals expressed opinions favorable to the conscription of wealth. For example, on August 31, 1917, a writer for the *Washington Standard* in Olympia, Washington had this to say:

History of former wars has shown, as everyone knows, that quite a number of people, although actually a very small percentage of the population, made enormous wealth out of each war, while the great body of the people of the country not only fought the war but had to pay for it, too. That is not right, of course, and in this present conflict, when the nation has rightly adopted the democratic idea of compelling the young men of the country to do their patriotic duty whether or no, so the ordinary person thinks that wealth, and particularly war-created wealth, should be compelled to serve likewise.[66]

Though the opinion expressed in the *Washington Standard* was reflected in many other papers, it is also abundantly clear that some people vigorously opposed the idea of a conscription of wealth, and that the concept was contested. On September 3, 1917, the *Grand Forks Herald* published a piece in which it was suggested that the phrase "conscription of wealth" made "a convenient mouthful for the professional agitator."[67] However, this and other critiques point to the underlying power of conscription of wealth arguments. Opponents may have disliked the phrase, but they readily emphasized its effect on mass opinion. Speaking of the phrase "conscription of wealth," a writer from the *New York Tribune* made the following commentary: "It is heard everywhere, on the street and in the press. To the unthinking masses the epigram, 'You conscript men's bodies, why not their money?' has a great appeal."[68] This quote laments the power of a phrase in the same way that those on the left today might lament the effect of conservative anti-tax slogans of recent years. It is a further indication of mass opinion.

In the end, in the United States the conscription of income and wealth view won the day. Policy outcomes responded with a tax system that was unimaginable prior to the war. The top rate for the income tax reached 77 percent; the top rate for the inheritance tax was raised to 25 percent; and legislation vastly increased the use of the excess profits tax.

FRANCE

The history of debates about progressive income taxation in France is a complex one. We can attribute this to the unsettled inheritance of the French Revolution. During the Revolution, strong support emerged in some quarters for progressive taxation of the rich, and this at a much earlier date than in many other countries. Yet, the Revolution did not result in the creation of a modern income tax, either progressive or proportional.[69] Instead of opting for a tax on assessed incomes, revolutionary and post-revolutionary governments chose to create taxes on external indicators of income and/or wealth. The four taxes created during this period would subsequently become known as the *quatres vieilles*, or the "four old ones." Many have attributed France's late adoption of progressive income taxation to the legacy of the quatres vieilles and more generally to the resistance against "inquisitorial" forms of taxation.[70]

The inquisitorial claim was indeed a major argument levied by the political right in France against the income tax during the nineteenth century. However, as occurred in the United Kingdom, Canada, and the United States, French participation in World War I altered the arguments made in favor of taxing the rich. The arrival of powerful new compensatory arguments helps suggest why France shifted within a period of only six years from having a top marginal rate of income taxation of 2 percent to having a top rate of 50 percent. Debates in France differed from those in the UK, the United States, and Canada in several important ways. Ability to pay arguments in favor of tax progressivity arrived on the scene only belatedly in France. Correspondingly, compensatory arguments played a much more important role throughout the period we consider. In fact, both advocates and adversaries of progressive income taxation used compensatory arguments.[71]

Between 1790 and 1791 the Constituent National Assembly voted to create three taxes on indicators of income or wealth: the *contribution foncière*, a tax on land and certain types of property; the *contribution des patentes*, a tax on professions; and finally the *contribution mobilière*, a tax on the rental value of lodgings. To the extent that these three *contributions* did tax income or wealth, it was in a proportionate and not a progressive fashion. In step with the radicalization of the Revolution, pressure subsequently grew for establishing progressive taxation. The Convention (the successor assembly to the Constituent) voted in favor of the principle of progressive taxation on March 18, 1793.[72] At the time supporters used ability to pay arguments to justify this measure. However, war mobilization in 1793 also led to the creation of new arguments that the rich should be taxed to compensate for war sacrifice. During the Revolution, the Convention did not implement a permanent progressive tax scheme. What it did do is vote a series of forced loans that were based on a progressive scale. There was also substantial ad hoc taxation of the rich at the local level.[73] According to standard accounts, this arbitrary feature of progressive taxation during the revolutionary era helped color future French opinion about progressive taxation of any sort.

After the end of the Revolution all attempts to implement direct and progressive taxation of income were abandoned, but in 1798 the French government did establish a tax on doors and windows. This would join the three contributions voted in 1790–1791 and would become the fourth of the quatres vieilles. Some would claim that the incidence of this tax was progressive. However, the final point to remember about the quatres vieilles is that their combined incidence was very low. During the income tax debates of 1907, the French Ministry of Finance produced an estimate showing that French households with high revenues paid only about 2 percent of their annual income on these four taxes combined.[74]

Following the Revolution, the next significant attempt to create a permanent income tax did not come until the advent of the Second Republic in 1848. This effort turned out to be brief and unsuccessful. New discussion of the income tax would not occur again until the advent of the Third Republic in 1870. From that point onward the income tax would remain a prominent feature of political debate, but it would take forty-four years before France finally passed an income tax law. This occurred on July 15, 1914, on the eve of the First World War. In what follows we first consider what proponents and opponents of the income tax said during these five decades of debate.

After the establishment of the Third Republic in 1870 there was a flurry of proposals in the French Chamber of Deputies to establish a general income tax in France. This would be a tax on all income with an assessment. It would supplant or replace the system of the quatres vieilles that relied on external indicators of income and wealth. The deputy Louis Wolowski defended the idea of a proportional and general income tax in the following terms: "We ask that all revenues, whatever type they may be, pay equally. This is true equality and justice."[75] In other words a general income tax was the best way to ensure citizens were treated equally. Wolowski argued that the proposed tax of 3 percent would not be very heavy, nor would it be levied arbitrarily. He also defended the idea of having a subsistence minimum of revenue exempted, even if this would deviate from the principle of equal treatment. Finally, Wolowski referred to the English experience to suggest that an income tax could be used to levy very substantial revenues without this having a negative effect on economic activity.

If many in 1871 supported establishing an income tax, France's president, Adolphe Thiers, strongly opposed the idea. This was despite the fact that he had been supportive of the idea in 1848. A speech Thiers gave in December 1871 is credited with leading to the failure of the income tax proposal.[76] Like others, Thiers argued that the proposal would lead to arbitrary taxation. However, the most fascinating, and most detailed, part of his speech involved a comparison with the United Kingdom and a compensatory argument *against* the income tax. Thiers suggested that because the United Kingdom had an open economy, albeit with trade taxes, and because the burden of trade taxes fell heavily on the poor, it was natural that the rich in the United Kingdom should be taxed via an income tax. France, according to Thiers, had a much more closed economy, so the poor logically suffered less from trade taxes. He also argued that many indirect taxes in France were on luxuries and that the rich were taxed more heavily via the doors and windows tax. Therefore the compensatory argument in favor of the income tax did not make sense for France. Summing things up, Thiers concluded with this:

> Wealth in England owed something to the country; it was natural that the burden of the income tax should be placed on wealth. In France, in contrast, the propertied and comfortable classes do not owe something to the French people because they are [already] paying three quarters of the taxes. There, sirs, is the strongest argument, from the point of view of truth, I would say honestly, that can be invoked against the income tax in France.[77]

Whether the assessment by Thiers of the relative burden of taxation in France and England was accurate is a question that lies beyond the scope of our study. Certainly, some of the subsequent speakers (including Wolowski) disputed his figures.[78] Thiers's argument further reinforces the idea that compensatory arguments can have a particularly powerful impact in the political arena. If the compensatory argument for an income tax in England made sense, then it was crucial to show why the same argument should not also apply in France.

In addition to compensatory arguments against the income tax, criticisms that the tax would be arbitrary and that it would require a fiscal inquisition were a permanent feature of French debates between 1870 and 1914. These same fears had been expressed in other countries, but they appeared more vociferously in France, perhaps due to a reaction to the revolutionary experience. One of the most eloquent expressions of this idea can be found in a speech made in 1896 by Léon Say, a long- time opponent of the income tax and of tax progressivity. In the speech Say used a common French distinction at the time between "real" taxes that were levied on an object versus "personal" taxes that were levied directly on people:

> Everyone knows that real taxes are a guarantee established by the Revolution in favor of the people; it is because the people did not want to present themselves naked in front of a very fiscal and very authoritarian government that our fathers from 1789 sought to do away with personal taxes. With the instrument of progressive taxation in their hands the socialists will more easily arrive at their dream of a new distribution of wealth.[79]

With such arguments claiming the Revolution's legacy, efforts to establish an income tax in France faced substantial headwinds. However, as time went on, and France became more of a European outlier by not having an income tax, there were renewed efforts to establish one.[80] Following an election victory for the left in 1906, France's finance minister, Joseph Caillaux, launched a new effort to establish a progressive income tax. He would ultimately be successful even if the law establishing the tax would not pass both chambers of the legislature until 1914.

Finance Minister Caillaux first presented his income tax bill in 1907. Opponents of the tax emphasized many of the same themes that they had in the past regarding the desirability of France's existing "real" taxes and the need to ensure as much individual liberty as possible. However, it was the arguments made by proponents that were the most interesting for several reasons. When compared with proponents of progressive taxation elsewhere, proponents in France seem to have relied less heavily on ability to pay arguments. French parliamentary speakers who favored the income tax instead relied more heavily on compensatory arguments. The types of compensatory arguments employed varied. Caillaux, a representative of the center left, suggested that progressive income taxation was needed to compensate for the unequal incidence of existing taxes. Jean Jaurès, the prominent socialist, suggested that progressive taxation was instead necessary to compensate for unequal privileges in society more generally. This argument by Jaurès differs from the type of compensatory arguments we emphasize in this book because they depend on state action.

In making his compensatory argument Caillaux referred to the need to use income taxation to compensate for the incidence of indirect taxation. Appealing to the principle of equal treatment, Caillaux also referred implicitly to the fact that the existing system of the quatres vieilles was ineffective at taxing new forms of income in an industrial society:

> Sirs when we study in the most general terms the history of our fiscal system, we see that there have always been two vices in our system of taxation, like two weeds in a garden that return continually. It is first a privilege, profiting certain classes, or profiting certain localities, or certain parts of the territory. It is in second place the extension of indirect taxes to the detriment of direct taxes, which is after all a form of privilege. We see that all the movements that have taken place in our history against the existing tax system have always been dominated by the need to restrain privilege and by the desire to insure a greater role for direct taxes by restricting indirect taxes within a circle that they should not exceed.[81]

Jean Jaurès did not dispute the claims made by Caillaux. However, in arguing for the income tax bill, Jaurès suggested that it was necessary to compensate for a much broader set of privileges that he thought had emerged in French society. These were privileges that went beyond just the tax system or even beyond state action. Jaurès made his points by referring to the revolutionary heritage and the need to renew with it. For Jaurès the revolutionary heritage was not about the avoidance of "personal" taxes or fiscal inquisition; it was instead about the abolition of privilege:

> This is the real truth of the Revolution. And today, after one hundred and twenty years, the peasants and the workers find themselves faced with new privileges: privileges of capital, privileges of great fortune, privileges of lords of real estate and of great industry, privileges of creditors and of banks. And, as happened one hundred and twenty years ago, they are demanding equality, and not illusory or theoretical equality, but equality with the practical means to realize it, and there can be no equality in the fiscal order without a general income tax, with taxation, and assessment, with exact knowledge of revenue. It is we who are faithful to the spirit of the Revolution, to the true spirit of France.[82]

As we have said, the argument by Jaurès went beyond Joseph Caillaux's claim that there was a need to compensate for privileges granted by the state. For him it was also necessary to compensate for "privileges" that involved the simple functioning of the market economy. Did this argument help lead to the creation of the income tax? The final income tax law of 1914 only provided for a top marginal rate of 2 percent. This may have helped to compensate for the existing inequality due to indirect taxation and the uneven incidence of the quatres vieilles. It was, however, a level of taxation entirely inadequate for compensating the effect of the privileges and inequalities of which Jaurès spoke. It would only be in the context of war that French governments would shift toward taxing income (and wealth) much more heavily. The war context would give France's socialists a new argument for taxing the rich. Instead of arguing against privilege and inequality in society as a whole, they could now make a case for why great fortunes had emerged as a result of privileges accorded by the state itself.

French fiscal policies during the First World War differed from those of other Allied countries. France, at least initially, relied almost solely on borrowing to a greater extent than was the case in the United Kingdom or the United States. This can be explained in part by the fact that the war was taking place on French soil and severely disrupting the economy. However, the choice to shy away from collecting new tax revenues was a subject of partisan conflict. Those on the left pressed the government to draw more revenue from taxation, and in particular from the rich. Heavy reliance on borrowing meant that discussions of appropriate levels of taxation were postponed till the latter stages of the war and till after the war's end.

In the period before World War I it was deputies from the center left, such as Joseph Caillaux, who had been the principal authors of progressive tax proposals. During and after the war, socialist deputies further to the left began to play a much more prominent role in tax debates. As they did so they hammered home two ideas that we have seen elsewhere. The first was that some were earning very substantial profits from the war, and the tax system should be used to compensate for this. The second was that if labor was to be conscripted then capital should be conscripted as well. The English phrase "conscription of wealth" came to be referred to as the *conscription des fortunes.*[83]

A look at the French Socialist Party's "Program of Action" agreed on in April 1919 is one good way to see how France's Socialists used the wartime context to reinforce arguments they had long made in favor of redistributive policies. The introduction to the Program includes the following statement: "The war has proven that class antagonism is very much the law of current Society, because while creating new rich and new poor, the war has increased both fortunes and misery, concentrating capital, as well as the international proletariat."[84] The Program of Action involves many specific policy proposals, and those regarding where new revenue can be found are described in the following terms:

> The Socialist Party declares that these extraordinary or permanent resources, must be sought: In the severe revision of contracts

and war profits, by special laws and the return to the state of abusive profits; in the conscription of fortunes, every bit as legitimate as the conscription of men; in a tax on excess profits. In the strict collection of the income tax and inscription taxes, with greatly increased progression.[85]

Clearly, the context of mass mobilization for war provided the French Socialist Party with powerful new arguments for taxing the rich. The same thing is apparent when we look at the arguments made in the French Chamber of Deputies. A particularly important tax debate occurred in the spring of 1920. At this time France's lower house, the Chamber of Deputies, had a right-wing majority, elected in the fall of 1919. France's Senate remained more evenly distributed between left and right. The debates of 1920 ultimately resulted in the French government implementing a top marginal income tax rate of 50 percent. This followed on several increases that had happened during the war itself.

In the 1920 debate a right-wing government made explicit the need to tax the rich more heavily than the rest. A speaker responsible for presenting the work of a parliamentary committee did so in part by explicitly emphasizing ability to pay and taxation of luxury. However, he also clearly emphasized that war profits were an issue to be dealt with. The speaker first suggested that France ought to merit some sort of international compensation because the war had been fought on its territory. However, he also had this to say about distributive issues within France: "But, in the interior itself, too many scandalous profits spread themselves out insolently and rejoice on the tombs and on the ruins."[86]

Needless to say, these were strong words coming from a representative from the political right. Though the specific issue at hand was war profits, it is hard not to see how such claims might color attitudes toward the rich more generally. Though the government opposed the idea of a conscription of wealth or a special tax on capital, it did propose to double the top marginal rate of income taxation from 20 percent to 40 percent. In the end, after consideration by the Senate the top rate was set at 50 percent, a very dramatic increase on the prewar era. In the new environment it was also the case that some economists who had opposed income taxation prior to the war now advocated a conscription of wealth.[87]

Consider next the stance taken by the Socialists in the 1920 debate. Vincent Auriol, a future president of France, presented an alternative Socialist Proposal that would have addressed not only the income tax but also a 3 percent annual tax on capital in lieu of a one-off conscription of wealth. The proposal would have also involved a substantial strengthening of France's weak tax administration so as to improve revenue collection. The weakness of state capacity for collecting the income tax was a perennial issue at this time.[88] Auriol suggested that the government proposal was inadequate for compensating the sacrifices that the government had asked of citizens during the war:

> To this people for which during the war you exalted the sentiments of justice and of right, you give the spectacle of the most cruel iniquity. You have spoken of solidarity; you give the example of egoism. You speak of fiscal courage, and thanks to you the comfortable classes will practice fiscal cowardice.[89]

In the end, in a chamber dominated by the right, the Socialist proposals saw little chance of becoming law. Even so, the context of war sacrifice prompted the right to concede to a great increase in the progressivity of the income tax. This was accompanied by the maintenance of a war profits tax established in 1916 and by an increase in the top rate of inheritance taxation. For a Socialist like Vincent Auriol this seemed like a defeat, but it was in fact a fundamental shift in the way that the French state taxed the rich.

CONCLUSION

World War I is especially well suited for comparing fairness arguments before and after the conflict because the timing of the conflict was an exogenous shock. Further, the war created new inequities by requiring large numbers of citizens to fight. It also generated increased profits across many sectors of the economy. In the UK, France, Canada, and the United States these new war-induced inequities changed fairness debates about taxation. In each case not only did policy change, but fairness arguments shifted to an emphasis on new compensatory arguments. Across the political spectrum, politicians, bureaucrats, and other elites argued for higher taxes on the rich in order to compensate for these new inequalities. As we have shown from local newspapers, the same was the case with mass opinion.

CHAPTER SEVEN

THE ROLE OF WAR TECHNOLOGY

Thus far we have said that mass warfare matters for taxation, but we have offered no explanation for when and why states engage in wars of mass mobilization as opposed to more limited engagements. Over the last two centuries countries like the United States have shifted from engaging in wars where only a small part of the population has been mobilized, to a period of mass mobilization, and then back to smaller scale mobilizations since that date. The scale of mobilization matters because when only a small fraction of a country's population is mobilized, it is hard to suggest that the rich should make a special sacrifice if most others are not sacrificing either.

There are two key reasons why the material we present in this chapter is critical for this book. The first is to help better understand the deeper reasons why steeply progressive taxes happened when they did, and why it may be more difficult to build political support for them today. The second is to suggest that the process driving taxation of the rich has been far from accidental. It has instead depended on long-run trends in international rivalry and war fighting technology.

The era of the mass army, and therefore the conscription of wealth, was to a great extent technologically determined. It depended on a state of technology in which men and supplies could be moved en masse by rail yet where the remote delivery of explosive force was not yet advanced enough to avoid the need for mass infantry. The era of the mass army of course also depended on the fact that there were sizeable powers that saw themselves as rivals. These basic facts have clear implications for how we think about taxation of the rich and about social stratification more generally. When changes in technology or international rivalries produce a shift toward a war strategy of mass mobilization, this will press states to take actions that reduce social stratification. Taxation of the rich is one such policy. Current technological trends suggest a continued turn away from mass mobilization strategies, which will drive countries further and further from a context where "conscription of wealth" arguments can be used to justify heavy taxation of the rich.

THREE HISTORICAL EXAMPLES

Waging war means projecting armed force, and often over a considerable distance. For most of human history projecting force meant sending soldiers to the field of battle. It also meant mobilizing the resources that soldiers would use to fight: armor, weapons, ships, and food. In some cases these resources were substitutes for soldiers, so one heavily armed knight might be expected to have the same impact as multiple infantrymen. In other cases these resources were complements, so for example a ship in the classical era required many rowers to propel it. Over the course of history, the scale of military mobilization has depended heavily on the type of technology that states use to wage war. There is also good reason to believe that the scale of mobilization has then influenced inequality. In societies where the choice of technology leads to the great mass of citizens being mobilized, there have been pressures for social leveling.[1] Technology compatible only with smaller armies has in contrast been associated with greater social stratification. It's worth considering a few examples to show the generality of this phenomenon. In so doing we distinguish between two ways that technology has mattered. In some cases exogenous changes in technology, due to invention, have allowed states to fight wars in new ways. In other cases a change in the nature of a state's opponents has led to a shift from employing one existing technology to another. Both of these changes are at work today.

Classical observers argued that when states employed a military technology requiring broad mobilization of the population, it was associated with a more democratic form of rule. Aristotle provided a succinct description of this phenomenon in section seven of book six of *The Politics*. In his words: "Where a territory is suitable for the use of cavalry, there is a favorable ground for the construction of a strong form of oligarchy: the inhabitants of such a territory need a cavalry force for security, and it is only men of large means who can afford to keep and breed horses." In contrast Aristotle argued: "Light-armed troops, and the navy, are drawn from the mass of the people, and are thus wholly on the side of democracy."[2]

But why should having a navy be associated with less social stratification? The short answer to this is that in the classical era, naval vessels were rowed as well as sailed, and in naval warfare it was useful to have as much massed manned power as possible for this purpose. Athens is the prime example where reliance on naval power is said to have led to a democratic form of rule, though the city made a deliberate choice to have a navy rather than having this be imposed by technology. A fascinating text by an author known to posterity only as "The Old Oligarch" describes why mass mobilization should go hand in hand with a more egalitarian society. Though the Oligarchic's identity is unknown, he almost certainly hailed from the wealthier class of Athenians. The text provides a clear argument why mass mobilization should result in more equality—because this is the fair thing to do:

> So, first of all, I will say this, that it seems fair enough that in Athens the poor and the common people should have more power than the noble and rich, because it is the common people who row the ships and so render the city powerful; indeed the steersmen, boatswains, pursers, look-out men, and shipwrights render the city powerful, far more than the hoplites, the noble and the good. Since this is so, it seems fair that they should all share in the offices of state by the processes of lot and election, and that anyone of the citizens who wishes should have the right to speak.[3]

Over the course of history changes in military technology have also pushed toward increased social stratification, an outcome opposite from that observed in Athens. One excellent example of this involved the way in which the exogenous introduction of a new technology, the iron stirrup, helped lead to feudalism in Europe. The historian Lynn White proposed this theory.[4] In the two centuries after the fall of the Roman Empire in the West, when warfare occurred, it took place predominantly on foot. The reason for this was that for horsemen, with the primitive saddles of the day it was difficult and dangerous to expect to wield a sword or spear from a mount. Though the Dark Ages were certainly not the best of times, this style of warfare fit with a social structure in the Germanic kingdoms of Western Europe in which there were relatively few official class distinctions. In the Frankish kingdom all free men had both the right and the duty to bear arms.

The arrival of the iron stirrup, an import from Central Asia, changed the way European warfare was waged, and if White's thesis is correct, it also changed society. The iron stirrup allowed horsemen to brace themselves effectively so that they could wield a sword, or especially a lance. As a natural extension of this, mounted warriors increasingly adopted armor to protect themselves. With these developments Western Europe was on the way to having armed forces in which heavily mounted warriors would play a critical role. Now, in the economic conditions of the day, maintaining a warhorse together with everything associated was a very costly venture. Military equipment for one man fighting in this manner was estimated to have cost at least ten oxen. We lack accounts from that time of the sort provided to us by the Old Oligarch for Athens. Nonetheless, some likely believed that if only a few were in a position to engage in this new style of warfare, then these few should enjoy special privileges. The eventual outcome was that the introduction of the iron stirrup helped give birth to a feudal system in Europe with rigid class distinctions. One should certainly not see this as a story with a single cause. There were also other factors pushing toward feudalism, and White's thesis has been much debated.[5] All the same, it is a fascinating example of the conscription of wealth in reverse.

Europe has not been the only world region in which technology has helped determine the ways states fight wars and therefore social structure. China during its initial period of unification provides us with a particularly stark example. In this case it was not technology that changed; it was instead a change in the type of opponents fought that prompted the Chinese state to shift between two existing technologies of war fighting. This in turn had consequences for social stratification. Prior to its unification under the Qin (221–206 BC) and Han (206 BC–AD 220) dynasties, China experienced intense warfare between several regional states. These states increasingly adopted a strategy of fighting with mass armies of peasant conscripts. The leaders of the state of Qin were the most advanced in this regard. Unlike in the case of Athens, mass mobilization in states like Qin was not accompanied by the extension of political rights to the broad populace. However, it is clear from numerous sources that benefits were offered to the peasantry in exchange for their service. States like Qin engaged in important agricultural improvements. They provided land grants to peasant soldiers, subsidized food and clothing, and helped to stabilize grain prices.[6] This does not change the fact that the Qin was, to say the least, an extremely repressive state, but the provision of social benefits to those who fought is still noteworthy.

If the state of military technology under the Qin dynasty helped push in the direction of lower social stratification, changes under the Han dynasty would push in precisely the opposite direction. After the Qin dynasty's quick collapse, the Han dynasty maintained many of the same institutions and policies including universal military conscription. But over time this situation changed. As a "universal" empire the Han dynasty faced no challenge from another large state. It instead found itself battling with nomadic tribes on its frontiers. The ideal military force for waging this type of conflict was an elite army of well-trained horsemen, rather than a mass army of peasant conscripts. Moreover, a mass peasant army could increase the risk of internal rebellion. In AD 31, the Emperor Guangwu issued an edict abolishing universal military conscription.[7] This decision changed the way China fought wars; it also had direct social implications. No longer needing the peasantry to fight, the Han state retreated from the sort of social interventions that had been initiated by the Qin.[8]

The experiences of Han dynasty China, Classical Greece, and Europe during the Dark Ages are obviously very distant from that of the more contemporary period that we consider in this book. However, precisely because they are so distant, they suggest that the link between military technology and policies that reduce social stratification is a very general one.

THE RAILROAD AND THE MODERN MASS ARMY

With the broad historical context in mind, let us now return to the industrialized world over the last two centuries. Is it possible that changes in military technology, and thus mobilization, have led to similar social change?

To answer this question we need to consider how wars were fought in Europe at the outset of the nineteenth century, the starting point for this book. Warfare had evolved substantially since medieval times with well trained and drilled national armies composed mostly of infantry using firearms. However, in other ways things had not changed that much at all. Armies still marched to battle on their feet. Anything they ate had to be carried with them, foraged for on location, or supplied from the rear using horse-drawn wagons. The supply problem placed an upper bound on the size of an army that could be maintained in any one location at a given time. Though it is popular to think of the Napoleonic era as having been a watershed, for all of Napoleon's tactical innovation, he was still bound by the same logistical challenges that had constrained armies since ancient times. If Napoleon knew that an army marches on its stomach, he also knew that this constraint could only be satisfied by effective foraging or by painfully slow provision of supplies from the rear.

The beginnings of a solution to the logistical problem arrived only four years after Napoleon's death—a railway with cars propelled by a steam locomotive.[9] The advent of the railroad, as well as the invention of the telegraph, fundamentally changed Western and other societies. Outside the circle of military historians it is less frequently appreciated that the arrival of the railroad also permitted a drastic increase in the scale of warfare.[10] Railroads could move men rapidly, and they could also move the supplies to feed them. For the first time large armies could be fed without having to forage for food. The first passenger railways, dating from the 1820s, were still very primitive transport systems, and it was several decades before innovations in rails, locomotives, and car design led to railroads that could carry large numbers of troops over substantial distances. The first significant military use of railways was made by Napoleon's nephew, Napoleon III, during his army's Italian campaign of 1859.[11] Railroads were, of course, heavily used in the American Civil War (1861–1865). This war in many ways presaged the destructiveness of European conflicts to come. As we noted previously, it also saw the beginnings of compensatory arguments for taxing the rich.

To assess the impact of the railroad on the scale of military mobilization, together with our co-author, Massimiliano Onorato, we analyzed military mobilization in thirteen great powers between 1600 and 2000.[12] For each country for each year of war we estimated the total strength of a nation's armed forces, not including forces from colonies that may have served under the flag of the colonizer, nor home defense units that are not part of the regular armed forces. We used information on the actual strength of the armed forces as opposed to what is referred to by military historians as an army's "paper strength." Governments have a natural incentive to exaggerate the size of their armed forces, and this needs to be taken into account.

We expect a country that engages in mass mobilization for war to have an army that is large in absolute terms while also representing a significant fraction of the total population. Figure 7.1 shows average military sizes over twenty-five-year periods across the thirteen great powers for the last four centuries. In order to consider maximal army capabilities, we consider army sizes during war years only. There was a general increase in army size from 1600 to 1900, followed by a dramatic increase in the first half of the twentieth century. Figure 7.1 also presents evidence on army sizes relative to a country's total population. We call this measure "military mobilization." This measure starts off somewhat high in the beginning of the seventeenth

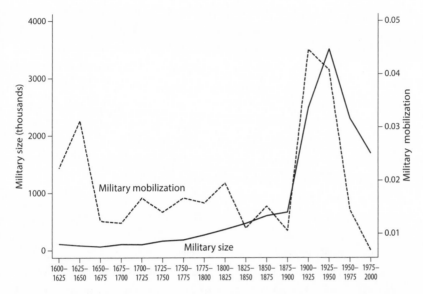

Figure 7.1. Military Size and Mobilization, 1600–2000. This figure reports the twenty-five-year averages for the absolute size of the military and mobilization rates for great power states in war years from 1600 to 2000. See Onorato, Scheve, and Stasavage (2014) for sources.

century. This is almost entirely due to the ability of a few small powers (Sweden in particular) to raise large armies with foreign soldiers. These were not mass mobilized citizen armies of the sort we would see in later centuries. More generally, the average scale of military mobilization remained relatively constant during the seventeenth, eighteenth, and nineteenth centuries. In other words, army sizes may have increased, but total population increased in the same proportion. Now consider what happened during the twentieth century—the scale of military mobilization rose drastically only to decline almost as dramatically toward century's end.

How do we know it was the arrival of the railroad that led to this dramatic increase in military mobilization? There were, after all, many things that changed between the nineteenth and twentieth centuries. To consider this we collected data on the overall size of national rail networks and investigated whether this was correlated with the scale of military mobilization. The idea here is that the greater the size of a country's rail network, the easier it would be keep a mass army supplied. To deal with the likelihood that a third factor might have influenced both army sizes and railroad networks, we also considered several other possibilities. One might think that richer countries could afford to mobilize a greater fraction of their population. One might also think that a spirit of nationalism would drive more people to serve in the armed forces. Since it has been argued that basic literacy is a necessary precondition for nationalist sentiment, we considered the effect of basic literacy.[13] We finally considered whether democracy made a difference for the scale of mobilization. It is plausible to suggest that people will be more likely to fight if they enjoy the right to vote and thus to influence choices made by their government.

Even accounting for the other factors, there is a clear and unambiguous correlation between the extent of a country's railway network and the scale of military mobilization. The same correlation is observed when using military size, as opposed to mobilization, as an outcome. Do these results reflect a causal effect of the railroad on the scale of military mobilization? We need to consider the possibility of reverse causality; governments may have developed railroads in order to be able to mobilize troops. It would be very difficult to argue that railroads were invented to allow for mass mobilization; they were instead a by-product of the Industrial Revolution. The invention of the steam engine made it possible to move goods by rail in a way previously thought impossible. Improvements in steel production allowed for rail networks of durable steel rails. Even so, one might still argue that once the steam locomotive and the steel rail were invented, governments improved and expanded their railroads in anticipation of the need to mobilize a mass army. There were certainly some instances where this did take place, as with Prussia during the second half of the nineteenth century. Yet the phenomenon does not appear to have been general. Daniel Bogart, an economic historian, has shown that when governments anticipated military threats, they often responded by nationalizing their railways, but they did not expand the scale of them.[14] Therefore, as long as we focus on the size of a rail network in our analysis, and not ownership, we can suggest that the correlation between railroads and military mobilization reflects the impact of the former on the latter.

In emphasizing the role of the railroad for mass mobilization, we are also challenging an important piece of received wisdom. Many scholars see the mass army as a product of the French Revolution and the creation of the idea of "the nation in arms."[15] By calling up the entire nation through a *levée en masse*, the French revolutionaries led Western Europe into a new style of warfare on an unprecedented scale. The evidence contradicts this notion. There is no apparent break in average army size in 1789 or any other year associated with the French Revolution. Even for France itself, there is little support for the claim that the revolutionary or Napoleonic eras were a watershed. It is true that the Napoleonic era saw important innovation in tactics. It is also true that the French revolutionaries briefly experimented with a system of universal conscription. But the increase in army sizes during this period paled in comparison with the change ushered in during World War I.

At the close of the seventeenth century, Louis XIV mobilized an army of 362,000 men. This was equivalent to 1.9 percent of France's total population at the time. During the year in which Napoleon launched his Russian campaign there were 800,000 men in service in France, or 2.7 percent of the population. Should we call this increase a watershed? It would make sense to do so if the Napoleonic increase was followed by a new plateau, but this is not what happened. Compare now the figures for mobilization under Louis XIV and Napoleon with mobilization during World War I. At its peak France had an army of 5.3 million men, or fully 16 percent of the total population at the time. If we are to speak of a watershed then this clearly took place in 1914, and it was arguably a product of the railroad. This French evidence is borne out in the data more generally. When we take the entire dataset and examine whether the French Revolution constituted a statistically significant break in army sizes, we fail to see that this is the case.[16] It is certainly still possible that the French Revolution gave birth to the idea of "the nation in arms," but it would not be until the advent of the railroad that this idea could be fully realized.

The railroad was not only important for the scale of military mobilization; it was also associated with a dramatic shift in the way that governments recruited armies. Apart from the brief French Revolutionary experience, European armies during the eighteenth and nineteenth centuries were generally recruited either by attracting volunteers, through periodic coercion of certain groups, or by a system of conscription that allowed for those with money to purchase a replacement. This is the type of system that existed during the U.S. Civil War. It was also the system used by France for much of the nineteenth century. The practice of purchasing a replacement seems contrary to modern sensibilities, and it certainly provoked protests at the time, but many advocates defended the French system by suggesting that the government should have no business in restricting a voluntary exchange between two individuals.[17] Margaret Levi has argued convincingly that governments eventually removed such possibilities for replacement in order to improve compliance with conscription.[18] If all were expected to be able to serve, then any resistance to conscription would be weaker. The shift to universal conscription was also spurred by the development of the railroad.

To see the link between the railroad and universal conscription, we compiled evidence for the thirteen great powers on the date at which they first adopted universal conscription as well as the date at which they abandoned it.[19] We then repeated the analysis we performed for military size and military mobilization while considering universal conscription as the outcome to be explained. The results show that the arrival of conscription with replacement or opt-outs was not correlated with the arrival of the railroad. The emergence of this type of conscription in most cases pre-dated rail transport. The situation with universal conscription was much different. The more extensive a country's railway network, the greater the likelihood that its government would shift to a regime of recruitment by universal conscription, a practice that would become the default strategy for raising a mass army. The arrival of universal conscription led also to demands for a conscription of wealth.

We have already made a number of caveats about our evidence and whether the correlation between the expansion of the railroad and mass armies can be given a causal interpretation. In addition, we make no claim that the railroad was the only technological innovation that led to the era of the mass army. There were prior or simultaneous developments, as well as subsequent developments with the internal combustion engine, that also pushed in this direction. We are simply using this as the most prominent example of an important technology that allowed governments to field armies on an unprecedented scale. Second, we also make no claim that the railroad was a sufficient condition for the mass army to develop. Transport by rail solved the supply problem, but the scale of mobilization also depended on the type of enemies that were being fought. If warfare during the first half of the twentieth century had been limited to large powers waging wars against smaller counterparts, or in colonial contexts, it is likely that the railroad would not have been associated with such a large increase in the scale of mobilization.

THE DEMISE OF THE MASS ARMY

Technological innovation in the nineteenth century helped make the mass army possible. Technological innovation in the twentieth century helped make mass armies less desirable to field. The era of the mass army depended on the existence of a particular technological state of affairs. In this state it was possible to transport men en masse and keep them adequately supplied, but the remote precision delivery of explosive force was not yet a reality. During the twentieth century this situation changed. It became feasible to deliver explosive force from a distance, and as time went on this delivery became more and more precise. Today those countries with advanced weapons systems can deliver explosives with precision measured in a few feet. This development has quite arguably spelled the end of the mass army and with it the potential for compensatory arguments involving the conscription of wealth. In the words of Major Leonard Litton of the U.S. Air Force, "It is no longer required to bring forces into the same geographical area to bring their effects to bear on the same target and, in fact, on the modern battlefield it may be dangerous as well."[20]

When it comes to the technology that led to the rise of the mass army, it seems fair to say that the development of the railroad was an essentially exogenous development, a product of the Industrial Revolution. In strong contrast, the technologies underlying the move away from the mass army have been an endogenous development, heavily influenced by investments from national militaries, and in particular that of the United States. The radar, the laser, and the satellite have been among the technologies that have helped allow for more precise targeting of munitions. This has led to an increased ability to deliver explosive force from the air. There is every reason to believe that for great powers, the arrival of the nuclear age has also had an effect in shifting states away from a strategy of mass mobilization. However, the development of nuclear weaponry has itself been aided by the same developments in delivery and guidance systems.

One might object to the previous argument by saying that destructive air power has been in place since World War II, and that was certainly a war of mass mobilization. What is sometimes not recognized is how much more accurate aerial bombing has become over time and how inaccurate it was some seventy years ago. The most common metric for judging the accuracy of payloads delivered from the air is circular error probability. For a given device the circular error probability is the radius around a target within which payloads will fall 50 percent of the time. In 1944 while using the Norden bombsight, the most advanced technology of the time, American B-17 crews were able to deliver conventional bombs with a circular error probability of 1,000 feet.[21] That may have been sufficient to wreak havoc on the civilian population, but it wasn't very precise for hitting specific military or industrial targets.

Fast forward to the Vietnam War. While this was a war fought mostly with conventional (i.e., unguided) bombs, the United States did also make the first use of a laser-guided bomb in the conflict. In raids conducted in 1968 using M117 bombs equipped with laser-guided bombs, a circular error probability of seventy-five feet was achieved.[22] One of the most fascinating elements of this story involving the United States introducing the laser-guided bomb is that its use had a rapid impact on the thinking of Soviet military planners.

The Soviet military had access to North Vietnamese reports on how effective laser-guided bombs proved to be. For an army whose European military strategy relied upon the idea of a mass armored push across the continent, this was a serious challenge.[23] Today, with the third generation of laser-guided bombs, the GBU-24 Paveway III series first introduced in 1983, under ideal conditions a circular error probability of 3.6 feet can be achieved. While Paveway III bombs are expensive, in 2008 in Iraq the United States deployed a less expensive weapon, the LJDAM GBU-54, that still has a low circular error probability. In sum, precision has increased remarkably, and it has also become less expensive. To complete the discussion of air power we would of course also need to include cruise missiles and various forms of rockets. Given these developments, it is not surprising to see that great powers, such as the United States, have mobilized successively smaller numbers of soldiers in recent conflicts.

We investigated whether the arrival of precision weapons spelled the end of the era of the mass army. To do this we constructed a measure that takes a value of one for each year in which a government had access to cruise missiles and zero otherwise.[24] We then examined whether this was correlated with either army size or the scale of military mobilization. As we would expect if precision weapons led to smaller armies, we found a negative correlation between access to cruise missiles and both military size and the scale of mobilization. We should be very cautious, however, before suggesting that this result proves that the arrival of precision weapons caused the end of the era of the mass army. As we mentioned earlier, if the railroad was an essentially exogenous invention, precisions weapons certainly cannot be characterized in the same way. The underlying technologies that allowed for their development, such as gyroscopes, radar, and satellites, were developed in a context of intense military competition between the major powers. So, even if there is good reason to believe that precision weapons caused the end of the mass army, our statistical tests do not unambiguously demonstrate this fact.

Aside from the development of precision weapons, the other obvious reason why great powers no longer fight wars of mass mobilization is that since 1945 they have ceased to fight wars against each other. When they are deployed today, great power armies are much more likely to find themselves fighting insurgencies against which a mass army is less effective. The Han dynasty of two thousand years ago found that in such circumstances it makes sense to switch away from mass armies toward a more capital-intensive form of warfare. In recent decades the United States appears to have been arriving at the same conclusion.

IMPLICATIONS FOR THE FUTURE

The era of the mass army, one where countries have mobilized a substantial fraction of their citizens to fight, was dependent on a specific state of technological development. As the precision of weapons delivered from the air has increased, it has become unnecessary, and perhaps undesirable, to mobilize a mass army for conflict. It seems unlikely that technological trends will push in the opposite direction anytime soon. Given the nature of enemies that a country like the United States, or other large industrial powers, are likely to face going forward, it seems even more unlikely that mass mobilization will take place. What does this imply about taxing the rich? The twentieth-century conditions that created powerful compensatory arguments for taxing the rich are unlikely to be repeated anytime soon. These conditions were far from accidental; they were driven by long-term trends involving international rivalries and military technology.

CHAPTER EIGHT

WHY TAXES ON THE
RICH DECLINED

What happened after mass mobilization ended, and what was the impact on tax policy? We know there has been a general movement to lower top rates of income and inheritance taxation in recent decades, but it took some time after 1945 before this process began. In fact, the postwar era is often described as one where there was a consensus in favor of a certain set of economic policies, of which progressive taxation was a key element. Our goal in this chapter is to consider this "postwar consensus" and the subsequent shift away from taxing the rich. We first ask whether there was a postwar consensus to begin with and whether it was linked to compensatory claims about war sacrifice. We then investigate the movement away from taxing the rich, examining the role of beliefs about the economy, globalization, and the evolution of fairness arguments.

While compensatory arguments were common during the Second World War, they were also common in the aftermath of the conflict. After 1945 war debts needed to be paid, and substantial reconstruction was needed. As after the First World War, the money for these efforts needed to come from somewhere. As part of this context, it was suggested that those who had fought needed to be recognized with benefits while those who profited from the war should be taxed. For all these reasons compensatory arguments were made suggesting that the rich needed to pay. However, even in the immediate postwar period the consensus on taxing the rich was far from complete. Perhaps the term "consensus" is even inappropriate. There were early signs, certainly in the United States, that many individuals favored much less progressivity of income taxation. This suggests that, as in any other period, the postwar era was one where tax fairness was contested.

If the strength of compensatory claims after 1945 solidified support for taxing the rich, we also need to ask why this support eventually diminished. There are two explanations most commonly offered for the movement away from taxing the rich. These involve fears for economic growth and the constraints of globalization. We argue that these factors may have contributed to downward political pressure on top rates, but they are not the whole story, and they probably are not even the biggest part of the story. The other, more important, factor impacting taxation of the rich has been that proponents of progressive taxation no longer have access to the same sort of compensatory arguments that they could make in 1945. Different compensatory arguments can be made today, but they have a smaller impact. In today's debates about progressive taxation, observers often fail to appreciate this fact.

WAS THERE A POSTWAR CONSENSUS?

The idea of consensus is exaggerated, but there is no doubt that the postwar context made it possible for proponents of progressive taxation to make powerful compensatory arguments in favor of taxing the rich. These centered on the idea that those who had sacrificed during the war should be compensated, while those who had profited from the war should be taxed. These were of course exactly the same arguments that had been made in the immediate wake of World War I. Much more than in World War I, compensatory arguments also concentrated on the need to spend on war veterans and all those who had sacrificed during the war. In most cases the compensatory arguments made by political parties of the left after 1945 did not focus specifically on the top rates of income or inheritance taxation. They were more general in form, but it was clear that wealth was still the target.

Consider first the situation in a victorious country like the United Kingdom. Two months after the German surrender, a general election was held in which the Labour Party won a large majority in the House of Commons. It is well known that this paved the way for the establishment of Britain's welfare state. Labour's victory also helped solidify Britain's policies involving heavy taxation of high incomes and large fortunes. It is instructive to consider the type of arguments made in the Labour Party's election manifesto because these clearly involved compensatory themes. In its very first paragraph the manifesto made the following statement:

> The gallant men and women in the Fighting Services, in the Merchant Navy, Home Guard and Civil Defence, in the factories and in the bombed areas—they deserve and must be assured a happier future than faced so many of them after the last war. Labour regards their welfare as a sacred trust.[1]

In other words, the policies that Labour would advocate were desirable precisely because people deserved them after their wartime sacrifices. In its manifesto the party continued by emphasizing its belief that after World War I those who had profited from the war had been insufficiently taxed. Moreover, it was said that these same interests came to control economic policy during the 1920s and 1930s and guided them in a manner conducive to the most fortunate. Yet the party reminded voters that because of its direct ministerial role during the Second World War, war profits had been taxed more heavily:

> The interests have not been able to make the same profits out of this war as they did out of the last. The determined propaganda of the Labour Party, helped by other progressive forces, had its effect in "taking the profit out of war." The 100 percent Excess Profits Tax, the controls over industry and transport, the fair rationing of food and control of prices—without which the Labour Party would not have remained in the Government—these all helped to win the war. With these measures the country has come nearer to making "fair shares" the national rule than ever before in its history.[2]

In its manifesto the Labour Party then proposed that such policies should be maintained so as to ensure fair burden sharing. We know that Labour won an election landslide in 1945 despite Winston Churchill's personal popularity at the close of the war. This in itself provides a good indication that the arguments in the Labour manifesto had an impact. This view is also supported by the reports of a British Institute of Public Opinion survey conducted on July 31, 1945, immediately after the election result became known. When asked whether they believed that the election result indicated that the British public wanted the Labour government to introduce sweeping changes, and not simply to govern more efficiently, 54 percent said yes while only 30 percent said no.[3]

Consider next the situation in an occupied country such as France. The political force that took control in France during the liberation of the country was the Conseil National de la Résistance, a group that included members from different political parties and unions. On March 15, 1944, the Conseil agreed to a common program entitled "Les Jours Heureux," or "Happy Days."[4] The program specified how the resistance and French population should act in order to bring the war to a close. It also specified an economic program for the postwar period. In a country like France, where the collaboration with the occupying forces had been extensive, compensatory arguments hinged less on the need to recognize those who had fought than on the need to extract resources from those who had benefitted unfairly. The Conseil's program called, among other things, for the establishment of a progressive tax on war profits.

After the liberation, in October 1944 the provisional French government announced a tax on all "illicit" profits that had accrued during the war. This included profits from the black market or from any commercial transactions with enemy forces.[5] The logic therein was clearly compensatory. If the nation had grown poorer under occupation, then some had grown richer, and therefore they should be taxed. Following this decision, the French government also implemented a series of nationalizations of key industries. While the motivation for these nationalizations was partly one of perceived efficiency, support for this measure was also attributable to the perception that several of these industries had earned high profits under the occupation. So, for example, the car maker Renault was nationalized in part because during the occupation it had produced vehicles for the Wehrmacht.[6] Though the measures adopted by the French government after the liberation focused more on taxing war profits than on raising top rates of income or inheritance taxation, there seems little doubt that perceptions that many of France's wealthy had collaborated with the enemy helped color attitudes toward the rich for some time to come.

As a third example, consider the situation in a defeated country like Germany. Here questions of compensation would turn neither on the issue of how to recognize the victors, nor on how to sanction those who had profited from the presence of an enemy regime. In 1945, Germans instead set about the task of debating how to compensate the many who suffered material losses during the war.[7] There was a strong sense on the part of those who had suffered war damages that they had sacrificed for the war while others had earned profits even in the midst of defeat. For a number of years after 1945 the idea of how to compensate individuals, or equalize the burdens of defeat, took place. In the end, these led to the passage of a *Lastenausgleich*, or burden sharing, law in 1952. The law involved a substantial redistribution of wealth from the more fortunate to the less fortunate. It established a 50 percent levy on real assets that was to be paid over a term of thirty years, resulting in what was in essence a property tax.

Consider finally the situation in a country like Sweden, which had not participated in the war. Though Sweden had not seen sacrifice of the sort made by citizens of belligerent countries, the Swedish economy was nonetheless seriously disrupted as a result of the more general economic dislocation that the war entailed. The Swedish government also mobilized a large military, not knowing whether it would succeed in maintaining its neutrality. In this context the Swedish Social Democrats, like other parties of the left in Europe, made use of compensatory arguments in order to try to build support for redistributive economic policies. In July 1945, Gunnar Myrdal gave a campaign speech arguing that after the sacrifices that the state demanded of citizens during the Great Depression and the war, the postwar period would be one of harvest time wherein past sacrifices would be recompensed.[8] The phrase "harvest time" would subsequently gain popularity in Sweden.

In sum, for a variety of different countries in different situations in 1945, the aftermath of war influenced debates about collective burden sharing. This included redistributive measures to compensate those who had sacrificed while taxing those who enjoyed a more profitable position. These debates about postwar compensation often did not focus directly on asking what the top marginal rate of income or inheritance taxation should be. Even so, there seems little doubt that this context had a major impact on how people thought about the fair position of the rich in society.

After 1945 powerful compensatory arguments supported taxing the rich. However, there was also a complementary factor. Once tax rates had gone up during wartime they became the new status quo legislation, and the status quo can be difficult to reverse. A status quo of higher revenues helped fuel a debate about whether these higher revenues could be used to fund new welfare state expenditures.[9]

Was there a "postwar consensus" in favor of taxing the rich? A first reason to think otherwise is that even in 1945, measures adopted by some governments were a subject of debate. Take the case of the 1945 general election in the United Kingdom. While the Labour Party advocated development of an extensive welfare state, the Conservative Party warned ferociously about the dangers of socialism.[10] Likewise, in Germany if there was broad agreement that those who had suffered war damage should be compensated, the extent of this compensation was hotly debated. It was for this reason that Germany did not pass its burden-sharing law until 1952.[11]

The other evidence suggesting we should be careful before jumping to the conclusion that there was a postwar consensus comes from polling data in the United States. Consider again the Gallup polls that asked respondents whether they thought that the amount of federal income tax they were currently paying was fair. We pointed out in chapter 3 that during the war itself, a strikingly high fraction of respondents said that the amount of taxes they paid was fair. Though wealthier respondents were somewhat less likely to respond in the affirmative to this question, even among this group fully 77 percent said their taxes were fair.[12] These numbers are striking, but it is not completely clear how much they say about distributional considerations. The ideal question for our purposes would have been a specific query about taxing the rich and whether it was deemed fair.

As we discussed in chapter 3, between the end of the war and the next time the question was asked (February 1946), the overall percentage of respondents saying they paid a fair amount of income tax dropped from 85 percent to 65 percent.[13] The change in perception was slightly larger among the wealthy, with the fraction saying their income taxes were fair dropping from the wartime peak of 77 percent to a peacetime level of 54 percent.

There is also additional evidence that at least in the United States, the "postwar consensus" in favor of taxing the rich was not as strong as some might think. In response to the very high top marginal tax rates implemented by the Roosevelt administration, at various points from 1938 through the 1950s conservative groups advocated implementing either statutory or constitutional limitations on the amount of income taxes that the federal government could require an individual to pay.[14] In the case of the constitutional initiatives, a significant number of state legislatures voted in favor of holding a constitutional convention to discuss an amendment to limit income taxation. The resolutions passed by individual states (and also proposed in Congress) varied in form. Some called for limiting the top marginal rate of income, inheritance, or gift taxation to 25 percent, others limiting the effective rate to 25 percent, and some also allowed for exceptions in time of war.[15] Proponents of these tax limitation proposals argued that high income taxes would hinder economic growth. In the heightened rhetoric of the Cold War there was also an attempt to associate high marginal rates with Communism. They finally appealed to more basic notions of equal treatment. This demonstrates that even during the heyday of the postwar income tax, standards of fairness were contested.

To gauge public sentiment on the question of income tax limitation, in May 1952 the Gallup organization asked a sample of 2,097 individuals to respond to the following question by either agreeing, opposing, or expressing no opinion:

Many wealthy people now pay as high as 90 percent of their income in Federal income taxes. Would you favor or oppose Congress passing a law so the Federal government could not take more than 25 percent, or one fourth, of any person's income in taxes except in war-time?[16]

Fully 92 percent of respondents chose to express an opinion about the issue, with a narrow majority of 51 percent in favor of an income tax limitation. Is it really possible that as early as 1952 a majority of Americans supported such a drastic reorientation in income tax policy? We should be cautious before jumping to such a conclusion. The question is slightly misleading because even though the top marginal rate of income taxation exceeded 90 percent at this time, as we showed in chapter 3, effective tax rates for even the top 1 percent or the top 0.01 percent were substantially lower than 90 percent. It is also the case that this question was asked by the Gallup organization on only one occasion. If it had been asked several times in different contexts this would have given us a better gauge of public sentiment.[17]

The polling evidence on tax fairness and tax limitations suggests that we should be wary of accepting the idea that there was a postwar consensus with regard to progressive taxation. At the same time, the Gallup poll evidence, with its limitations, is hardly sufficient for us to dispense with the idea that the postwar era was one of strong support for taxing the rich. These results also cover only one country, and it is possible that the political legacy of war faded more quickly in the United States than in those countries whose very existence had been threatened by the war.

The conclusion we draw is that the postwar period was one where support for taxing high incomes and top fortunes was reinforced by powerful compensatory arguments. By having access to these arguments supporters of progressive taxation were in a better position. However, their ideas were still contested, and the "consensus" in favor of taxing the rich was far from complete.

DID FEARS FOR GROWTH LEAD TO LOWER TAXES?

There is a common perception that the move in recent decades to reduce top tax rates has been motivated by fears for economic growth. If the rich are taxed too heavily, then they will work less and invest less. Therefore everyone will suffer. According to one variant of this interpretation, sometime in the 1970s or 1980s, observers began to realize just how heavily high top tax rates weighed on the economy, whereas prior to that date such concerns had been underemphasized. There is no doubt that recent advocates of reducing taxes on the rich have made efficiency arguments of this type. The real question is whether they have been saying anything different from what critics of progressive taxation have been saying all along. Criticisms of the effect of progressive taxation on growth have been present for five centuries. So the real question is, has there been anything new about these critiques in recent decades?

Looking back at the twentieth century, arguments about the economic effect of taxing the rich were made even when taxes on the rich were at their wartime peak. In 1942 the *Wall Street Journal* ran a series of articles entitled "The New Poor" that described how the ceiling that the Roosevelt administration placed on executive salaries was negatively impacting the economy. While the exaggerated title for this series may not have been the best choice, the articles did also have another constant refrain—ultimately the rich used their income to employ others:

> Mr. Smith. $100,000 salaried president of a nationally known company will have to make some readjustments in his living, but they will be much less severe than those required of the 12 personal employees which the shot at his salary will knock off his payroll.[18]

Another way to consider efficiency arguments is to see whether and when they have appeared in election manifestos of parties from the right of the political spectrum. It is not surprising to see that manifestos from the Thatcher era in the United Kingdom laid heavy emphasis on the high costs of taxation. The Conservative Party manifesto of 1979 emphasized that "lower taxes on earnings and savings will encourage economic growth."[19] It may seem more surprising to see that Conservative Party manifestos in the immediate wake of the Second World War made exactly the same point. Consider the language used in the Conservative Party manifesto of 1950:

> Socialism has imposed a crushing burden of taxation amounting to eight shillings of every pound earned in this country.

Enterprise and extra effort have been stifled. Success has been penalised. Thrift and savings have been discouraged. A vote for Socialism is a vote to continue the policy which has endangered our economic and present independence both as a nation and as men and women.[20]

Similar ideas to those expressed in 1950 can be found in all Conservative Party manifestos up to 1979. The idea that taxes were inimical to growth did not begin with the Thatcher revolution. Therefore, one needs to ask why this rhetoric had so much more impact in 1979 than it did in 1950.

Turning to the United States, we see a very similar phenomenon. Few would be surprised to hear that the Republican Party platform of 1980 placed heavy emphasis on the inimical effects of high taxation. It concluded: "Tax rate reductions will generate increases in economic growth, output, and income which will ultimately generate increased revenues."[21]

In its election manifesto of 1952, with reference to the work of successive Democratic administrations, the Republican Party made the following statement: "We charge that they have choked opportunity and hampered progress by unnecessary and crushing taxation."[22] So it seems that in the United States as well, the idea that taxation was harmful to growth had existed for some time.

If Republicans in the United States and Conservatives in the United Kingdom were much more successful at cutting taxes in 1980 and 1979 than in 1950 and 1952, it was not because they were pointing to previously unrecognized costs of taxation. Such arguments were present all along; something else changed between the 1950s and the 1980s.

One possibility is that economic performance in wealthy countries like the United States and the United Kingdom turned negative in the 1970s and that in this context, arguments about the negative effects of high taxes on growth became more persuasive. We tested this possibility in two ways. First, we considered whether after 1973 (often considered a pivotal year due to negative supply shocks to the world economy) governments tended to cut top tax rates when experiencing a contraction in real gross domestic product from one year to the next. We found no evidence that governments that experienced recessions tended to cut tax rates more than other governments. We next asked whether countries that experienced more of a general growth slowdown after 1973 tended to cut top tax rates. The idea here is that it may not have been recessions but a general decrease in the trend rate of growth that prompted people to reassess the wisdom of taxing the rich. We found no evidence to support this claim either.[23]

DID GLOBALIZATION MAKE IT IMPOSSIBLE TO TAX THE RICH?

We have shown that arguments about economic costs from taxing the rich have existed since the Renaissance. In the modern era, political parties of the right, and others, consistently emphasize these costs, but this is not a new feature of the debate over taxation. Yet globalization presents an alternative way in which the economic constraints on taxing the rich may have changed quite dramatically. Over the last decades flows of capital have become increasingly globalized, simultaneous with decreased taxes on the rich. Does the parallel nature of these trends mean that there is a causal link between the two developments? It may be that globalization has prompted states to compete increasingly with one another, offering lower tax rates to attract as much economic activity as possible. It may also be that globalization has simply allowed individuals to move their wealth beyond the reach of their home country. In what follows we review existing work on globalization and corporate taxation. This is one way in which taxation of the rich may have been affected. We then consider the same question for the personal income tax as well as the inheritance tax.

Much of the work on globalization and tax competition has focused on the issue of corporate taxation.[24] If corporations can shift activity from one jurisdiction to another without too much cost, this may place pressures on all states to moderate their levels of corporate taxation. There are a number of factors that might lower this cost, such as if a corporation already has multiple branches in multiple countries. It will also be less costly for corporations to shift activity when countries do not place restrictions on the movement of capital. This is the norm today among the advanced industrial countries, but it certainly was not always the case. The theory of corporate tax competition also predicts another striking phenomenon: as it becomes less costly for corporations to shift their activity, smaller countries will lower their corporate taxes to a greater extent. Smaller countries have a smaller domestic tax base relative to the global tax base. Therefore, they should have a greater incentive to lower their corporate tax rate so as to attract as much economic activity as possible.[25]

Corporate tax rates have dropped as capital has become more mobile, but this in itself does not suffice to demonstrate a causal link. There may be other broad trends common to all countries that produced the shift. For a better test we can make use of the fact that countries have not moved toward greater capital mobility and lower corporate taxation in lockstep. Some countries liberalized capital flows before others and some also reduced corporate taxes at earlier dates than others. Also, the end point in terms of corporate tax rates has not been the same. Making use of this fact, scholars have found clear evidence that as countries liberalized capital flows, they tended to reduce corporate tax rates. Their evidence parallels that from a number of other recent studies, though the conclusions of these other studies are certainly not unanimous.[26]

The other main evidence suggesting that globalization has affected corporate taxation comes from the distinction between large and small countries. The standard theory of corporate tax competition predicts that smaller countries should adopt lower tax rates, and the gap between large and small should increase as it becomes easier for companies to relocate capital and operations. This is in fact precisely what we see. Smaller countries tax corporations more lightly on average, and the difference between large and small countries has increased over time.[27] This pattern of change over time also supports the theory.

The preceding discussion applies only to taxation of *corporate* income. The next question is whether the same theory and the same results might also apply for taxation of *personal* income, the type of tax that we have considered. Some scholars suggest that this has indeed been the case. In a 2009 study James Hines and Lawrence Summers demonstrated that small countries tend to derive less of their total revenue from personal income taxes than do larger states.[28] However, it is not clear that the total share of revenue from income taxes is the appropriate measure to use here. It is less plausible that globalization would have an impact on tax rates for individuals who aren't high earners.[29] Why might high earners be affected? Here we need to introduce the fact that high personal incomes may be earned either through returns on capital or through returns on labor. In the case of capital income, the key question is whether financial globalization has made it easier for individuals to place their wealth abroad in a manner that makes it costly or impossible for a home government to track. Faced with this dilemma, home governments may prefer to lower statutory rates of personal income taxation so as to continue to retain some revenue. The adoption by the Nordic countries of a dual income tax, with a lower tax rate for capital income, provides one example of a policy reform that was in part initiated because of this constraint.[30]

We examined what effect capital mobility may have had on top income tax rates using the same strategy we suggested previously for corporate taxation. Instead of focusing only on the broad trend over time, we asked whether in any given year, countries with lower restrictions on capital have had lower top tax rates. The database of income tax rates allows us to do this in a way that previous studies have not. To conduct our test we made use of the index constructed by Dennis Quinn to measure legal restrictions on the movement of capital in or out of a country.[31]

At first blush we might think that capital mobility has indeed had an impact on top income tax rates. In 1950 the average value of the Quinn index was 34.2, whereas the average top rate of income taxation was 64 percent. By 2010 the average value of the Quinn index was 97.5, essentially complete capital mobility in all twenty countries, and the average top rate of income taxation had fallen to 37 percent. However, there were of course many things that changed between 1950 and 2010 apart from capital mobility. To learn more, we need to look at whether it was the case that within each time period, countries with more capital restrictions also had higher top rates of income taxation. In fact, this was not the case. In 1950 those countries with below average capital mobility also had lower top tax rates on average. This directly contradicts the theory. An even more convincing way to test this argument is to use the same difference-in-differences logic that we have adopted elsewhere in this book. Using this approach we found no evidence of a correlation between the Quinn index of capital account restrictions and top statutory rates of income taxation.[32] We see the same result when substituting effective rates for statutory rates. We also reach an identical conclusion when using the top inheritance tax rates data instead of the income tax data. It would seem that, although capital mobility may have induced countries to cut their taxes on corporate income, this has not carried over to their taxes on personal income or inheritance—or at least not yet.

The preceding analysis applies only to capital income. In the case of labor income, the question is whether individuals might be willing to move not their capital but themselves in order to take advantage of lower tax rates elsewhere.[33] Most observers seem to believe that individuals are less likely to relocate themselves as opposed to their capital. However, when countries do offer personal income tax reductions, evidence suggests that the effect on individual mobility decisions can be large. This has been demonstrated by Henrik Kleven, Camille Landais, and Emmanuel Saez in a study of the market for European soccer professionals. This is a fairly particular market, but a recent example of tax preferences for highly skilled professionals offered by the Danish government leads to a similar conclusion.[34] So, even if high earners may be more likely to move their capital than themselves, there is evidence that mobility of high earners can be a real phenomenon.

We have no adequate way of directly testing the effect of international migration possibilities on personal income tax rates. One might consider looking at official restrictions on immigration for high earners, but in the countries we consider, other features involving the internationalization of labor markets are likely to play a bigger role. As an indirect test, we can return to the question of whether tax rates are correlated with country size. We noted previously that smaller countries face a greater incentive to tax capital lightly in order to attract it. The same exact argument can apply for incentives to tax labor income. Small countries may be more likely to suffer outward migration from high earners if they tax labor income heavily. In addition, by taxing labor income lightly, they will also have a larger pool of potential labor to attract relative to their own domestic pool.

What does the evidence on country size and top rates of income taxation show? There is some evidence in the data that if one uses GDP or total population as a measure of country size, larger countries sometimes tax top earners more heavily. If this effect were driven by globalization, we would also expect to see that the correlation between country size and top income tax rates has grown over time, just as is the case with corporate taxation. In fact, the pattern has been precisely opposite. Across the twenty countries, it was only in the earlier decades, prior to substantial globalization, that there was a positive relationship between country size and the top personal income tax rate. This goes against the idea that international migration pressures have had a substantial effect on top income tax rates. It also further undermines the idea that capital mobility has had the same effect.

A final way to investigate whether globalization has influenced income tax rates is to explore whether tax rate decisions made by individual countries have become more interdependent over time. In a world with increasingly free flows of capital and labor we should expect to see that when making tax rate decisions, governments pay greater heed to decisions made by other states. Analysis of the top tax rate data suggests that decisions made by individual countries are indeed interdependent, but we failed to find evidence of increasing interdependence over time.[35]

We are not claiming that globalization has had no impact on taxation of the rich. To the extent that corporate taxation has a greater incidence on wealthy households, the evidence for this particular channel seems quite clear. However, when it comes to the income tax or the inheritance tax, the evidence of globalization's impact is much weaker. This is not to say that globalization will pose no constraint on taxing the rich going forward as high earners become more and more mobile. What it does suggest is that if we want to understand the shift away from taxing the rich that has already occurred, we need to look elsewhere. In the chapter's final section we show that the compensatory theory of progressive taxation can help provide an answer to this question.

CHANGING FAIRNESS CLAIMS

If neither fears for economic growth nor globalization can explain the movement away from taxing the rich, then what else has mattered? The final possibility we consider is that, as external conditions have changed, the type of fairness-based arguments that people can make about taxing the rich have also changed. We argue that while fairness arguments from the right have remained relatively constant in emphasizing equal treatment, the big change has been for parties of the left. As memory of the Second World War grew more and more distant, parties of the left no longer had access to the same sort of compensatory arguments that they used in the past. This left them in a position of having to defend taxes on the rich strictly by referring to ability to pay or by saying that such taxes were "fair" without providing an explanation of why they were fair.

To begin with we need to recognize that in recent decades, parties of the right have not only justified lowering taxes because of the effect on the economy. They have also made appeals to equal treatment and the idea that people have a right to keep what they earn. This was particularly clear with the Reagan and Thatcher "revolutions." So, in the case of the Conservative Party manifesto of 1979, the party didn't only emphasize the effect of taxes on growth; it also suggested the following: "We shall cut income tax at all levels to reward hard work, responsibility and success."[36]

In 1980 the Republican Party platform in the United States struck a very similar tone. In a sentence immediately following a reference to taxes and growth, it suggested the following: "The greater justification for these cuts, however, lies in the right of individuals to keep and use the money they earn."[37] Again, the reference is to the deservingness of those who earn their money. As we saw in chapter 2, since Matteo Palmieri in 1429, proponents of equal treatment have objected to the ability to pay doctrine for precisely this reason.

Consider now what types of fairness arguments parties of the left used in response to the Reagan and Thatcher movements. Opposing tax cuts, the Labour Party manifesto of 1979 called for a new tax on the wealthy, and it referred to fairness as a reason for this policy. However, the exact nature of the fairness argument was somewhat vague, suggesting simply that "the tax system must be fair and be seen to be so."[38] The Labour manifesto of 1983 struck a similar tone, emphasizing the idea of "fair shares" but without saying why high taxes on the rich were fair.[39] Now consider the position adopted by the U.S. Democratic Party in its 1980 platform. It called attention to the need to preserve the progressive character of the U.S. tax code while also emphasizing the importance of fairness. However, no more specific fairness-based argument was offered.[40] The 1984 Democratic Party Platform did the same.[41] It was almost as if for both Democrats in the United States and Labour supporters in the United Kingdom, arguments in favor of taxing the rich had evolved toward simply saying this was "fair" without any explanation of why it was fair. Had Democrats and Labour simply forgotten how to make a convincing fairness argument? The more likely possibility is that external conditions had changed and with it the type of arguments that could be made. Compensatory war sacrifice arguments simply no longer worked.

One way to chart the gradual disappearance of war sacrifice arguments is to pick up on a fact we considered earlier. The term "equality of sacrifice" was often used in late-nineteenth-century debates as a synonym for the ability to pay doctrine. The term would gain more of a mass appeal beginning in World War I, but with a new meaning. In the wartime context, equality of sacrifice didn't mean that the rich should pay more because they had more; it meant that the rich should sacrifice for the war effort just like the rest of the population. We can consider the evolution of wartime compensatory arguments by looking at subsequent use of the phrase. Figure 8.1 shows

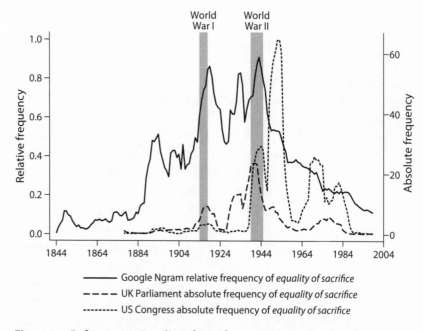

Figure 8.1. References to Equality of Sacrifice, 1844–2000. This figure reports the seven-year moving average for references to *equality of sacrifice* from Google Ngrams, the United Kingdom's parliamentary debates reported in Hansard, and U.S. congressional debates reported in the Congressional Record.

the frequency with which authors referred to equality of sacrifice in three different venues. The first involves the number of references by year in either house of the UK as recorded in the UK Hansard. The second involves the number of references to equality of sacrifice in the Congressional Record. For purposes of comparison, we also report a time series from Google's Ngrams tool. This captures the relative frequency of all references to equality of sacrifice in the Google Books database.

There is substantial variation between the three series in figure 8.1, but it is variation around a common theme. In the half century after John Stuart Mill's first use of the term, equality of sacrifice was referred to very little. Then, the phrase became most heavily used during the two world wars. Finally, in recent decades use of the phrase has declined precipitously, almost vanishing in fact.

In the end, compensatory claims are powerful arguments for progressive taxation, but they cannot be invented at will. External factors instead determine how credible these claims are. In the late nineteenth century basic consumption goods provided a base for taxation. This created the possibility of arguing that an income tax was necessary to compensate for the regressive incidence of the former. In the twentieth century inequalities in war participation made it possible to argue that the rich should be taxed heavily to help restore a degree of equal sacrifice. But as the war faded from memory, such arguments became less credible.[42]

COMPENSATORY ARGUMENTS TODAY

Compensatory arguments based on war sacrifice are no longer as relevant for taxing the rich as they once were. The mass army appears to be a thing of the past. Countries such as the United States still fight wars, but they are more limited engagements in which the rich are not sacrificing, but the great bulk of the population isn't really sacrificing either. In this case there may be strong fairness reasons for compensating those who have sacrificed in Iraq or Afghanistan. What is not clear is why this compensation should be funded through a tax specifically on the rich. A more general levy would seem to be what fairness would dictate. Given this, do compensatory arguments for taxing the rich still have any relevance at all?

There is a wealth of public opinion data on taxation for the United States, and some of it can be used to track opinions over time. At various points since the 1940s the Gallup organization has asked people whether they think the federal income taxes they pay are fair. However, there is not more detailed historical evidence asking people to provide justifications for *why* they thought their taxes were fair or unfair. In our own survey evidence we considered whether people used fairness justifications for their preferred tax policy. Here we explore in more detail what people actually said in that survey when they referred to fairness.

The respondents made a variety of different fairness-based arguments. As an example of equal treatment claims, consider this statement by a respondent: "I do not think it is just to charge a higher percentage of taxation to a group just because they earn more money. I want a fair tax." Likewise, a second respondent said, "Increasing all taxes the same is only FAIR." Finally, a third argued that it was "not fair to punish people because they are successful." Overall, among the respondents who justified their tax preference on fairness grounds, 28 percent adhered to an equal treatment standard.

Other respondents expressed a different opinion based on ability to pay logic. Though critics of the ability to pay principle have long suggested that it is too difficult to implement, many of the respondents did not share this opinion. For them the logic of ability to pay was obvious and easy to state. As one respondent argued, "the rich can afford to carry more of the load." Another suggested, "I think that people who have more money also have the responsibility to help more, since they have the greater ability to do so." Among the respondents who referred to fairness, 35 percent subscribed to this ability to pay logic.

The final fairness category we consider involved those who referred specifically to compensatory reasons for taxing the rich. These were less commonly expressed than either the equal treatment or ability to pay arguments. This fact in itself is interesting. It suggests that in the current environment there is not as much of an opportunity for making compensatory arguments as in the past.

What type of compensatory arguments did people make? Some people justified taxing the rich based on the type of compensatory argument made in the late nineteenth century: "People in the low income bracket already pay enough in taxes via sales, excise, Social Security, Medicare and other payroll taxes. Leave these people alone, they are struggling enough."

A second idea expressed was that the rich should be taxed more heavily because economic gains were tilted unfairly toward them. One respondent argued, "I think the wealthier folks whose income is higher and who very generally speaking probably make money at the expense of poorer people, should have a higher tax burden." This is a compensatory argument akin to that made for the case of war profits. It emphasizes that there is something unfair about the way in which income is generated. It is unclear though whether the respondent had in mind compensating for inequitable actions taken by the state.

Finally, some people argued for compensation on the grounds that the rich benefitted from other types of tax privileges, or as one person claimed, "People earning less than $25,000 don't need higher taxes. People making more than $200,000 tend to get more tax deductions and ways to avoid paying taxes." This clearly involved taxing higher earners more heavily in order to compensate or counterbalance the effect of other state actions.

It is clear from these statements that for some people, the compensatory logic still operates when thinking about taxing the rich. The suggestions are that the rich are less burdened by other types of taxation, and they find it easier to benefit from deductions and loopholes. Given this situation, these respondents believed that some degree of fairness might be restored by having the rich pay a higher rate of tax than everyone else. These are the same type of compensatory arguments that have been made since the fourteenth century, as we saw with the example of medieval Siena. To be credible today, compensatory arguments may need to follow this pattern from earlier centuries, as the twentieth-century compensatory claims involving mass warfare are unlikely to be repeated anytime soon.

CHAPTER NINE

WHAT FUTURE FOR TAXING THE RICH?

Much debate about taxing the rich has focused on the current situation and specificities of the United States. If the U.S. Supreme Court recently removed restrictions on campaign financing, this must somehow help explain why the rich are so lightly taxed in the United States today. Some people explain the reduction in taxes on the rich by referring to other short-term developments. Conservatives often say that U.S. voters have learned the lessons of economic efficiency, while liberals claim that voters have somehow been hoodwinked. Current developments may be important, but we have learned a lot more by looking at taxation of the rich over the long run across multiple countries, and this suggests something about the future course of tax politics in the countries that we have already studied. Debates about taxation will hinge on differing interpretations of what it means to treat people as equals.

THREE WAYS TO TREAT PEOPLE AS EQUALS

Fairness can mean many different things, but one common feature of fairness in taxation is the belief that people ought to be treated as equals. We have distinguished between three different versions of treating citizens as equals in taxation. The first, *equal treatment*, is the idea that everyone should pay the same rate because this mimics basic democratic rights such as each person having a vote of equal weight. The second version, *ability to pay*, is the idea that the rate of tax you pay ought to be conditioned on the resources you have at your disposal. The third variant, the *compensatory* theory, is the idea that the rate of tax you pay ought to depend on whether the state has taken other actions that have put you in a privileged position.

Since at least Renaissance Florence, opponents of progressive taxation have argued that it violates the norm of equal treatment in a republic. Evidence shows that many twenty-first-century survey respondents seem to think exactly the same thing. We even see this view among people who would otherwise have had more income if a progressive rate structure was adopted. We also saw very ample evidence of equal treatment arguments in our review of nineteenth- and early-twentieth-century debates about taxation. Equal treatment arguments clearly resonate in the political arena.

An alternative version of treating citizens as equals is to levy differential tax rates based on ability to pay. If the rich have more, then they shouldn't only pay a greater quantity of taxes; they can also afford to pay a higher tax rate. Though the ability to pay doctrine was not presented in formal mathematical terms until the end of the nineteenth century, it existed as a principle nearly four centuries prior to that date, as is evident from Francesco Guicciardini's proponent of progressive taxation in the *decima scalata* and in eighteenth-century debates about taxing "luxury." Today the ability to pay doctrine provides part of the foundation for modern optimal tax theory in the field of economics, although in optimal tax theory the objective is to maximize aggregate welfare rather than seeing that everyone makes the same sacrifice when it comes to taxation.

The ability to pay doctrine is intuitive, and many people have clearly subscribed to it over time. Nineteenth-century advocates of ability to pay used the doctrine to argue for progressive taxation. Many twentieth-century observers, such as Edwin Seligman, took it as given that the emergence of the ability to pay doctrine explained why many countries were moving to implement progressive income taxes. We also see evidence of support for ability to pay in the contemporary survey evidence. The ability to pay doctrine has resonated with many citizens and it will continue to do so.

Ability to pay arguments matter for many, but they seldom carry the day. The findings from chapters 3 and 4 show that top tax rates over time have not been altered in response to prevailing levels of inequality. If they had been altered in this manner, it would be clear in the data that as inequality rose, the top tax rates would also rise. This isn't what happened. Also, the massive increase in top tax rates associated with war mobilization cannot be explained by ability to pay. If ability to pay concerns were the reason why governments implemented these policies, then we should see statements in parliamentary debates reflecting this fact. Instead, what we saw was a dramatic decrease in the use of ability to pay arguments during the war itself. Something else was at work.

The ability to pay doctrine has been subject to two persistent criticisms, one of which has been better founded than the other. Critics suggest first that the doctrine offers no clear plan for saying just how much more in taxes the rich can afford while still making the same sacrifice as everyone else. But as we discussed previously, many people, including survey respondents, believe in ability to pay in practice, and, in any event, the direction that such arguments imply for taxing the rich is clear enough. Critics suggest, second, that the ability to pay doctrine takes no account of how money is earned in the first place. This may be the main reason why we see no clear correlation between levels of inequality and how heavily governments choose to tax the rich. Whether people want to see the rich taxed heavily in a period of high inequality depends on the broader context and how they think inequality was generated in the first place.

The third way to treat people as equals, the compensatory theory, takes direct account of the broader context for state action. If the state has treated people unequally on one dimension, then taxation should be used to compensate for this. At many moments throughout history, compensatory ideas have influenced what people think about taxing the rich. In fourteenth-century Siena, the city council deemed that if some taxes fell heavily on one group, then other taxes should be set so as to fall on alternative groups. During the nineteenth century similar arguments were made in favor of an income tax. If the weight of indirect taxation was lighter for the rich than for the rest, then an income tax should be designed and implemented so as to counteract this effect. Finally, compensatory arguments help explain why governments during the twentieth century adopted very high top tax rates at a time of mass mobilization for war. Wartime governments certainly needed new revenues to fund their expenditures, but this doesn't explain why they chose to increase taxation by so much on those at the very top. It is the power of wartime compensatory arguments that explains why they made this choice.

In considering compensatory arguments, we have shown that people will be most convinced to use the tax system to compensate for the effect of inequalities generated by the state itself. Moreover, in the political arena compensatory arguments are most commonly used in reference to current or recent inequalities created by the state. In principle one could think of using the tax system to compensate for state actions further in the past, or for a long history of unequal treatment by the state. Though a few nineteenth-century theorists considered using progressive taxation to achieve precisely this objective, such arguments have not been common in the political arena. Our evidence does not say exactly why this is the case, but it may be because the facts about past inequalities may be more open to dispute.

The compensatory theory is of course also related to a broader discussion about the role of good fortune (luck) as opposed to virtue (effort) in determining how rich someone is. This is a very prominent subject of discussion among those who work on the politics of redistribution. It is established from survey evidence that citizens of most European countries are more likely to say that doing well economically depends on luck, whereas American survey respondents emphasize the role of effort. This fact is then used to explain why the United States has a smaller welfare state than most European countries. But, as we have emphasized repeatedly, the United States is hardly exceptional today in taxing the rich less heavily than was once the case. Moreover, it is also entirely likely that Americans in

the immediate postwar era believed every bit as much in the importance of effort, yet very high top marginal tax rates prevailed in the
United States. When citizens think about taxing the rich, they think
not just about whether the rich have been lucky, but more specifically about whether the rich were lucky to receive privileges awarded
by the state.

THE TOP TAX RATES PEOPLE WANT TODAY

What do our findings imply for today's debates about taxing the
rich? Much of the popular discussion focuses on rising inequality
and the fact that those at the very top seem to be reaping most of the
gains. Many conclude that the rich ought to be taxed more heavily.
It's not hard to see why people take this view. If you subscribe to the
ability to pay view of taxation, then the rich should be paying more.
If you simply dislike inequality, you would think the same. Contemporary surveys in the United States do often show that people
are worried about rising inequality, and they wish the government
would do something about it, including by taxing the rich. This latter fact is usually demonstrated by questions asking whether taxes
on people earning $250,000 a year or more (or sometimes $1 million) should increase, though the surveys typically don't ask how
much taxes should increase. The surveys also do not ask whether
people believe that taxes should be raised by increasing statutory
rates, or by reducing exemptions to increase effective rates, a critical
issue that we will consider below.[1] These considerations lead naturally to the question of why there seems to be so little in the way of a
policy response to today's inequality. Although it is understandable
to point to any number of contemporary political developments
or shortcomings of American democracy, we have seen that there
just isn't much historical evidence that inequality alone prompts
governments to tax the rich.

How can we reconcile the historical record with recent surveys?
One way is to conduct a survey that asks respondents what tax rates
they prefer rather than simply whether taxes should be increased
without any indication whether the increase should be through

reducing exemptions or raising rates, and if the latter, what the extent of the desired change should be. If people favor raising tax rates on the rich by a couple of percentage points, this is entirely different from the thirty- or forty-percentage-point increase that would be necessary to get top rates back to where they stood for much of the twentieth century.

In work with Cameron Ballard-Rosa and Lucy Martin, we fielded a survey with 2,250 individuals that was representative of the American population. As part of this investigation each respondent was asked the following question:

Consider the taxes paid in the US by those families making X each year. Please select from the list below which marginal tax rate you would most like to see families making X each year pay: 0, 5, 10, 15, 20, 25, 30, 35, 40, 50, 60, 70, and 80 percent.

There is a possibility that survey respondents might confuse the marginal tax rate, the rate applying to the last dollar of income, with the average (or effective) tax rate, which is obtained by dividing total taxes paid by total income. In order to limit this possibility we provided respondents with a definition of the marginal tax rate.[2] The levels of income considered for X in the survey were designed to closely track the cutoffs in the current U.S. income tax schedule.

All respondents were asked to provide a preferred rate for the more than $375,000 category. Each of the respondents was then asked to provide a preferred rate for one of the other (randomly assigned) income levels. Put all these responses together and we have a view of how the American population would like to see the rich taxed relative to the rest. The responses to this survey question are shown in the box plot in figure 9.1.[3] The median preferred marginal rate for a household making more than $375,000 a year is 30 percent (with a mean preferred rate of 33 percent). This is below the marginal rate of 39.6 percent that such a household would actually pay in the United States today. We can also see that the bulk of the responses range from 20 percent to about 40 percent.

The obvious lesson from this survey is that there is little support for the idea that Americans would like to see much higher top tax

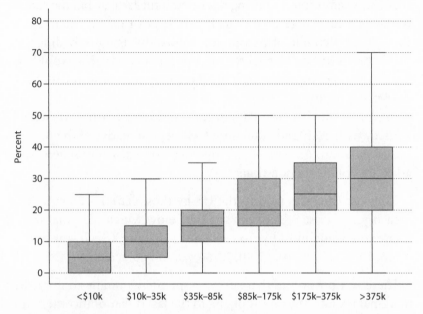

Figure 9.1. Marginal Tax Rate Opinions, United States 2014. This figure plots the distribution of preferred tax rates in the United States for six income categories approximating current U.S. tax groups. The survey was conducted by YouGov in June 2014. See online appendix and Ballard-Rosa, Martin, and Scheve (2015) for details about the survey. For each income group, the box indicates the interquartile range and the line in the middle of the box indicates the median.

rates, but they aren't getting the policies they want. While we believe that this survey question provides us with a more precise view of opinions on taxation than do the alternative questions often used in existing work, we also conducted a much more extensive series of survey experiments using an entirely different question wording and methodology but arrived at very similar conclusions with respect to preferred rates of taxation.[4]

One possible reason people don't want higher tax rates is that the individuals in our survey fail to understand how high inequality is today and how much it has increased in recent years. This is a common argument. A recent survey experiment helps adjudicate this question. The experiment provided a large sample of individuals with a "treatment" that involved provision of accurate information about the income distribution in the United States today. It then observed whether this prompted individuals to support a higher marginal tax rate on those with high incomes. There was indeed such an effect, but its magnitude was very small. Individuals who received the treatment supported a top marginal rate of income taxation only one percentage point higher than did members of a control group that did not receive the treatment.[5]

The second reason people may not want higher tax rates today is the one we have emphasized throughout this book. Over the last two centuries the most politically powerful arguments in favor of heavy taxation of the rich were compensatory claims made in a context of mass mobilization for war. As we saw in chapter 8, as countries like the United States transitioned away from an era of mobilization, parties of the left were deprived of the compensatory war sacrifice arguments that had proven so powerful. They relied instead on the idea that taxing the rich was necessary because it was fair, but they often lacked strong arguments for why it was fair—witness the Labour and Democratic Party manifestos from the 1980s that we reviewed in chapter 8. Under pressure from political parties of the right, top tax rates were lowered dramatically. The end result, at least in the United States, is a situation where top tax rates today are just about where most people would like to see them.

What does this conclusion suggest about the future for taxing the rich? The truth may be that at least in the United States, there simply isn't much support for adopting very high top rates of the sort that prevailed in the immediate postwar era, at least not enough support to overcome whatever advantages the wealthy may have in the political process. Building such support would require the construction of a new compensatory argument, outside of a wartime context, which would suggest how the rich have benefitted from state privilege while others have sacrificed. Now, there certainly have been cases where this has been true of late. To see this we need look no further than the bailout of large banks that preceded the Great Recession. But even this involved a privilege enjoyed by only a fraction of the better off, those with large stakes in these banks, as opposed to the rich as a group. To put it differently, it is not clear why Silicon Valley should be taxed just because Wall Street was bailed out. Moreover, a great many citizens opposed the Wall Street bailout to begin with, so their preferences were focused less on compensating for it than on simply opposing it. Drawing on this history we can see that, much as was the case in the nineteenth century, successful compensatory arguments today would need to emphasize inequities within the tax system itself.

THE DEBATE GOING FORWARD

When people today think about taxing the rich there is often a tendency to compare current conditions with those that prevailed in the decades following the end of the Second World War, an era with very high top marginal tax rates. We ourselves have made such comparisons many times over the course of this book. Yet as we have also pointed out, the era of the two world wars and their aftermath was a particular one because of mass mobilization. Mass mobilization occurred because of interstate rivalry and because states found themselves in a particular state of technological development where it was both feasible and desirable to field a mass army. Today, the question is what fairness-based arguments for or against taxing the rich remain relevant in a new era of limited mobilization. In the absence of compensatory arguments, future debates will follow the usual divide between those who appeal to ability to pay as a reason for taxing the rich and those who appeal to equal treatment in order to oppose it while also emphasizing efficiency costs. This debate is unlikely to result in much deviation from current trends in tax rates. We suggested at the end of chapter 1 that change with regard to taxing the rich would instead depend on the ability of proponents to do one of two things. First, they could use compensatory arguments compatible with an era of peace. Second, they could appeal to the logic of equal treatment to oppose those situations where, because of exemptions or special privilege, the rich are taxed less heavily than others. We close by considering these two possibilities.

When we ask whether compensatory, or even equal treatment arguments, in favor of the rich are relevant today, we should recall the tone of the debate during the nineteenth and early twentieth centuries. In other words, we need to look back prior to the era before mass mobilization for war fundamentally changed tax debates.

One thing we see clearly in early debates is that proponents of the income tax didn't only refer to ability to pay; they also appealed to equal treatment. Prior to the establishment of general income taxes, direct taxes were often levied on land, or on presumed income from land. In rapidly industrializing societies this meant that whole new categories of mercantile income went untaxed. Taxes on external manifestations of wealth, such as doors and windows, suffered from many of the same flaws. Under these conditions, Joseph Caillaux argued in France in 1907 that a general income tax was necessary to reestablish equal treatment. He saw the establishment of a general income tax as continuing the work of the French revolutionaries by abolishing new sources of privilege that had emerged since 1789. Caillaux also suggested that each time privileges within a tax system are abolished, they gradually reemerge, necessitating periodic efforts to see that equal treatment is maintained.

Now consider how the logic of Joseph Caillaux's argument applies in the twenty-first century. Today the advanced industrial countries have a general income tax applying to a broad-based definition of income. However, the U.S. tax code in particular provides a great many reasons why reported income may not be taxed at the full rate one would expect. There are deductions. There are exemptions. There are opportunities to class income as capital gains that are subject to a lower rate of tax. These features of the tax code today could arguably be said to play an analogous role to the special privileges of the past. They are also currently producing a system whereby, after a certain point, the higher one's income the lower the effective rate of tax one is likely to pay. In the presence of such a system, there are arguments in favor of taxing the rich that don't have to rely on the principle of ability to pay. One can simply insist on respecting equal treatment.

To see this we can use information produced by the Internal Revenue Service on effective tax rates across different income categories. Data from 2011 show that up until an income of $2 million per year, the more people earn, the higher the effective rate that people tend to pay.[6] However, as incomes increase above $2 million per year, the effective income tax rates filers face actually decrease. The IRS calculated that on average in 2011, those earning between $1.5 million and $2 million a year faced an effective income tax rate of 25.2 percent. In contrast, on average those earning more than $10 million per year faced an effective income tax rate of only 20.5 percent. Had those making more than $10 million per year been obliged to pay the same effective tax rate as those making between $1.5 million and $2 million, this would have brought in about 15 billion extra dollars in revenue. This is a tiny fraction of the total federal budget (less than one-half of 1 percent), but it is not an inconsequential sum. It is equivalent to roughly twice the total salaries of all kindergarten teachers in the United States today.[7]

Equal treatment logic can also apply to payroll taxes and the question of whether to raise the ceilings applied to them. In the United States in 2014, the social security tax was levied on employees at a rate of 6.2 percent up to $117,000 in annual earnings. This limitation clearly results in a regressive incidence. The story of regressive payroll taxes in a number of European countries is even more dramatic. In France the lowest earners pay approximately 25 percent of their income in payroll taxes, while the highest earners pay less than 5 percent.[8]

We are not saying that these equal treatment arguments are ones that necessarily should be made, or that it is the whole story. For the income tax many deductions and exemptions exist for good reasons, and there are efficiency arguments for taxing capital gains less heavily than regular income. Likewise, ceilings on payroll taxes can be justified if one claims that these are not part of general taxation but instead separate payments for services rendered that are not financed out of the general government budget. What we are suggesting is that rather than focusing on high top statutory rates, supporters of taxing the rich will probably be more successful if they look elsewhere in the tax system and appeal to equal treatment.

Let's consider next the current relevance of compensatory arguments. For centuries people have emphasized that if one tax has an unequal incidence across citizens, then another tax can be used to balance things out. We saw this in an example from fourteenth-century Siena. During nineteenth-century debates this same compensatory argument was levied in support of the income tax. Robert Peel used it in the United Kingdom in 1842 to support reintroducing the income tax. John Stuart Mill advocated an income tax targeted at higher incomes for precisely the same reason. We also saw evidence from the United Kingdom that by the first decade of the twentieth century, thanks to the existence of a progressive income tax, the overall burden of taxation across different income groups was essentially flat. This was not an ideal outcome as far as ardent advocates of taxing the rich were concerned, but it was certainly better than the regressive tax system based on indirect taxation that had existed prior to that date. In sum, compensatory arguments appear to have made a difference even outside of a wartime context.

Now think about whether it might be possible for proponents of taxing the rich today to use peacetime compensatory arguments. Such claims can still be made because lower income groups continue, as has always been the case, to bear the principal burden of indirect (or consumption) taxation. As Steven A. Bank has emphasized, this also has direct implications for the fairness of "flat tax" schemes on income. He suggests flat tax schemes should take into account how much citizens pay from all sources and not just from one tax.[9] In European countries, value added taxes constitute a very significant fraction of the taxes paid by poorer households, and this is true even though basic necessities are taxed at special, low rates. In France today those with the lowest incomes pay fully 15 percent of their income in consumption taxes whereas the highest earners pay only 5 percent of their income in such taxes.[10] The regressive incidence of consumption taxes creates a potential argument for taxing the rich more heavily so as to restore equal treatment. The United States does not have a value added tax. However, individual states and localities within the United States do of course implement general sales taxes. All the evidence suggests that even though basic necessities are often exempted from these sales taxes, their overall incidence is still regressive.[11] This again provides a compensatory argument for a progressive income tax. It could also provide an argument for having progressive rates apply to consumption taxes.[12]

All of the above examples suggest ways in which future debates about taxing the rich *might* deviate from a simple dispute between those who claim that the rich can afford to pay more and others who emphasize equal treatment and efficiency. Overall, this could lead to some degree of increased taxation of the rich in the coming years. But it is very unlikely to lead to a repeat of twentieth-century patterns. To have that happen one of two things would need to occur. The first possibility is that there might be massive political or economic shocks that put new compensatory arguments on the table, just as happened in 1914. Alternatively, proponents of progressive taxation would need to make a credible and compelling claim that current government policies are heavily biased toward the rich. That prospect seems uncertain and sure to be contested. In the end, one thing that is certain is that taxation of the rich will continue to be a fundamental source of social conflict, and when we seek to understand this conflict, we can learn a great deal from history.

NOTES

CHAPTER 1: WHY MIGHT GOVERNMENTS TAX THE RICH?

1. See for example "How to Fix Our Appalling Tax Code" by Dave Camp, *Wall Street Journal*, February 25, 2014.
2. See Dworkin (1977), p. 370 as well as Anderson (1999).
3. Theoretically, this insight can be used to justify many different types of tax systems, including those where all pay the same rate. Historically, however, ability to pay has most often been used to justify why the rich should pay a higher rate of tax than the rest of the population.
4. For contributions on the U.S. case see in particular Bank, Stark, and Thorndike (2008) and Brownlee (2004), as well as Alstott and Novick (2006) and Kennedy (1980). For the British case, see Daunton (2002, 1996) and Cronin (1991) in particular. See also Feldman and Slemrod (2009).
5. The twenty countries are Australia, Austria, Belgium, Canada, Denmark, Finland, France, Germany, Ireland, Italy, Japan, Korea, the Netherlands, New Zealand, Norway, Spain, Sweden, Switzerland, the United Kingdom, and the United States.
6. Although we think our conclusions are general, this does not mean that fairness debates do not work differently across different types of countries. Even in the sample, we will point out some important differences, for example between democratic and non-democratic countries, that are predicted by our arguments. We would expect further differences in the importance and dynamics of fairness considerations in tax debates by characteristics such as the ability of states to deliver whatever the public goods are for which the revenue is being raised. We will address this possibility for the countries in the sample in what follows, but these issues may generate even greater differences for the politics of taxation in countries outside the sample, especially in the developing world.
7. For several recent contributions to this literature, see Alesina and Glaeser (2004), Beramendi (2012), Beramendi and Anderson (2008), Hacker (2008), Hall and Soskice (2001), Hays (2009), Huber and Stephens (2001), Iversen and Soskice (2006, 2009), Kenworthy and Pontusson (2005), Lieberman (2003), Mares (2003), Moene and Wallerstein (2001), Pontusson (2005), Przeworski and Wallerstein (1988), Rehm (2011), Rodden (2010), Roemer (1998, 1999), Rueda (2007), Steinmo (1993), Swank (2002), and Timmons (2005).
8. It would be misleading to claim that we have a complete picture of the incidence of taxation on different social groups in medieval and early modern Europe. However, the consensus among historians of the period is that European wars, especially after

1300, were mainly fought with money raised by indirect taxes on common consumption goods. These would have fallen less heavily on the rich than on other social groups. Molho (1996), p. 104 makes this claim for Florence, and Blockmans (1987) provides compelling evidence for cities in the Low Countries. O'Brien and Hunt (1993) discuss how England relied increasingly on indirect taxation after becoming engaged in continental wars beginning in 1688. The autonomous city of Siena provided one exception to the general European pattern, as Bowsky (1969) shows that it relied extensively on direct taxation. The French monarchy also relied heavily on direct taxes, and in particular the *taille*. However, the overall incidence of taxation in France was extremely low by modern standards. In the year 1607, total taxes amounted to 31,437,671 livres tournois (Chaunu 1977). Using a population estimate of 18.5 million people (http://www.ggdc.net/maddison/maddison-project/data.htm), this would amount to 1.7 livres tournois per capita. This would be equivalent to about 3.4 days of wages for a building laborer in Paris at the time. (Data reported by the Global Price and Income History Group, original collection by Robert Allen, http://gpih.ucdavis.edu/Datafilelist.htm.)

9. Data on tax revenues as a percentage of gross domestic product are from Mauro et al. (2013).

10. This idea, introduced by Peacock and Wiseman (1961), has recently been explored extensively by Beetsma, Cukierman, and Giuliodori (2013).

11. Guicciardini (1994, p. 49).

12. In concluding his review of the history of progressive taxation in 1908, Edwin Seligman observed the following. "From the above review it is evident that the tendency toward progressive taxation is almost everywhere on the increase. Whether we deplore it or not, democracy is asserting itself more vigorously and it is precisely in the most democratic countries like Australia and Switzerland that the movement in favor of progressive taxation is the strongest." Seligman (1908), p.124.

13. Shultz (1926, p. 282).

14. See in particular the contributions by Acemoglu and Robinson (2006, 2000) and by Boix (2003). Some have also proposed a partisan variant of the hypothesis; instead of a hypothetical median voter choosing policy, parties of the left (representing lower income groups) and parties of the right (representing upper-income groups) vie for power with different proposals. It then matters who ends up holding political power. See Przeworski and Sprague (1986) and Roemer (1997) for a formalization. The original political economy model of suffrage expansion and redistribution was produced by Allan Meltzer and Scott Richard in 1981, building on earlier insights by Romer (1975) and Roberts (1977). Meltzer and Richard considered an economy populated by individuals having different incomes who must choose the rate for a proportional tax on income that is used to fund a lump-sum redistributive transfer to each citizen. One way to think of this is as the simplest possible type of progressive tax policy—though the tax rate is the same for all individuals, the rich can end up paying a greater proportion of their income once the lump-sum transfer is taken into account. Under this scenario the preferences of voters are naturally ranked by income; the richer a voter, the lower the tax rate they prefer. Meltzer and Richard demonstrated that if one starts with a society in which the franchise is limited to the rich, then as the suffrage is expanded this would lead to higher taxation and more redistribution from rich to poor. Strictly speaking, the Meltzer-Richard model does not give us a general result about democracy and taxation of the rich. To get that we would ideally need to move to a model with a more complex (and more realistic) tax system where voters are choosing an income tax schedule, something like we see in the United States today where the federal income tax has multiple brackets. Or, to make the theoretical prediction truly general, we should allow

voters to choose from a set of *any* possible tax schedules. The problem is that once we do this, we cannot necessarily rank preferences over taxation by income. Take a society with three groups: the rich, the poor, and the middle class. A middle-class person might prefer a tax system that soaks the rich, or might prefer one that soaks the poor. It is also possible to have a scenario where the poor and rich vote for an outcome that soaks the middle class. There have been various attempts to find a way out of this conundrum, but no definitive solution has yet been found. See Roemer (1999), Carbonell-Nicolau and Ok (2007), Carbonell-Nicolau (2009), and Iversen and Soskice (2006) on this point. In the end, most scholars have a strong intuition that democracies with universal suffrage should tax the rich more heavily, even if there is no general theoretical model that shows this will necessarily be the case.

15. See Aidt and Jensen (2009).
16. See the online appendix at http://press.princeton.edu/titles/10674.html. This archive also has all materials needed to replicate the analyses in this book.
17. Many scholars, particularly in political science, have cited the Meltzer and Richard (1981) study when making this argument, but this is a rather fragile foundation. First, as we have noted, the Meltzer-Richard model involves the choice of a single tax rate on all, combined with a redistributive transfer. So it doesn't necessarily carry over to a context where separate tax rates are being chosen for separate groups. Second, even in the Meltzer-Richard context, concluding that greater inequality results in more redistribution depends on several additional assumptions that may or may not hold. It's theoretically possible in this model to have a shift to a more unequal society be characterized by lower taxes on the rich.
18. See Nelson (2004) on this point.
19. Guicciardini (~1520 [1867]).
20. Jean-Jacques Rousseau, *Discourse on Political Economy*, edited by Victor Gourevitch (1977, p. 19).
21. Emmanuel Farhi and Ivan Werning have constructed a theoretical model that suggests exactly how this might take place. If levels of wealth taxation are chosen sequentially by democratic vote, even wealthy voters may agree to be taxed today so as to avoid much more substantial redistribution in the future. See Farhi and Werning (2009). A further reason that governments might respond to greater inequality with higher taxes on the rich is that voters are simply inequality averse. See Lü and Scheve (2014) for one version of this argument. Although there is certainly laboratory and survey-experimental evidence consistent with the idea that people do not like too much inequality, it is not at all clear whether this motivation is sufficiently strong to lead to high taxes on the rich. The patterns of inequality and tax policy discussed in the text suggest that this motivation alone is not enough.
22. See Gilens (2012) and Bartels (2008).
23. See in particular Bonica, McCarty, Poole, and Rosenthal (2013).
24. For a good example of this view see Graetz and Shapiro (2005). Fairfield (2015) also presents evidence along these lines by studying the success of economic elites in preventing tax reform across issues and countries in Latin America.
25. See Bonica et al. (2013) for an insightful review of campaign finance, lobbying expenditures, taxation, and inequality in the United States today. See Birnbaum and Murray's *Showdown at Gucci Gulch* (1988) for a discussion of lobbying in connection with the tax reform act of 1986.
26. See Acemoglu and Robinson (2008).
27. For a classic contribution that does attempt to answer this question, see Slemrod (2002). For more recent evidence see Giertz, Saez, and Slemrod (2012).
28. See Alt (1979) and Fisman, Jakiela, and Kariv (2014).

29. See, for example, the statement by Michael Boskin (2000) that Francis Edgeworth ignored the possibility that high taxes on the rich could give them an incentive to supply less labor.
30. Edgeworth (1897), p. 553.
31. Our emphasis on war, compensatory arguments, and taxation of the rich is closely related to arguments that highlight the link between warfare and the provision of political or civil rights. Mass mobilization for war has led to important changes in the status of women and of ethnic or racial minorities, based on the simple notion that if a group lacking full rights participated in the war effort, then they ought to be granted the same rights as everyone else. For a particularly stark example of this, see the study by Philip Klinkner and Rogers Smith (1999) on the status of African Americans during war and peace. The same argument has been made for the establishment of democracy more generally. See Ferejohn and Rosenbluth (forthcoming). As we discuss in chapter 7, in ancient Athens it was argued that if the lower classes rowed the boats to power the Athenian navy, then they should be granted the same political rights as everyone else. While we emphasize how mass warfare created opportunities for new fairness-based arguments, we do not pretend that the only effect of warfare has been via this fairness channel. When a population is mobilized to fight, this can mean that citizens find it easier to use violence and to mobilize after a war's end. A recent and persuasive statement of this phenomenon is provided by Jha and Wilkinson (2012). This phenomenon has been important in a wide variety of historical contexts, but it seems unlikely that it is driving the effect of mass mobilization wars on tax policy. We show variation in the effect of war on taxing the rich across countries—e.g., a stronger effect in democracies for which the norm of treating citizens as equals is stronger—that cannot easily be explained by the fact that wars arm citizens. Another main effect of mass warfare independent of fairness is an improvement in state capacity. Throughout history warfare has arguably been associated with improvements in the capacity of states to tax. This is an argument most closely associated with Charles Tilly that has been studied more recently by Tim Besley and Torsten Persson. See Tilly (1975, 1990) and Besley and Persson (2009). However, this improvement has meant an increased ability to tax all social classes and not just the rich. Finally, fighting a war provides a qualitatively different public good than does providing defense in normal times, and this likely impacts support for taxation. While we will present evidence consistent with this view, this argument suggests broader support for taxes on all income groups and not just the rich.
32. See Levi (1997). This is also related to Levi's claim in *Of Rule and Revenue* (1988, p. 53) that "rulers can increase compliance by demonstrating that the tax system is fair."
33. http://www.dailykos.com/story/2013/05/14/1208899/-Whatever-Happened-to-the-Conscription-of-Wealth
34. This is of course a persistent theme in his work, best illustrated by Piketty (2014) and Piketty (2001).

CHAPTER 2: TREATING CITIZENS AS EQUALS

1. Hall and Rabushka (1981, p. 185).
2. See Regent (2014) for a recent historiographical discussion. Guicciardini's text was also referred to by Friedrich Hayek in his *Constitution of Liberty* (1960 [2011]), p. 430. In addition to presenting Guicciardini's arguments against (but not for) progressive taxation, Hayek also followed earlier work by Guicciardini suggesting that the *decima scalata* became a tool of the Medici to oppress other members of the Florentine elite (see Guicciardini, "Del Reggimento di Firenze").

3. Translated by Bruce Edelstein (Guicciardini ~1520 [1867], p. 355). There also exists a prior English translation of Guicciardini's text (~1520 [1959]), but we judged it to be less faithful to the original Italian.

4. "On this matter I say that, as the poor man suffers from a tax, so does a rich man, and so it disorders his necessary expenses, as for the poor; for ordinary expenses are not the same for all, but rather they differ according to the different ranks of the citizens; and so it is necessary for the rich to have high expenses in order to maintain their rank, as a small expense is necessary for the poor, and for me, being of average wealth, an average expense is necessary." Translated by Maria Carreri.

5. This "equal treatment" account would later be cited by Friedrich Hayek in his *Constitution of Liberty*. See Hayek (1960 [2011]), p. 430.

6. Matteo Palmieri (1429 [1982], pp. 141–142). Translated by Bruce Edelstein. For further discussion of this passage and of Palmieri's opinions on taxation, see Ricca-Salerno (1881, pp. 32–33) and Isenmann (1995).

7. For general discussions of the luxury debate, see Hont (2006) and Shovlin (2006). See also the closely related work of Pocock (1985) on "virtue" and "commerce." Eich (2013) sees debates about luxury taxes as presaging later debates about progressive taxation.

8. Jean-Jacques Rousseau, "Discourse on Political Economy," edited by Victor Gourevitch (1997), pp. 32-33.

9. For the context of Saint-Lambert's piece, see Hont (2006) and Shovlin (2006).

10. The full text is: "The subjects of every state ought to contribute towards the support of the government, as nearly as possible, in proportion to their respective abilities; that is, in proportion to the revenue which they respectively enjoy under the protection of the state. The expence of government to the individuals of a great nation is like the expence of management to the joint tenants of a great estate, who are all obliged to contribute in proportion to their respective interests in the estate. In the observation or neglect of this maxim consists what is called the equality or inequality of taxation." *The Wealth of Nations*, Book V, Chapter 2, paragraph 25.

11. On this point see Hont (2006), Ignatieff and Hont (1983), and Eich (2013).

12. The complete passage is as follows: "The necessaries of life occasion the great expence of the poor. They find it difficult to get food, and the greater part of their little revenue is spent in getting it. The luxuries and vanities of life occasion the principal expence of the rich, and a magnificent house embellishes and sets off to the best advantage all the other luxuries and vanities which they possess. A tax upon house-rents, therefore, would in general fall heaviest upon the rich; and in this sort of inequality there would not, perhaps, be any thing very unreasonable. It is not very unreasonable that the rich should contribute to the public expence, not only in proportion to their revenue, but something more than in that proportion." *Wealth of Nations*, Book V, Chapter 2, paragraph 71.

13. John Stuart Mill, *The Principles of Representative Government*, Book V, Chapter 2, paragraph 7. "For what reason ought equality to be the rule in matters of taxation? For the reason that it ought to be so in all affairs of government. As a government ought to make no distinction of persons or classes in the strength of their claims on it, whatever sacrifices it requires from them should be made to bear as nearly as possible with the same pressure upon all, which, it must be observed, is the mode by which least sacrifice is occasioned on the whole. If anyone bears less than his fair share of the burthen, some other person must suffer more than his share, and the alleviation to the one is not, *cæteris paribus*, so great a good to him, as the increased pressure upon the other is an evil. Equality of taxation, therefore, as a maxim of politics, means equality of sacrifice. It means apportioning the contribution of each person towards the expenses of government so that he shall feel neither more nor less inconvenience from his share of the payment than every other person experiences from his. This standard, like other

standards of perfection, cannot be completely realized; but the first object in every practical discussion should be to know what perfection is."

14. The full passage is as follows: "Setting out, then, from the maxim that equal sacrifices ought to be demanded from all, we have next to inquire whether this is in fact done by making each contribute the same percentage on his pecuniary means. Many persons maintain the negative, saying that a tenth part taken from a small income is a heavier burthen than the same fraction deducted from one much larger: and on this is grounded the very popular scheme of what is called a graduated property tax, viz. an income tax in which the percentage rises with the amount of the income." John Stuart Mill, *The Principles of Representative Government*, Book V, Chapter 2, paragraph 10, 3rd edition 1852.

15. Ibid., paragraph 11, third edition 1852. For Bentham's contribution see Jeremy Bentham (1794, p. 388). As Seligman (1908) observes, Bentham was not the ultimate originator of the idea of exempting a subsistence minimum from taxation, and he provides several earlier sources.

16. John Stuart Mill, *The Principles of Representative Government*, Book V, Chapter 2, paragraph 12, 3rd edition 1852.

17. This was the case of the window tax. See Mill's letter to the *Examiner*, January 13, 1833, entitled "Necessity of Revising the Present System of Taxation."

18. John Stuart Mill, *The Principles of Representative Government*, Book V, Chapter 2, 3rd edition 1852.

19. See Edgeworth (1897) and Pigou (1928).

20. Matthew Weinzierl (2014) has recently presented survey evidence suggesting that citizens prefer to apply a fairness standard rather than a welfarist one when choosing a tax scheme. See also Young (1990, 1995) and Roemer (1996) on the relationship between the concerns of contemporary economists and modern approaches to fairness in resource allocation.

21. See Lionel Robbins (1932, p. 125).

22. See Simons (1938).

23. Pigou (1928, p. 156).

24. Thomas Piketty (1995). Bénabou and Tirole (2006). See Fong (2001) for empirical support as well as Alesina and Angeletos (2005) for a comparison of attitudes between the United States and Europe.

25. See Murphy and Nagel (2002).

26. Another way to think about the implications of Murphy and Nagel's argument is that deciding on a normatively appealing tax system requires a compelling theory of distributive justice. Here it is worth noting that a great deal of contemporary work on distributive justice since Rawls (1971) has focused on egalitarian accounts, and a central question is what should be equalized in a just society (see, e.g., Sen, 1980; Dworkin, 1981a, 1981b; Cohen, 1989; and Roemer, 1998). Murphy and Nagel's argument in part suggests that it is not possible to talk about fairness or equality in a tax system without answering the larger distributive justice questions of what should be equal in a just society.

27. See Bowsky (1969, 1981). The quote is located on page 191 of Bowsky (1981). The emphasis is ours.

28. House of Commons, Select Committee on Income and Property Tax, testimony by John Stuart Mill, May 20, 1852. House of Commons Papers vol. 9, p. 299. See also the discussion in *Principles of Political Economy* V 3.15.

29. Several of these contributions are reviewed by Seligman (1908, pp. 145–147), and for a more detailed review see Gaston Gros (1907), pp. 556–577.

30. John Rawls (1971, pp. 246–247).

31. Speech by citizen Pierre-Gaspard Chaumette, procureur general de la commune March 9, 1793. *Archives Parlementaires* p. 6. Author's translation. This speech is also cited by Seligman (1908, p. 32) using an incorrect abbreviation of the text that derives from Gomel (1902, pp. 389–391). See Gross (1993, 1996) for a broader discussion about progressive taxation during this period.

32. See Seligman (1908, p. 145) and Walker (1883, pp. 453–455).

33. On this point see the review by Seligman (1908, pp. 142–145) as well as Walker (1883, pp. 453–455).

34. Except of course the case of a progressive tax on consumption.

35. See Camerer and Fehr (2004) on ultimatum game results.

36. See Camerer and Fehr (2004).

37. See Engl (2011).

38. See Fisman, Jakiela, and Kariv (2014). Their results show that one-third of their subjects can be characterized as purely fair-minded, 15 percent can be characterized as purely self-interested, and that the remaining 52 percent were intermediate between these two classifications.

39. See Henrich et al. (2010).

40. This is demonstrated in the context of the dictator game by Oxoby and Spraggon (2008) and in the case of the ultimatum game by Carr and Melizzo (2013). See also Cappelen et al. (2007) for related results.

41. See Reuben and Riedl (2013).

42. See, e.g., Gilens (1999), Luttmer (2001), Fong (2001), Alesina and Angeletos (2005), Alesina and Glaeser (2004), Durante, Putterman, and van der Weele (2014), and Cavaille and Trump (2015), among many others. It should be added that there is debate in this literature about the importance of self-interest in determining economic policy opinions. Our view is that there is considerable evidence that self-interest, other-regarding preferences, and fairness concerns all inform preferences with substantial heterogeneity across policies and individuals in the weight given to these considerations.

43. The survey was carried out online by YouGov, which employs matched sampling to approximate a random sample of the adult population.

44. The possible increases for those making between $25,000 and $200,000 were 1.1, 1.25, or 1.5 percentage points. The possible increases for those making more than $200,000 were 2, 3, and 4 percentage points.

45. Further details about the survey are available in the online appendix.

46. Examples include "Everyone should pay the same" and "Rich and poor should pay equally." Note that this category includes cases where people simply say taxes should be equal, as well as cases that explicitly say the government should treat people the same.

47. This "reason" essentially repeats the preference of the respondent for the progressive choice without providing a justification. Examples include "The rich should pay more" or "Lower taxes on the poor."

48. Of the 500 respondents, 73 did not answer this question at all or provided an incoherent answer. Further, 16 respondents gave multiple reasons and it was not possible to code a primary argument. Our description of the pattern of arguments is therefore for the 411 respondents for which we could classify a primary argument.

CHAPTER 3: THE INCOME TAX OVER TWO CENTURIES

1. Seligman (1911, pp. 42–53). See Conti (1984) for a more detailed description of the Italian case and Clamageran (1868) for France.

2. The *Comparative Income Taxation Database* (Genovese, Scheve, and Stasavage 2014) also includes the amount from which the top marginal rate applies, the law governing the tax, and the source of this information (original legislation or secondary literature). The data and codebook are available at http://data.stanford.edu/citd. The countries included in the sample are Australia, Austria, Belgium, Canada, Denmark, Finland, France, Germany, Ireland, Italy, Japan, Korea, the Netherlands, New Zealand, Norway, Spain, Sweden, Switzerland, the United Kingdom, and the United States.

3. This observation does not have much substantive importance. As we discuss in further detail below, we also collected data on local income taxes. Once these taxes are included, Switzerland looks more like the rest of the sample.

4. The data on local income tax rates are not comprehensive for an entire country. Rather, we collected data on local rates assuming the taxpayer lived in the largest city. We then determined if there were income taxes levied at the municipal or provincial level and what these rates were.

5. The tax rates for 1925, 1950, 1975, 2000, and 2010 are based on the nominal GDP per capita. We constructed the full schedule graphs for countries in the *Comparative Income Taxation Database* for which we were able to obtain rates and thresholds for all of the brackets. We concentrate on national income tax schedules at six 25-year intervals: 1875, 1900, 1925, 1950, 1975, and 2000, to which we add the full schedules from the last year in the database (2010). We report not the raw schedules but the schedules in terms of multiples of GDP per capita. Since we do not have reliable information on which thresholds of GDP apply to which percentiles of the population for each country-year in the database, we relied on Piketty (2001), who reports the income thresholds for individuals in France in the 10th, 50th, 90th (and, for some years, 95th and 99th) percentiles. Piketty's thresholds are the values we use to generate multiples of GDP per capita for the other countries. We calculated France's multiple per percentile per year by dividing the threshold by GDP per capita, and then averaged the multiples for all the available years (see Piketty 2001, pp. 671 and 672, col. 8–10 of table D12 and col. 4–6 of table D13; the years in these tables range from 1950 to 1998). We find that the average multiples for France by income group are: 0.48 for 10th percentile; 0.83 for 50th percentile; 1.66 for 90th percentile; 2.12 for 95th percentile; and 3.87 for 99th percentile. We round up to 0.5, 1, 1.5, 2, 4, and use these values to find the income thresholds that correspond to the tax rates in the full schedules in other countries. We also include a high multiple of 100 to capture the very top rates in all country series. The remainder of this note discusses the sources of schedules for each of the six countries under consideration, and the decisions that characterized the calculations of the tax rates in terms of multiples of GDP per capita. *France, 1925–2010.* The schedules for France start in 1925, because the national series start on July 15, 1914. The sources of the full schedules are the following: for 1925, we use the legislative text of August 1926, also reported in Piketty (2001), table 4.2, at p. 263; for 1950, we follow Piketty (2001), table 4.5, at p. 296; for 1975, we follow Piketty (2001), table 4.5, at p. 297; for 2000 and 2010, we use the OECD Income Tax Database (2014).

The GDP per capita for France up to 1998 is the nominal national GDP divided by total population based on Mitchell's *International Historical Statistics*. GDP is in millions of old francs up until 1949, then between 1958 and 1960 the French franc was revalued, with 100 existing francs making one nouveau franc. GDP is in billions of new francs from 1950 until 1998. From 1999 onward, nominal GDP per capita is from Eurostat (2014) and is in euros.

The 1925 tax rates are structured around the 25 "tranches de revenue" in the law. Piketty (2001, p. 263) reports thresholds for these rates aggregated for the years 1919–1935, so the multiples of GDP per capita (which we obtain for the year 1926) are indicative. The 1950 tax rates are based on a rescaled version of nominal GDP per capita because, while Mitchell's GDP values are in millions of francs in 1950, the thresholds in Piketty are still reported in the "old" francs, so we scaled the GDP multiplying it by 100 to concord with the thresholds. The tax rates of 1975, 2000 and 2010 are based on the multiples of the nominal GDP per capita.

Germany, 1925–2010. The schedules for Germany start in 1925, because the national series starts on March 29, 1920. The sources of the full schedules are the following: for 1925, we rely on Dell (2008), table at p. 119; for 1950, we use the brackets from the first postwar income tax law of 1958, and rely on the thresholds in the Bundesministerium der Finanzen (BMF) 2013 review of historical rates, which shows tax benchmarks based on the tax formula of the fiscal law (https://www.bmf-steuerrechner.de /uebersicht_ekst/); for 1975, we use the thresholds of the BMF review; for 2000 and 2010, we use the OECD Income Tax Database (2014) and the BMF 2013 review.

The GDP per capita for Germany up to 1990 is the nominal national GDP divided by total population based on Mitchell's *International Historical Statistics*, where GDP is in millions of marks (Deutsche Mark, DM). From 1991 onward, nominal GDP per capita is from Eurostat (2014) and is in euros (ex post).

The 1925 tax rates were calculated by transforming the nominal GDP in DM to GDP in Reichsmark, which was the national currency between 1924 and 1958 and is the value the thresholds are reported in. The value of Reichsmark in DM was 1 Deutsche Mark = 1 Reichsmark for first 600 RM, 1 Deutsche Mark = 10 Reichsmark thereafter, so we multiplied GDP by 10 in order to calculate the multiple of GDP per capita used to find the rates (Information on the value of Reichsmark in terms of DM was retrieved from the Deutsche Bundesbank: http://www.bundesbank.de/Redaktion/ DE/Standardartikel/Statistiken/kaufkraftvergleiche_historischer_geldbetraege.html?view =render%5BDruckversion%5D; accessed June 24, 2014.) The 1950 (or precisely 1958) and 1975 tax rates are based on a rescaled version of nominal GDP per capita because the rates reported in the BMF review are in euros: we know the exchange rate of DM to euros from up to 1975 from the Federal Reserve Bank of St. Louis; we then found the euro value of 1958 nominal GDP per capita, which we used to find the rates (see ex-post exchange rates of USD, DM, and euros at http://research.stlouisfed.org/fred2 /data/EXGEUS.txt; accessed June 24, 2014). The tax rates of 2000 and 2010 are based on the multiples of the nominal GDP per capita, though note that the schedules in this year are formula-based and the Bundesministerium reports selected middle schedules as orientation.

New Zealand, 1900–2010. The schedules for New Zealand start in 1900, because the national series start on October 11, 1892. The sources of the full schedules are the following: for 1900, we rely on the brackets of the Land Tax and Income Tax Act, 1892; for 1925, 1950, and 1975, we rely on McAlister et al. (2012) and their supplementary appendix; for 2000 and 2010, we use the OECD Income Tax Database (2014).

The GDP per capita for New Zealand up to 1999 is calculated from millions of New Zealand dollars of national nominal GDP divided by population in millions. The data come from Statistics New Zealand. For the year 2000 we retrieved the nominal GDP per capita from the IMF World Economic Outlook Database (WEO 2000). For the year 2010, we retrieved the nominal GDP per capita from the statistics of the NZ government (statistics available at https://www.nzte.govt.nz/en/invest/statistics/; accessed June 24, 2014).

The 1900 and 1925 tax rates were calculated based on thresholds that in the 1892 fiscal law are expressed in fractions of New Zealand pounds, i.e., in schillings. We transformed GDP from NZ dollars into NZ shillings relying on the fact that 1 NZ pound = 2 NZ dollars, and that 1 NZ pound = 20 schillings, so we divided GDP per capita in NZ dollars by 2 and multiplied by 20 (information from Reserve Bank of New Zealand at: http://www.rbnz.govt.nz/notes_and_coins/coins/0094086.html; accessed June 24, 2014). The 1950 tax rates are expressed in New Zealand pounds, so we calculated the rates per multiples of GDP by transforming GDP in New Zealand dollars into New Zealand pounds, thus we multiplied the GDP per capita by 2, because £NZ 1 = $2 NZ. The tax rates of 1975, 2000, and 2010 are based on the multiples of the original nominal GDP per capita.

Sweden, 1875–2010. The schedules for Sweden start in 1875, because the national series start in 1862. The sources of the full schedules are the following: for 1875 and 1900, we rely on Du Rietz, Johansson, and Stenkula (2010), working paper version, appendix D, p. 55; for 1925, we rely on Du Rietz et al.'s rates at p. 57, where we use their base amounts (lower due to their account of average tax cap) multiplied by the withdrawal percentage for 1925 (see table D.6); for 1950 and 1975 we use Du Rietz et al.'s tables at pp. 58 and 59, respectively; and for 2000 and 2010, we use the OECD Income Tax Database (2014).

The GDP per capita for Sweden up to 2000 is the nominal national GDP by expenditure at purchaser prices from Rodney Edvinsson, http://www.historia.se/. From 2001 onward, nominal GDP per capita is from Eurostat (2014).

The tax rates of 1875 and 1900 are based on the multiples of Edvinsson's nominal GDP per capita. The 1925 tax rate relies on Edvinsson's GDP per capita, adjusted to the fact that after 1919 the SEK was recoined (20 Kr coins became 10 SEK). The tax rates of 1975, 2000, and 2010 are based on the multiples of the nominal GDP per capita.

UK, 1875–2010. The schedules for the United Kingdom start in 1875, because the national series start on January 9, 1799. The sources of the full schedules are the following: for 1875 and 1900, we rely on discussion in Mitchell (1988) and Mallett and George (1929, p. 399); for 1925, we rely on the brackets in the Finance Act 1925, Part II (p. 10); for 1950, we rely on the Finance Act 1948, Part III (change in ordinary rates) and IV (extraordinary rates); for 1975, we use the schedules from the Crown's National Archives (see HM Revenue and Customs Archives, http://webarchive.nationalarchives. gov.uk/+/http://www.hmrc.gov.uk/stats/tax_structure/00ap_a2c_2.htm; accessed June 24, 2014); for 2000 and 2010, we use the OECD Income Tax Database (2014). The nominal GDP per capita of the UK from 1875 to 2010 is based on nominal national GDP from Williamson's "Measuring Worth" project (see Measuring Worth project at http://www .measuringworth.com/; accessed June 24, 2014). The GDP is million pounds and is divided by population. These values are consistent with the Bank of England's data from the report "The UK recession in context: what do three centuries of data tell us?", the IMF World Economic Outlook Database (WEO 2000), and more recent data from the OECD (2014).

The tax rates of 1875 and 1900 are based on the multiples of the nominal GDP per capita. The tax rates of 1925 and 1950 (or more precisely 1948) are based on multiples of the nominal GDP per capita that we calculated by multiplying GDP by 10 in order to scale it to the decimal value that the pound had between 1925 and 1960. The tax rates of 1975, 2000, and 2010 are based on the original nominal GDP per capita.

United States, 1925–2010. The schedules for the United States start in 1925, because the national series, although starting in 1863, only has permanent schedules from October 3, 1913, onward. The sources of the full schedules are the following: for 1925, 1950, and 1975, we use the IRS official schedules in nominal GDP; for 2000 and 2010, we use the OECD Income Tax Database (2014), which we checked with the IRS schedules.

The nominal GDP per capita of the United States from 1925 to 2010 is from Williamson's "Measuring Worth" project (Officer and Williamson, 2006). The data are consistent with the IMF World Economic Outlook Database (WEO 2000) and, for recent years, the United Nations Statistics (2014).

6. The multiples we select are based on the income thresholds in France approximating the 10th, 50th, 90th, 95th, and 99th percentiles reported in Piketty (2001). For France, on average a 0.5 multiple corresponds approximately to the 10th percentile, a 0.8 multiple to the 50th percentile, a 1.7 multiple to the 90th percentile, a 2.1 multiple to the 95th percentile, and a 3.9 multiple to the 99th percentile. In figure 3.3, we round to 0.5, 1, 1.5, 2, 4, and use these values to find the income thresholds that correspond to the tax rates in the full schedules in other countries. We additionally include a high multiple of 100 to capture the very top rates for each schedule. For most countries and years, a multiple far less than 100 is needed to reach to the top marginal rate. However, because a large multiple is necessary for Sweden in 1925 and the United States in 1925 and 1950, we use 100 to ensure that we have the top rate in the figure for all countries and years.

7. At this time in New Zealand, if an individual's income passed a threshold with a higher statutory rate, the higher rate applied to all income earned by that individual rather than only to the income above the threshold, unlike the case of contemporary income tax systems. This meant that individuals with incomes well above the highest threshold faced a lower marginal rate than those with incomes near the threshold.

8. Further inspection of the full schedules suggests that this conclusion comes with some qualifications. For example, there is important variation in the rate of increase of the statutory marginal rates among cases with similar top marginal income taxes. This type of variation can matter for how the income tax system influences the income distribution, and it is not captured by the top statutory rate measure. Our claim is simply that the top rate is a reasonable proxy for the overall progressivity of the system.

9. We constructed the graphs for selected countries in the *Comparative Income Tax Database* for which we were able to find a long series of effective rates. The statutory top marginal income tax rates are defined and reported in the database. The effective rates constitute the income tax rates after credits and bonuses of individuals in the top 0.01 percent of the national income distribution (0.05 percent for the Netherlands and United Kingdom). We retrieved the effective tax rates from the sources cited below. The countries under consideration are Canada, France, the Netherlands, Sweden, the UK, and the United States. With the exception of Canada and Sweden, we compare national level statutory and effective rates. For Canada and Sweden, we compare rates that include sub-national income taxes.

The graphs compare the statutory and effective series from the years where they are both available. We also report the Pearson correlation coefficient (ρ) as a measure of the strength of the relationship between the two series. The remainder of this note discusses the sources for effective rates for each of the six countries under consideration, and the decisions that characterized the calculations of these rates if they were not available from secondary sources.

For Canada, 1920–1997, we used the effective rate series for the top 0.01 percent income share presented by Saez and Veall in Atkinson and Piketty's 2009 book, table 6F.1, pp. 301–302.

For France, 1915–1998, we used the effective rate series for the top 0.01 percent income share presented by Piketty (2001), table B-20, pp. 636–637.

For the Netherlands, 1946–1999, we used the effective rate series for the top 0.05 percent income share presented by Salverda and Atkinson in Atkinson and Piketty (2007), table 10.6, pp. 455–456. The figure reports data from 1946, though Salverda and Atkinson report some effective rates for earlier years due to a break in the time series.

For Sweden, 1903–1990, we used the effective rate series shared by Roine and Waldenström and presented in the chapter "Top Incomes in Sweden over the Twentieth

Century" in Atkinson and Piketty (2010). The 0.01 percent income series is illustrated at p. 323. The tax rates were computed using tax tables in Söderberg (1996) and the Swedish National Tax Board.

For the UK, 1937–2000, we used Atkinson's chapter "The Distribution of Top Incomes in the United Kingdom, 1908–2000" (pp. 83–114) in Atkinson and Piketty (2007). We divided the total tax amount of the top 0.05 percent (top available fractile, although for a smaller amount of years Atkinson shows top 0.01 percent incomes) by their taxable income. We collected the pre-tax income share from table 4.1, pp. 93–94, the post-tax income share for the same fractile at table 4.2, pp. 104–105, and then the total household income and total tax deducted at columns 3 and 4, table 4B.1, pp. 126–127. Using these measures we calculated the total pre-tax income of the top 0.05 percent, the total post-tax income of the top 0.05 percent, and then the effective tax rate by dividing the difference between these two figures by total pre-tax income.

For the United States, 1916–1995, we constructed an effective rate series relying on the Piketty and Saez chapter "Income and Wage Inequality in the United States" (pp. 171–173) in Atkinson and Piketty (2007) and each of the annual Internal Revenue Statistics of Income Reports (http://www.irs.gov/uac/SOI-Tax-Stats-Archive). Note that prior to 1944, "income" means net income and after 1944, income means adjusted gross income (AGI). Generally speaking, net income equals adjusted gross income less allowable itemized personal deductions. Both concepts include gross income less such items as (1) allowable trade and business deductions; (2) travel, lodging, and other reimbursed expenses connected with employment; (3) deductions attributable to rents and royalties; (4) deductions for depreciation and depletion allowable to beneficiaries of property held in trust; and (5) allowable losses from sales of property. However, net income subject to normal tax is net income less exemptions such as applicable personal exemptions for taxpayers and their dependents, dividends on stock in domestic corporations (through 1935), interest on some U.S. obligations and the earned income "credit" (for 1934 through 1943). Net income subject to surtax is all net income through 1933 and net income less the personal exemptions for taxpayers and their dependents thereafter.

We constructed the effective tax rates for the top 0.01 percent incomes by dividing total income tax paid by the top 0.01 percent income holders and the total income for the top 0.01 percent of taxpayers. We first consulted Piketty and Saez to retrieve the total number of tax units in the United States in the given year. Next we consulted the basic statistics of each of the IRS reports, and identified the table that lists numbers of returns in each income class as well as total net income/adjusted gross income for each income class and total income tax liable. Starting from the richest returns we added up income and tax liability until we arrived at the number of tax units from Piketty and Saez. Since this number was often reached in the middle of an income class, we prorated the total income and total tax liability within this class. Using the above we calculated effective rates for the top 0.01 percent for every year. The specific tables used in the IRS reports were: 1916 pp. 18–19; 1917 pp. 26–27; 1918 pp. 34–35; 1919 pp. 41–42; 1920 pp. 46–47; 1921, pp. 40–41; 1922 pp. 79–83; 1923 pp. 59–63; 1924 pp. 104–108; 1925 pp. 87–93; 1926 pp. 74–79; 1927 pp. 68–72; 1928 pp. 74–78; 1929 pp. 61–65; 1930 pp. 69–73; 1931 pp. 60–64; 1932 pp. 66–70; 1933 pp. 68–71; 1934 pp. 57–60; 1935 pp. 74–77; 1936 pp. 84–88; 1937 pp. 117–121; 1938 pp. 17; 1939 pp. 8–9; 1940 pp. 78–82; 1941 pp. 76–80; 1942 pp. 92–95; 1943 pp. 124–129; 1944 pp. 65–67; 1945 pp. 69–71; 1946 pp. 63–65; 1947 pp. 65–67; 1948 pp. 65–67; 1949 pp. 75–77; 1950 pp. 35–37; 1951 p. 25; 1952 p. 18; 1953 p. 23; 1954 p. 33; 1955 pp. 6, 18; 1956 p. 20; 1957 p. 20; 1958 p. 24; 1959 p. 23; 1960 p. 32; 1961 pp. 32–33; 1962 pp. 32–33; 1963 pp. 33–34; 1964 p. 10; 1965 p. 8; 1966 p. 6; 1967 p. 7–8; 1968 p. 6; 1969 p. 9; 1970 pp. 7–8; 1971 pp. 6–7; 1972 pp. 6–7; 1973 pp. 4–7;

1974 pp. 6–9; 1975 pp. 5–6; 1976 pp. 7–10; 1977 pp. 7–9; 1978 pp. 6–8; 1979 pp. 9–11; 1980 p. 36; 1981 p. 34; 1982 p. 38; 1983 p. 6; 1984 pp. 10–12; 1985 pp. 12–14; 1986 pp. 16–18; 1987 pp. 20–22; 1988 pp. 18–20; 1989 pp. 18–20; 1990 pp. 16–18; 1991 pp. 19–21; 1992 pp. 29–30; 1993 pp. 29–30; 1994 pp. 30–31; 1995 pp. 27–28.

10. See Piketty and Saez (2007). We should note that the effective tax rates series in their paper differs from the one reported here because they adopt a different concept for gross income, and this is linked to the fact that they are also considering the incidence of corporate taxation.

11. None of our conclusions are substantially affected by focusing on overall universal rather than universal male universal suffrage. As is the case with unitary states, for federal states, such as Germany, our universal male suffrage measure takes account only of suffrage laws established at the national level and applying to the national legislature, provided that such laws exist. We also take account of available information involving restrictions on certain categories of men, such as African Americans in the United States prior to 1965. In cases where a country established universal suffrage before becoming fully independent from another power, we use the date of the state's independence to code this variable. Unless otherwise noted below we used either Caramani (2000, p. 53) or Mackie and Rose (1974) to code this variable. Dates of establishment of universal suffrage for the countries in the sample are as follows: Australia 1902, Austria 1897, Belgium 1894, Canada 1921, Denmark 1918, Finland 1917, France 1848, Germany 1871, Ireland 1922, Italy 1913, Japan 1925, Netherlands 1918, New Zealand 1879, Norway 1905, South Korea 1948 (source: Croissant, 2002), Spain 1869–1875 (1888), Sweden 1911, Switzerland 1848, United Kingdom 1918, United States of America 1965.

12. The before and after approach, however, requires us to believe that had a country not adopted universal male suffrage or democracy, tax policy would have remained constant. It also requires us to believe that universal male suffrage was adopted for reasons unrelated to other factors influencing the top rate of income taxation. These are strong assumptions, but examining the time series evidence is nonetheless informative.

13. The main statistical results in this book remain unaltered if we instead adopt an earlier date for universal male suffrage in the United States.

14. In the online appendix we address some of the potential limitations of the before and after comparisons by conducting a complete set of regression analyses averaging the data over five-year periods and estimating ordinary least squares regressions with country and time period fixed effects and time varying control variables as well as a wide number of alternative specifications. There is no evidence in these further analyses of a significant positive correlation between universal suffrage and the top rate of income taxation.

15. It is worth noting that there are a few cases that appear to be more consistent with the democracy hypothesis. For example, Austria increased its top marginal income tax rate from 0 to just below 5 percent in the same year (1897) that it adopted universal male suffrage.

16. See the online appendix.

17. See Mares and Queralt (forthcoming) for an analysis of voting in parliament on the income tax in 1842. Rather than emphasizing democracy, they highlight the conflict between landowners, who preferred income taxes to direct taxes on land, and the newly emerging industrial class, who preferred the opposite. This intersectoral conflict is also observed in parliamentary debates about the income tax. Its implication is that even an interpretation that the expansion of the franchise contributed modestly to the low rates of income taxation that we observed during the nineteenth century is too generous to the democracy hypothesis. This is consistent with our more general claim that the expansion of the franchise did not typically drive countries to adopt high income taxes on the wealthy.

18. According to the data in Flora (1983 vol.1, p. 149), in the election of 1910, 62.4 percent of males of eligible age could vote.

19. This definition and data is from Boix and Rosato (2001). The definition is a modification of the definition used by Przeworski et al. (2000) to a context where the suffrage may be restricted. The countries in the sample are coded as having competitive elections for the following years: Australia 1901–2013; Austria 1920–1932, 1946–2013; Belgium 1894–2013; Canada 1867–2013; Denmark 1901–2013; Finland 1917–2013; France 1848–1851, 1870–1939, 1945–2013; Germany 1919–1932, 1946–2013; Ireland 1922–2013; Italy 1946–2013; Japan 1952–2013; Netherlands 1897–2013; New Zealand 1856–2013; Norway 1905–2013; South Korea 1960, 1988–2013; Spain 1931–1936, 1977–2013; Sweden 1911–2013; Switzerland 1848–2013; UK 1885–2013; United States 1800–2013.

20. This null finding for competitive elections also holds in the main fixed effects regression analyses that we report in the online appendix. We also considered other potentially important features of democratic political institutions. For example, we investigate whether it is the introduction of direct elections for the lower house that moves countries to tax high incomes at higher rates. Finally, we also consider the effect of having an unelected upper house, which might tend to veto redistributive policies. Again, for the most part, these analyses do not suggest a systematic impact of these institutions on tax policies. A partial exception to this argument is that there is some mixed evidence that the absence of an unelected upper house leads countries to adopt tax policies with higher rates.

21. As in the case of universal suffrage, a simple pooled comparison across all years does yield the expected partisan differences, with left country-years having an average top rate of 49.6 percent and non-left country-years having an average rate of 23.5 percent. The problem, of course, is that this comparison takes no account of the fact that left governments appeared in the twentieth century rather than the nineteenth, and there are many other factors that differed between the two centuries.

22. Canada, Ireland, South Korea, and the United States are not coded as having labor or socialist left parties that are in government. There are also no transitions to left parties for Switzerland because left parties never control a majority of the seats in the executive.

23. See the online appendix for further evaluation of the partisan hypotheses. Among other things, this analysis allows us to relax some of the assumptions of the evidence discussed here. The results are quite similar with there being some mixed evidence consistent with the partisan hypothesis, but the magnitude of the effect is relatively small and the result is sensitive to econometric specifications.

24. This could occur if high top rates prompt top earners to reclassify earnings as something other than income, if they exert less effort to receive higher salaries, or if they substitute leisure for labor.

25. The data were accessed from http://topincomes.g-mond.parisschoolofeconomics.eu/ and are discussed in detail in Atkinson and Piketty (2007, 2010) as well as other publications in the top incomes project.

26. The correlations between the top 1 percent income share and top rate are: 0.06 for 1925, 0.47 for 1950, -0.36 for 1975, and -0.17 for 2000. Obviously, the negative correlations for 1975 and 2000 are substantially stronger than for the top 0.01 percent income share measure, but the key point is that the correlations are not stable over time for either measure.

27. In other words, we conducted a pooled Granger test including country fixed effects and time effects modeled either with a common time trend or year dummies. See the online appendix for a full description and results.

28. Sokoloff and Zolt (2006) present an historical analysis of the role of inequality in the formation of tax systems. Their study suggests that large variations in inequality across the Americas did not lead to significant differences in national-level tax patterns. They

do find, however, that greater inequality was associated with *less* progressive taxes at the state and local level. See also Zolt (2009). On the effect of tax rates on inequality, see Roine, Vlachos, and Waldenström (2009) for a separate analysis that suggests that tax progressivity reduces top income shares.

29. Note that with the exception of a brief period for France under German occupation, all of the countries in figure 3.8 were democracies for the years considered, and so the lack of a positive correlation between inequality and top income tax rates is not due to a lack of democracy.

30. See, e.g., Atkinson and Piketty (2007, 2010) and Piketty (2014).

31. As discussed below, we generally use 2 percent of the population in the military to indicate whether a country is "mass mobilized" for war. Although the data on population mobilization for the full sample do not start until 1816, France and the United Kingdom slightly surpassed the 2 percent level of mobilization for selected years during the Napoleonic Wars. These countries, as well as others, surpassed this level for selected conflicts prior to the beginning of the nineteenth century. Nonetheless, as we discuss in chapter 7, World War I marks a significant departure in the extent of mass mobilization for war. It is thus a natural starting point for evaluating this argument. One plausible alternative would be to start with the American Civil War. This conflict was marked by high levels of mobilization and the early use of railroads to transport men and supplies. As we have already discussed, it also featured an early adoption of an income tax in the North.

32. In 1848, a deputy to the German Federal Assembly proposed a progressive income tax with a top rate of 33.3 percent. Also in 1848, Pierre-Joseph Proudhon proposed to the French Constituent Assembly that it establish an income tax with a top rate of 50 percent. See Seligman (1911, pp. 235, 279).

33. *Economist*, March 10, 1883.

34. See the findings of Aidt and Jensen (2009) on this point.

35. For one early discussion of the effect of the increase in taxation on the distribution of incomes and wealth, see Bowley (1930).

36. The United States did increase its top marginal tax rate prior to World War I, from a prior rate of 7 percent to 15 percent in 1916. However, the increase upon entering the war was dramatically larger, moving from 15 percent to 67 percent in 1917.

37. See Perry (1955, p. 162).

38. See Atkinson and Piketty (2007, p. 95).

39. See Piketty (2001, p. 556) and Saez and Veall (2007).

40. In 1911 in Sweden and 1918 in the Netherlands.

41. See, for example, Andre (1975) on labor unrest in Sweden in the 1917–18 period, particularly in the wake of the Russian Revolution.

42. For the Netherlands, van Zanden (1997) emphasizes the lack of movement toward progressive taxation as right and center-right governments in the interwar period maintained a system based primarily on indirect taxation and relatively low top income tax rates. This raises the possibility that progressive income taxes failed to develop early in the Netherlands because the left was not yet in government. But among the war mobilization countries that adopted progressive tax systems, such as Canada, France, and the UK, parties of the left were not in power either.

43. Even U.S. entry into the war does not seem likely to be a result of such a selection mechanism. President Woodrow Wilson won the 1916 election on the slogan "He kept us out of war" and likely would have never entered the war if it were not for Germany's decision to implement unrestricted submarine warfare.

44. The four mobilization cases are Canada, France, the United Kingdom, and the United States. The four nonmobilization countries are Japan, Netherlands, Spain, and Sweden.

These countries were selected based on available data and in order to have a balanced number of mobilization and nonmobilization countries.

45. See Scheve and Stasavage (2010) and the online appendix for information on the calculation of these rates.

46. See the online appendix for an econometric evaluation of the proposed interaction between war mobilization and democracy. The evidence reported there is consistent with the impact of war mobilization being larger in democracies, though this result is somewhat sensitive to the specification. In general, we do not have that many non-democratic countries in the sample, and therefore our tests for this interaction are underpowered.

47. Again, this describes nineteenth-century mobilization for the sample, beginning in 1816. Some countries did surpass the 2 percent threshold in the Napoleonic Wars and before. See chapter 7 for a more complete discussion. Although we cannot include the Napoleonic Wars in our statistical analysis due to data limitations, it is in many ways an intermediate case consistent with our argument. While countries mobilized larger armies than in previous conflicts, the mobilization levels were much lower than in the conflicts of the early twentieth century. There was some movement toward taxing the rich, as exemplified by Britain's adoption of the first modern income tax, but these conflicts did not radically transform the politics of tax fairness as later mass mobilized conflicts would do.

48. More specifically, it would mean that our analysis relies on a comparison between mobilizers and nonmobilizers whose choice of tax rates was affected by the tax rates chosen by mobilizers. Ideally, we would be comparing mobilizers with non-mobilizers who were making strictly independent choices.

49. We have focused on the role that democracy, partisanship, inequality, and mass warfare have played in the timing of income tax innovations. Although we have discussed these independently, we have examined their influence simultaneously as well. These analyses allow us to control for each factor and we arrive at identical conclusions. See the online appendix for detailed results. See also Velez (2014) for an independent analysis that extends Scheve and Stasavage (2010) and also finds that mass mobilization wars cause a substantial increase in tax progressivity.

50. The other logical possibility is, of course, that the observed correlation between mass mobilization and top rates of taxation is spurious and does not reflect a causal relationship. Considering this possibility requires us to identify those factors that might be correlated with both war participation and tax policy that could account for the correlations that we have documented. Some of these factors, such as democracy, partisanship, and inequality, have already been considered. On the one hand, given the modest, at best, correlations between these factors and top rates of income taxation, it is unlikely that these factors account for the relationship between mass war mobilization and top rates. On the other hand, our analyses reported in the online appendix explicitly control for these factors, and we still find a strong relationship between mass warfare and top rates. We also evaluate the potential importance of other factors that can be measured and that could bias our conclusions. These include electoral institutions, trade openness, economic crises, and policy diffusion. We find somewhat mixed evidence of significant correlations between economic crises, trade openness, policy diffusion, and top rates of income taxation but find robust evidence of a positive partial correlation between majoritarian electoral systems and top rates of income taxation (but little evidence of a significant interaction between inequality and political institutions). Incorporating these measures, however, does not substantially change our estimates of the impact of war mobilization. Still there could be other potential confounders that are much more difficult to measure and assess. Our

analysis in the online appendix can control for some of these, such as time constant unobserved heterogeneity at the country level, through the use of country fixed effects or common shocks like the Cold War through the use of period fixed effects. We also consider other methods to rule out some types of confounders and strengthen our causal interpretation. That said, a causal interpretation of the correlation that we document requires some assumptions, specifically those associated with difference-in-differences estimates.

51. One might also consider two further alternative explanations. First, progressive taxation may have simply been in vogue during the early twentieth century, and when faced with a wartime expenditure shock, governments resorted to it. In other words, it was a bit like a policy that was in search of an application. This argument is plausible, but it fails to fit the evidence. Governments that did not mobilize for World War I also faced substantial expenditures even if at a lower level than those that mobilized for war. There is no reason why, if it was in vogue, progressive taxation would not have been applied in these countries either. Certainly, this is what proponents of progressive taxation in these countries argued. A second possibility is that war may alter beliefs about the incentive effects of high taxes on income and wealth or that it may make policymakers discount these future effects, providing states with greater flexibility to tax the rich. This mechanism would not suggest that the effect of mass mobilization wars should be larger in democratic countries. Nor would it anticipate that governments would raise top tax rates after a war's end, and not only during the conflict itself.

52. For a model suggesting this alternative result see Shayo (2009).

53. These surveys have previously been considered by Campbell (2009).

54. See American Enterprise Institute, "Public Opinion on Taxes: 1937 to Today," 2012.

55. Another aspect of the necessity argument is that mass warfare disrupted trade and tariff revenue to such an extent that taxing high incomes and wealth was needed. To some extent our discussion in chapter 5 covers this possibility. That said, it is important to note that it was not necessarily those countries for which trade was most disrupted that rates increased the most (e.g., the United States). Further, this mechanism would not predict that the effect was largest in democracies as discussed above and documented further in the online appendix. It is also important to consider the fact that war mobilization seems to have continued to influence policymaking after the war. This is inconsistent with the disruption of trade being the primary mechanism. Finally, the war mobilization correlation remains when we control for trade openness.

CHAPTER 4: TAXING INHERITANCE

1. See Book 55, chapters 24 and 25, Harvard Loeb Classical Library.

2. See Johnston (1965), p. 153. Similar views were expressed in the United States when it first established a stamp tax on estates in 1798. See Stabile (1998), p. 126.

3. Piketty and Saez (2013).

4. See Congressional Budget Office, 2009.

5. Full details can be found in Plagge, Scheve, and Stasavage (2011) and in our 2012 *American Political Science Review* article entitled "Democracy, War, and Wealth: Lessons from Two Centuries of Inheritance Taxation."

6. See Poterba (2001).

7. See Kopczuk and Saez (2004).

8. See Seligman (1925). The precise quote is on page 25.

9. These results are presented in Piketty (2001, p. 237). They derive from Caillaux (1910, pp. 208–209). See a more complete discussion in chapter 6.

10. The data from the census bureau show that in 1860 the United States had a total national wealth of $16.2 billion, and $12 billion of this was subject to property tax. Taxes collected amounted to $94.2 million, or 0.8 percent of the assessed value of wealth subject to ad valorem (property) taxation or 0.6 percent of total national wealth. In 1912, the United States had a total national wealth of $187 billion and $69.5 billion of wealth was subject to property taxes. Taxes collected amounted to $1.35 billion, representing 2.0 percent of wealth subject to ad valorem (property) taxation or 0.7 percent of total national wealth. The change between 1860 and 1912 was that tax rates had gone up, but the fraction of property subject to property taxation had shrunk. These two effects offset each other so that total taxes divided by total national wealth stayed roughly the same. See Bureau of the Census (1913), pp. 24–25, 747, 750.

11. See Du Rietz and Henrekson (2014).

12. Take the case of someone who held a stock of wealth for thirty years before dying, and for simplicity we will assume that they neither earned income on this nor did they draw on it for consumption. Now assume that the top marginal rate of wealth taxation from 1948 (1.8 percent) applied for each of the thirty years. Then assume that at death the wealth holder's heirs paid the top marginal inheritance rate from 1947 (70 percent) on the entirety of the remaining sum. Finally, consider what marginal inheritance tax rate would have had to be in place in order to leave the heirs with the same sum in the case where there had been no prior wealth tax. The answer is 82.6 percent. So the difference between 70 percent and 82.6 percent is significant, but not dramatic.

13. See Eichengreen (1989) for a review.

14. See Jens Beckert (2004) for an important survey of historical debates about inheritance in the United States, France, and Germany.

15. See Shultz (1926) for an example.

16. New Zealand had the highest marginal inheritance tax rate in 1913, followed by the United Kingdom at 15 percent.

17. The figure is drawn from Flora (1983, p. 339).

18. See Graetz and Shapiro for a discussion of lobbying over the Estate Tax in the United States (2005). See also Batchelder (2008) for a survey of issues surrounding the U.S. Estate Tax.

19. This is a point that has been previously emphasized by Duff (2005).

20. For the details, see Roine and Waldenström (2014). Roine and Waldenström (2014) also present a comprehensive analysis of the determinants of both top income and wealth shares over the long run. See also the earlier study by Ohlsson, Roine, and Waldenström (2007).

21. This analysis around World War I drops Finland from the list of ten countries for which we have wealth inequality data because it was not independent until the middle of the conflict. We include all ten countries for which we have data in the analyses that follow.

22. This fact does not, however, exclude the possibility that the correlation is spurious due to other factors simultaneously influencing wealth inequality and top inheritance tax rates across countries.

23. The figures for the other cases do not change our conclusions. These six cases were chosen to most closely follow, subject to data availability, those presented for the income tax.

24. As an aside, it might seem obvious that higher inheritance taxes will reduce wealth inequality. There is, however, a debate between economists about this. The key issue revolves around the idea of whether individuals are concerned only about themselves or are acting to further the welfare of a family dynasty. If it is the latter, then when faced with high inheritance taxes, parents may simply save more so that they can still transmit a sufficiently large inheritance to their children after taxes are taken into account. Gary

Becker and Nigel Tomes first proposed this idea in a paper published in 1979. More recent work by Benhabib, Bisin, and Zhu has suggested that this effect would be more limited. See the details in Benhabib, Bisin, and Zhu (2011). Like Becker and Tomes, they develop a dynastic model with finitely lived agents. However, they assume, unlike Becker and Tomes, that capital income in the model is stochastic. This generates the different result for taxation.

25. See the online appendix.
26. Soward (1919, p. 130).
27. See Scheve and Stasavage (2012).
28. These averages do not include data from Ireland, Finland, Germany, Norway, and Australia since these states had universal male suffrage from independence.
29. Mass mobilization is defined as in the previous chapter: an active participant in the war with at least 2 percent of the population mobilized at some point in the conflict.
30. Figures on inheritance sizes are from Piketty (2001, pp.746–747).

CHAPTER 5: TAXES ON THE RICH IN CONTEXT

1. For the early history of capital levies, see chapter 11 in Soward (1919).
2. See Eichengreen (1989). See also the earlier study by Hicks, Hicks, and Rostas (1941).
3. See Rostas (1940). The Czech levy was the most successful, whereas the Hungarian and Austrian levies were plagued by implementation problems.
4. See Hicks et al. (1941).
5. See Pigou (1918), p. 145.
6. See Brandes (1997) for a history of war profits in America.
7. Gallup Poll number 63, January 1937, based on a sample of 2,400 adults.
8. British Institute of Public Opinion Survey number 52, November 1938, based on a sample of 1,171 adults.
9. See Hicks et al. (1941), pp. 5–6.
10. See Haig (1929) for the most extensive account and Hicks et al. (1941) for further discussion.
11. See Grotard (1996).
12. See Hicks et al. (1941 pp. 164–168).
13. See the analysis in Frydman and Molloy (2012). They show that there was an effect of salary increase limits, but the impact varied significantly from industry to industry. In some industries, exemptions from the rule were granted in order to aid in the prosecution of the war. Leff (1991) provides the political background to these measures.
14. See Atrostic and Nunns (1991) for a review.
15. See Samuel (1919).
16. See Seligman (1925), chapter 22 and p. 692 for the specific figures.
17. See Adler (1951) and Colm and Tarasov (1941). Adler's study is not ideal in that he used a slightly different methodology from Colm and Tarasov. Also, his highest income category was only $7,500 per year, so this study is not truly informative about top earners.
18. See Aidt and Jensen (2013).
19. See Amenta and Skocpol (1988) for the US case.
20. See Dudley and Witt (2004).
21. See Seligman (1925), chapter 23 for an example of this reasoning.
22. See Toma (1992).
23. See Grady (1968).
24. See also Tooze (2006) for the role of financial repression in Germany's financing of World War II.

25. Figure 3.12 in chapter 3 plots the top rate of income taxation and the size of government as measured by total revenues divided by GDP and provides a striking picture that variation in taxes on the rich over time are not well accounted for by the size of government.

CHAPTER 6: THE CONSCRIPTION OF WEALTH

1. It should be noted, however, that the top rate of inheritance tax had reached 8 percent in 1895.
2. Seligman (1911, p. 130). Full speech available at http://hansard.millbanksystems .com/commons/1842/mar/11/financial-statement-ways-and-means#S3V0061P0_18420311_HOC_23
3. Ibid.
4. See, for example, the debate on April 29, 1842 between John Roebuck, Peel, and the Chancellor of the Exchequer, Henry Goulburn, regarding the inequality of the tax. Roebuck argues that "He [Peel] had to maintain three propositions: first, that there was an inequality in this mode of taxation; secondly, that the tax, being unequal, it sinned against those great canons of taxation which had been laid down by every man whose opinion was an authority on the subject, and that therefore if it were within their power to take away that inequality, it was their duty to do so; and, thirdly, that there was a mode by which this inequality might at least be reduced (for he would not go further than that), and that therefore a necessity was imposed upon the right hon. Baronet [Peel] to follow out that proposition." Source: http://hansard.millbanksystems.com/commons/1842/apr/29/income-tax#S3V0062P0_18420429_HOC_20.
5. It should be noted, however, that the top rate of inheritance tax had reached 8 percent in 1895 and 15 percent in 1907, where it remained prior to the beginning of World War I.
6. "Appendix II: The Incidence of Taxation." Wednesday, January 27, 1909. (p. 103). Mr. Philip Snowden, Chairman.
7. "Appendix II: The Incidence of Taxation." Wednesday, January 27, 1909. (p. 105). Mr. Philip Snowden, Chairman.
8. "Appendix II: The Incidence of Taxation." Wednesday, January 27, 1909. (p. 107). Mr. J. Ramsay MacDonald.
9. See the discussion in Daunton (2001) and in particular p. 358.
10. *The Times*, June 24, 1914, p. 9, col. G.
11. Mr. Wardle, House of Commons Debate, May 18, 1916, Vol. 82 cc1664-782, http://hansard.millbanksystems.com/commons/1916/may/18/finance-bill#S5CV0082P0_19160518_HOC_306 .
12. Trades Union Congress resolution, September 1916, cited in Daunton (1996, p. 890). Ramsay MacDonald, who would later become the first Labour Prime Minister, published an informative pamphlet entitled *The Conscription of Wealth*. It outlines Labour's view of how the war should be financed and illustrates the compensatory logic.
13. *Economist*, March 31, 1917, p. 579.
14. Sprague (1917), p. 5. Note also that Sprague played an important role in the U.S. debate about funding the war, lobbying publicly for high income and profits taxes.
15. *Economist*, April 8, 1916, p. 663.
16. This was in part because the UK Treasury judged that the imposition of a levy of this type would significantly reduce the revenues generated from the recently adopted high top rates of income tax and estate duty. See Daunton (1996) on this subject.
17. http://hansard.millbanksystems.com/.

18. The coding definitions were: (1) Equal treatment—Responses specify a preference for the government treating citizens the same. The orientation of the speech has to be against the income tax or higher rates. (2) Ability to pay—Responses specify that the rich are better able to afford or will be less harmed by a tax increase than the poor. This could include "equal sacrifice" arguments if the interpretation of equal sacrifice is that taxing the rich more is justified because the utility loss will be equal across the rich and the poor. The orientation of the speech had to be for the income tax or higher rates. (3) Compensatory—Responses that suggest a tax policy is justified because of other inequalities, advantages, or sacrifices due to state policy. This could include reference to the burden caused by other taxes levied by the state. It could include statements about the conscription of labor in the war effort. It could also simply include general ways in which the state facilitates the incomes of the wealthy. The orientation of the speech had to be for the income tax or higher rates. All other arguments such as economic efficiency, bureaucratic efficiency, prudence, or other fairness arguments were coded in a residual category. If more than one of the three fairness arguments was made, we coded it according to which argument was predominant. The coding was done independently by three undergraduate research assistants. The results that we discuss below are evident for each of the three sets of codings. For presentation purposes, we combined the codings by assigning each speech to a category if two or three coders agreed on the coding. For the few speeches for which there was no agreement, we used multiple imputation. The results in figure 6.1 and discussed in the text are based on multiple imputation estimates. See online appendix for the further details about our coding procedures and estimation methods.

19. We independently verified the decreased use of ability to pay arguments with a complementary analysis. We searched all Hansard speeches from the first use of the term "equality of sacrifice" to 1930. We then read the speech and determined if it was about government finance. If so, we then asked the question whether the speech could be interpreted as an ability to pay argument. These data suggested first that, as expected, there were more references to equality of sacrifice in wartime. There were 32 references between 1880 and 1913 but 47 references between 1914 and 1918. More to the point, the frequency of references to ability to pay in the discussion of equality of sacrifice dropped dramatically during wartime. In the period between 1880 and 1913, 39 percent of equality of sacrifice references can clearly be interpreted in terms of ability to pay. This is quite a high figure because in a large number of cases the reference to "equality of sacrifice" may well have meant ability to pay in the speaker's mind, but the discussion was sufficiently generic that we could not tell. Now consider what happened between 1914 and 1918. Only 3 percent of "equality of sacrifice" references can be interpreted in terms of ability to pay. This is a very dramatic drop-off and is consistent with the data in figure 6.1 suggesting that arguments favoring taxing the rich—including the meaning of equality of sacrifice—moved from emphasizing ability to pay to focusing on compensatory considerations.

20. See Perry (1955, p. 69).

21. Ibid., pp. 72, 107.

22. In addition to concern about the popularity of a new tax, Liberals were concerned about the reaction of subnational governments that had adopted direct taxes. Moreover, Liberals and Conservatives both viewed Canada's low taxes as a policy good for attracting new immigrants.

23. "Sir John A. Macdonald's Address to the People of Canada, February 7, 1891," in Carrigan (1968).

24. Carrigan (1968, pp. 402–404).

25. As mentioned above, another perspective from which to understand motivations of both Conservative and Liberal governments not to resort to direct taxes is that both

parties often argued that Canada's low tax environment attracted industrious immigrants. See, e.g., discussion in Perry (1955, pp. 144–145).

26. See ibid., pp. 143–146, for a full discussion.
27. Cited in ibid., p. 151.
28. Ibid.
29. See Perry (1955).
30. The initial war profits tax was really a high profits tax that taxed 25 percent of profits above a 10 percent return on capital for individuals, firms, and partnerships and a 7 percent return for companies (Hicks, Hicks, and Rostas 1942, p. 171).
31. Perry (1955, p. 152).
32. *The Times*, July 30, 1915, p. 6, col. F.
33. White's April 24, 1917 speech in House of Commons printed in the *Globe*, April 25, 1917, p. 4.
34. It is true that the April 1917 budget did make the war profits tax progressive, raising the top rate to 75 percent on profits in excess of 20 percent of capital (Perry 1955, p. 155). This change followed the compensatory logic described for the initial establishment of the tax in 1916 with continued pressure on the government to prevent some citizens from benefiting from the war effort.
35. The Military Service Act was passed on July 6, 1917. Note that conscription was not implemented until a bitter election was fought in December 1917 primarily over the issue of conscription. Borden won a landslide victory running in coalition with many Liberal MPs under the Unionist Party label but against the Liberal Party's leader Wilfred Laurier.
36. Borden Papers, cited in Robin (1966), p. 63.
37. Robin (1966).
38. Cited in Perry (1955, pp. 155–156).
39. It should be noted that in its effort to assure victory in the election, the government enacted laws disenfranchising conscientious objectors and citizens born in enemy countries. It also passed legislation granting women related to soldiers the right to vote and allowing the votes of soldiers abroad to choose what constituency they voted in.
40. Liberal Party Platform in Carrigan (1968, p. 72).
41. Unionist Platform in ibid., p. 77.
42. The Union Party won the election by a landslide with almost all the seats won by the Laurier Liberals coming from Quebec. The government continued to push tax policy in a more progressive direction for the remainder of the war and the years immediately afterward. Many Conservatives, including White, had hoped that the income tax would be temporary, but in the early 1920s, war debt and pensions made many of the same arguments observed during the war still relevant if not as widely held.
43. There are many excellent accounts of the history of the U.S. income tax. These include Mehrotra (2013), Bank, Stark, and Thorndike (2008), Brownlee (2004), Joseph (2004), Weisman (2002), and Witte (1985). It is important to note that the role of war in the development of the U.S. tax system features strongly in these works. Our work differs in its account of when and why wars have mattered. We show that this relationship is connected to a more general phenomenon involving compensatory arguments, and we identify this effect in political debates about taxation around the world. We also present new comparative empirical evidence over two centuries.
44. The Confederacy also adopted an income tax and various other levies aimed at the wealthy and those viewed as profiting from the war. Many of these taxes were adopted late in the conflict and there were considerable problems in collecting them.
45. The U.S. Constitution states that direct taxes should be apportioned on the basis of population. The ambiguity and debate was whether or not the income tax was a direct tax as understood in the Constitution.

46. See Hill (1894).
47. Ibid., p. 418.
48. Cited in ibid., pp. 438–439.
49. Cited in ibid., p. 439.
50. Bank et al. (2008, p. 41). It is important to point out that conscription in the Civil War allowed the wealthy to buy substitutes, exacerbating the sense of inequality in the war effort. See also Bank (1996) on this point.
51. Cited in Bank et al. (2008, p. 43).
52. Cited in Hill (1894, p. 425). It should be noted though that Morrill was a reluctant supporter of the income tax overall and played an important role in getting it passed.
53. A partial exception to this was the War Revenue Act of 1898, which instituted a federal estate tax with graduated rates. This tax had a low top rate of 2.25 percent and was associated with the Spanish-American War. It lasted until 1902.
54. The compromise legislation did implement a modest corporate income tax, but overall legislation was a victory for Republican conservatives.
55. See Bank (1996).
56. For a detailed account of the Revenue Act of 1916, see Brownlee (1985).
57. Note that the Act introduced an estate tax that differed substantially in details from the inheritance tax implemented during the Spanish-American War. As noted in chapter 4, we use the terms inheritance tax and estate tax interchangeably in this book.
58. For example, William Jennings Bryan wrote in *The Commoner* that new taxes should be "on large incomes and inheritances, rather than on the incomes of those who will have to do the fighting if there is any fighting to be done." Cited in Brownlee (1985), p. 185.
59. This is not to deny that there was still significant opposition to these prewar reforms. There was widespread business and conservative Republican opposition. These arguments featured some simple equality arguments and many efficiency arguments about the impact of the new taxes on economic performance.
60. For example, Sprague also published his arguments from the *Economic Journal* in *The New Republic* in February 1917. This, of course, was before U.S. entry into the war, but the article was nonetheless extremely influential.
61. National Tax Association (1917, p. 215).
62. Ibid., p. 216.
63. See Bank et al. (2008, pp. 62–76) for further examples.
64. See Otto Kahn (1918).
65. "Resolution adopted at Nebraska State Convention of Non Partisan League." *The Commoner*, Lincoln Nebraska, July 1, 1918. See also "Nonpartisan League Platform" in the *Montana Nonpartisan*, Great Falls Montana, September 2, 1919, and "Labor Firmly Behind U.S. In Its War" in the *Grand Forks Herald*, September 3, 1917.
66. "Conscription of Wealth" in *Washington Standard*, Olympia, Washington. August 31, 1917.
67. "Conscripting Wealth," in the *Grand Forks Herald*, Grand Forks, North Dakota, August 14, 1918.
68. "Conscription of Wealth From England's Viewpoint," in *New York Tribune*, January 27, 1918.
69. As we saw in chapter 4, the Revolution did lead to the creation of a modern inheritance tax, even if this tax was not implemented until after the Revolution's end. This tax was set at very low marginal rates throughout the nineteenth century
70. See in particular Asselain (2006) on this point, as well as the comparison between France and the United States, in Morgan and Prasad (2009).
71. The most detailed history of French debates over progressive income taxation can be found in Marion (1931), though as he was a clear opponent of progressivity his text

should be read with that in mind. These debates have also been covered more recently by Delalande (2011), and a brief discussion of them can also be found in Seligman (1911). The unpublished dissertation by Owen (1982) provides a detailed account of the politics of income taxation in France in the early twentieth century.

72. See Gross (1996, p. 125).
73. See Gross (1996).
74. These results are presented in Piketty (2001, p. 237). They derive from Caillaux (1910, pp. 208–209).
75. Wolowski (1872, p. 14).
76. Adolphe Thiers (1871 [1896]). This interpretation is emphasized by Seligman (1911).
77. Ibid., p. 32. All translations from the French in this section are by the authors.
78. See Wolowski (1871).
79. Leon Say, cited in Marion (1931, vol. 6, p. 193).
80. For a description of the sequence of proposals, see Delalande (2011), Seligman (1911), and Marion (1931).
81. Journal Officiel. Chambre. Débats July 10, 1907, p. 1828.
82. Journal Officiel. Chambre. Débats July 11, 1907, p. 1872.
83. For a discussion of this period, see Owen (1982, chapter 4).
84. Parti Socialiste: Section Française de l'Internationale Ouvrière, *Programme d'Action du Parti Socialiste*, 1919, p. 5.
85. Ibid., p. 14.
86. Journal Officiel. Chambre. Débats April 12, 1920, p. 874.
87. This was the case with Just Haristoy (1918).
88. See Tristram (1999).
89. Journal Officiel. Chambre. Débats April 12, 1920, p. 882.

CHAPTER 7: THE ROLE OF WAR TECHNOLOGY

1. This is an argument emphasized by Andreski (1968).
2. *The Politics*, Book VI, Chapter 7, as translated by Ernest Barker (1946).
3. *The Constitution of the Athenians*, as translated by Robin Osborne (2004). It should be acknowledged that not all Greek city-states with large navies had constitutions allowing for broad political participation. See Scheidel (2005) on the case of Corinth. See Ober (2015) for a broader discussion of the political economy of classical Greece.
4. See White (1962).
5. See Roland (2003) for a review of the debate and an assessment.
6. See Hui (2005).
7. See Lewis (2000).
8. Hui (2005).
9. This was the date of the creation of the Stockton and Darlington Railway.
10. See in particular van Creveld (1977, 1989) on this question, as well as Pratt (1915) for an earlier version of the story.
11. This date is offered by Pratt (1915, p. 9).
12. Onorato, Scheve, and Stasavage (2014). For the period from 1815 to the present we used data from the Correlates of War Project. For the years between 1600 and 1815 we relied on existing estimates produced by military historians for individual countries. For full sources, see Onorato et al. (2014). The thirteen great powers are defined by Levy (1983) and are Austria-Hungary (1600–1918), China (1949–2000), France (1600–2000), Italy (1861–1943), Japan (1905–1945), Netherlands (1609–1713), the Ottoman Empire (1600–1699), Prussia/Germany/West Germany (1740–2000), Russia/Soviet Union (1721–2000),

Spain (1600–1808), Sweden (1617–1721), United Kingdom (1600–2000), and the United States (1898–2000).

13. See Posen (1993) and Darden (2013) on the link between literacy and nationalism.
14. See Bogart (2009).
15. See in particular Posen (1993) and Snyder (2000).
16. This result was obtained by including a dummy variable in our military size and military mobilization regressions that took a value of 1 in all years beginning in 1789. The full result can be seen in table 2 of Onorato et al. (2014).
17. See the discussion in Schnapper (1968).
18. See Levi (1997).
19. This evidence is presented in the appendix to Onorato et al. (2014).
20. See Litton (2000, p. 3).
21. See Gillespie (2006, p. 27).
22. See ibid., p. 110.
23. See Murray and Knox (2001).
24. See Onorato et al. (2014) for the sources.

CHAPTER 8: WHY TAXES ON THE RICH DECLINED

1. "Let Us Face the Future: A Declaration of Labour Policy for the Consideration of the Nation," Labour Party, 1945.
2. Ibid.
3. British Institute of Public Opinion, survey 123, question 13.
4. Conseil National de la Résistance, "Programme du Conseil National de la Résistance," March 15, 1944.
5. Journal Officiel, October 19, 1944.
6. See de Vries and Hoeniger (1950).
7. On this subject see in particular the contribution by Hughes (1999).
8. See Meidner (1993).
9. As we suggested in chapter 1, this idea is explored in a recent paper by Roel Beetsma, Alex Cukierman, and Massimo Giuliodori (2013), who build on earlier findings by Peacock and Wiseman (1961). It is also closely related to Paul Pierson's (1994) arguments about how welfare states create constituencies prepared to defend their programs, frustrating attempts at policy retrenchment.
10. This was in particular the case in a speech of Winston Churchill's that was broadcast on June 5, 1945.
11. See Hughes (1999) on these debates.
12. "Wealthy" here is defined as those individuals who were placed in the highest socioeconomic status category based on the interviewer's subjective assessment. Gallup polls in this early period had no direct questions about annual income.
13. American Enterprise Institute, "Public Opinion on Taxes: 1937 to Today," 2012.
14. See in particular the discussion in Martin (2013).
15. The legislative history of this movement has been covered by Theodore Meyer (1956).
16. USAIPO 0492 Question 9.
17. In USAIPO 0366 in 1946 Gallup did also find a majority in favor of an income tax limitation, but that was to limit the total tax take (i.e., the effective rate) to 50 percent of one's income rather than 25 percent.
18. "The New Poor: A Salary Ceiling Story of Mr. Smith and his Fellow Bank Directors," Wall Street Journal, November 11, 1942.
19. 1979 Conservative Party General Election Manifesto.

20. "This Is the Road: The Conservative and Unionist Party's Policy, Conservative Party, 1950."
21. Republican Party Platform of 1980.
22. Republican Party Platform of 1952.
23. See the online appendix for the analyses. In our analyses discussed in the chapter 3 notes and reported in the online appendix exploring the robustness of our estimates of the effect of mass mobilization on war, we controlled for various measures of economic crises (e.g., debt, banking, and inflation crises). Those estimates reveal some evidence that countries experiencing economic crises on average lower their top rates of income tax. However, this result is sensitive to econometric specification, and there is no evidence that the relationship between crises and reductions is stronger after 1970 than before—in fact the absolute values of the point estimates are larger before than after. Thus, even if there is something to the idea that countries respond to economic shocks by lowering top rates—and our evidence is mixed on this point—it is consistent with our conclusion here that there is not persuasive evidence that fears about economic growth account for postwar declines in top rates of income taxation.
24. See Auerbach, Hines, and Slemrod (2007) for a thorough review of issues related to corporate taxation today.
25. See the theoretical review by Keen and Konrad (2013).
26. Devereux et al. (2008). See Kumar and Quinn (2012) who analyze a broader panel of countries, concluding that capital mobility has had relatively little effect on corporate tax rates. Other studies include Hallerberg and Basinger (1998), Hays (2009), Quinn (1997), and Swank and Steinmo (2002).
27. See the evidence compiled by Steffen Ganghof (2006) on this point.
28. See Hines and Summers (2009).
29. Swank and Steinmo (2002) report a negative relationship between capital control liberalization and effective taxes on labor but argue that this is not consistent with the usual globalization hypothesis because the expectation is that capital control liberalization forces governments to shift taxes from internationally mobile capital to generally immobile labor. They interpret the correlation as indicating that globalization has sensitized policymakers to the efficiency costs of high labor taxes. They also report no relationship between capital control liberalization and effective taxes on capital and conclude that, although globalization seems to have played a role in the setting of statutory corporate taxes, there is little evidence that it has played a primary role in the determination of other tax burdens. Their results, especially the null result for effective capital taxation, resonate with our analysis below.
30. See the review by Sorensen (2010).
31. See Quinn (1997). The underlying data come from the International Monetary Fund's annual report on exchange restrictions. The Quinn index has a minimum of zero and a maximum of 100, and it is available for the period between 1950 and 2011.
32. See the online appendix.
33. See the theoretical discussion in Piketty and Saez (2013).
34. See Kleven, Landais, and Saez (2010), and Kleven, Landais, Saez, and Schultz (2013).
35. We established this using the test for cross-sectional dependence proposed by Pesaran (2004).
36. Conservative Party General Election Manifesto, 1979.
37. Republican Party Platform, 1980.
38. "The Labour Way Is the Better Way," Labour Party Manifesto, 1979.
39. Labour Party Manifesto, 1983.
40. Democratic Party Platform, 1980.
41. Democratic Party Platform, 1984.

42. Fairness claims can also explain lower taxes on the rich in recent decades in countries that did not mobilize for war. For example, in Sweden, Henrekson and Waldenstrom (forthcoming) provide an account in which the possibility of the very wealthiest avoiding inheritance taxes combined with equal treatment norms to lead to the end of the inheritance tax. They argue that tax avoidance reduced political support for the tax because there was a perception that the wealthiest citizens avoided the tax while the less wealthy paid the tax. This exemplifies a different way in which violating equal treatment norms can undermine support for taxing the rich.

CHAPTER 9: WHAT FUTURE FOR TAXING THE RICH?

1. For just one example, see "Americans' Views on Inequality and Workers' Rights," *New York Times*, June 3, 2015.
2. "Also, all tax rates refer to marginal rates—this means that all individuals only pay that rate on the portion of their income that falls into that income category."
3. Figure 9.1 graphs the weighted data. The raw data medians are qualitatively similar though somewhat higher for the highest income category. Given that even this higher raw median is only 35 percent, this difference does not change our conclusion that there is little support for substantially higher rates than current law.
4. As discussed above, a common alternative survey question employed both in the popular press and in academic work asks individuals whether they support increased taxes on individuals with incomes over some threshold—usually $250,000 per year. In the United States over the last several years, a majority of respondents often answered this question in the affirmative. This fact has been interpreted as evidence that citizens want a much more progressive tax system with substantially higher rates than they are getting. Moreover, some survey researchers might prefer this question because our question requires respondents to express a specific quantitative preference, which is a relatively harder task. This is a problematic position for several reasons. First, respondents to this more common question may not know how high taxes already are on top earners. Second, the question is binary and it is not possible to infer whether respondents support slightly higher or much higher taxes on top earners. At least some survey evidence suggests that only small minorities support increased top rates of more than 5 percentage points. This is consistent with our more general point here that there is little evidence that the public prefers much more progressive income tax policies than currently exist. Third, the distribution of responses to our question is not substantively different if the sample is limited to more numerate or educated respondents. Fourth, questions that refer to individuals above a certain threshold paying higher taxes do not distinguish between higher statutory rates and increased effective rates through the reduction of exemptions and other privileges in the tax system. See Ballard-Rosa, Martin, and Scheve (2015) for the details of an alternative analysis that suggests preferred income tax rates in the U.S. public similar to those we report here. This study implements a conjoint experimental design to identify the salient characteristics of public preferences about alternative income tax plans taking into account revenue needs/constraints and reports results for the top rate that are quite similar to the simple survey question discussed here. Overall, it does not seem that in the United States there is strong support for significantly higher income tax rates on high earners despite substantial increases in inequality over the last three decades.
5. The authors did, however, find that providing information about how few people are subject to the estate tax in the United States today was associated with support for a

substantially higher marginal rate of estate taxation. See Kuziemko, Norton, Saez, and Stantcheva (2013).

6. Internal Revenue Service, Statistics of Income.

7. Statistics on kindergarten teacher compensation are drawn from the Bureau of Labor Statistics for 2013, http://www.bls.gov/oes/current/oes252012.htm

8. See Landais, Piketty, and Saez (2011).

9. See Bank (1996).

10. See Landais et al. (2011, pp. 50–52).

11. One of the most detailed sources on this issue is the "Who Pays?" report on state level taxation by the Institute on Taxation and Economic Policy. According to this source, averaging across all fifty states, those individuals in the bottom 20 percent of earners pay about 7 percent of their income in sales and excise taxes, whereas those in the top 1 percent of earners pay less than 1 percent of their income in sales and excise taxes. Institute on Taxation and Economic Policy (2013).

12. We can also ask what equal treatment logic implies for proposals to establish a progressive consumption tax in the United States. The idea behind this tax is that individuals would submit a declaration at the end of each year showing how much they had earned and how these earnings had been devoted to either consumption or savings. They would then be liable for a tax on the portion consumed, with higher rates applying to higher levels of consumption. People with a wide range of political views have advocated such a tax (Frank 2011; Caroll and Viard 2013). The idea of a progressive consumption tax is most often justified on grounds of economic efficiency, encouraging saving and limiting the effect on work incentives from something like a progressive income tax. However, independent of efficiency considerations, we can see how the logic of equal treatment can be applied to justify a progressive consumption tax. Instead of trying to justify a progressive rate structure by referring to economic efficiency or ability to pay, it could be justified by the norm of equal treatment. This could be done if the rates on this tax are set so that individuals from different income categories all spend roughly the same fraction of their income on consumption taxes. Under these circumstances, referring to a "progressive" consumption tax would be a misnomer. The new tax would actually be an "equal treatment consumption tax."

REFERENCES

Acemoglu, Daron, and James Robinson. 2006. *Economic Origins of Dictatorship and Democracy.* New York: Cambridge University Press.

———. 2008. "Persistence of Power, Elites, and Institutions." *American Economic Review* 98: 267–93.

Acemoglu, Daron, and James A. Robinson. 2000. "Why Did the West Extend the Franchise? Democracy, Inequality, and Growth in Historical Perspective." *Quarterly Journal of Economics* 115: 1167–1199.

Adler, John. 1951. "The Fiscal System, the Distribution of Income, and Public Welfare." In *Fiscal Policies and the American Economy*, ed. Kenyon Poole. New York: Prentice Hall.

Aidt, Toke S., and Peter Jensen. 2013. "Democratization and the Size of Government: Evidence from the Long Nineteenth Century." *Public Choice* 157: 511–542.

Aidt, Toke S., and Peter S. Jensen. 2009. "The Taxman Tools Up: An Event History Study of the Introduction of the Personal Income Tax." *Journal of Public Economics* 93: 160–175.

Alesina, Alberto, and George-Marios Angeletos. 2005. "Fairness and Redistribution." *American Economic Review* 95: 960–980.

Alesina, Alberto, and Edward Glaeser. 2004. *Fighting Poverty in the US and Europe: A World of Difference.* Cambridge, MA: Cambridge University Press.

Alstott, Anne, and Benjamin Novick. 2006. "War, Taxes, and Income Redistribution in the Twenties: The 1924 Veterans' Bonus and the Defeat of the Mellon Plan." Yale University.

Alt, James. 1979. *The Politics of Economic Decline.* Cambridge: Cambridge University Press.

Amenta, Edwin, and Theda Skocpol. 1988. "Redefining the New Deal: World War II and the Development of Social Provision in the United States." In *The Politics of Social Policy in the United States*, ed. Margaret Weir, Ann Shola Orloff, and Theda Skocpol. Princeton, NJ: Princeton University Press.

Anderson, Elizabeth. 1999. "What Is the Point of Equality?" *Ethics* 109: 287–337.

Andre, Carl-Göran. 1975. "The Swedish Labor Movement and the 1917–1918 Revolution." In *Sweden's Development from Poverty to Affluence, 1750–1970*, ed. Steven Koblik, transl. Joanne Johnson. Minneapolis: University of Minnesota Press.

Andreski, Stanislav. 1968. *Military Organization and Society.* Berkeley: University of California Press.

Ardant, Gabriel. 1972. *Histoire de l'impôt.* Paris: Fayard.

Aristotle. 1948. *The Politics.* Edited and translated by Ernest Barker. Oxford: Clarendon Press.

Asselain, Jean-Charles. 2006. "Un siècle d'histoire fiscale de la France: Le mirage de l'impôt progressif sur le revenu." In *L'Impôt en France au XIXe et XXe siècles*, ed. Maurice Lévy-Leboyer, Michel Lescure, and Alain Plessis. Paris: Comité pour l'histoire économique et financière de la France.

Atkinson, Anthony, and Thomas Piketty. 2007. *Top Incomes Over the Twentieth Century*. Volume 1. Oxford: Oxford University Press.

———. 2010. *Top Incomes Over the Twentieth Century*. Volume 2. Oxford: Oxford University Press.

Atrostic, B. K., and James Nunns. 1991. "Measuring Tax Burden: A Historical Perspective." In *Fifty Years of Measurement: The Jubilee of the Conference on Research in Income and Wealth*, ed. Ernst Berndt and Jack Triplett. Cambridge: National Bureau of Economic Research.

Auerbach, Alan, James Hines, and Joel Slemrod. 2007. *Taxing Corporate Income in the 21st Century*. New York: Cambridge University Press.

Ballard-Rosa, Cameron, Lucy Martin, and Kenneth Scheve. 2015. "The Structure of American Income Tax Policy Preferences." Stanford University.

Bank, Steven A. 1996. "Origins of a Flat Tax." *Denver University Law Review* 73: 329–402.

Bank, Steven, Kirk Stark, and Joseph Thorndike. 2008. *War and Taxes*. Washington, DC: Urban Institute.

Bartels, Larry. 2008. *Unequal Democracy*. Princeton, NJ: Princeton University Press.

Batchelder, Lily. 2008. "What Should Society Expect From Its Heirs? A Proposal for a Comprehensive Inheritance Tax." New York University School of Law.

Becker, Gary S., and Nigel Tomes. 1979. "An Equilibrium Theory of the Distribution of Income and Intergenerational Mobility." *Journal of Political Economy* 87: 1153–1189.

Beckert, Jens. 2004. *Inherited Wealth*. Princeton, NJ: Princeton University Press.

Beetsma, Roel, Alex Cukierman, and Massimo Giuliodori. 2013. "The Political Economy of Redistribution in the U.S. in the Aftermath of World War II and the Delayed Impacts of the Great Depression—Evidence and Theory." University of Amsterdam.

Bénabou, Roland, and Jean Tirole. 2006. "Belief in a Just World and Redistributive Politics." *Quarterly Journal of Economics* 121: 699–746.

Bendix, Reinhard, and Stein Rokkan. 1962. "The Extension of National Citizenship to the Lower Classes: A Comparative Perspective." Paper prepared for the Fifth World Congress of Sociology, Washington, DC.

Benhabib, Jess, Alberto Bisin, and Shenghao Zhu. 2011. "The Distribution of Wealth and Fiscal Policy in Economies with Finitely Lived Agents." *Econometrica* 79: 123–157.

Bentham, Jeremy. 1794 [1952]. "Proposal for a Model of Taxation in Which the Burthen May Be Alleviated or Even Balanced by an Indemnity." In *Jeremy Bentham's Economic Writings*. London: Allen and Unwin.

Beramendi, Pablo. 2012. *The Political Geography of Inequality: Regions and Redistribution*. New York: Cambridge University Press.

Beramendi, Pablo, and Christopher Anderson. 2008. *Democracy, Inequality, and Representation*. New York: Russell Sage Foundation.

Besley, Timothy, and Torsten Persson. 2009. "The Origins of State Capacity: Property Rights, Taxation, and Policy." *American Economic Review* 99: 1218–1244.

Birnbaum, Jeffrey, and Alan Murray. 1988. *Showdown at Gucci Gulch*. New York: Vintage.

Blockmans, Wim. 1987. "Finances publiques Et inégalité sociale dans Les Pays-Bas au XIVe–XVIe Siècles." In *Genèse de l'état moderne*, ed. Jean-Phlippe Genet. Paris: Editions du CNRS.

Blum, Walter J., and Harry Kalven, Jr. 1952. "The Uneasy Case for Progressive Taxation." *University of Chicago Law Review* 19: 417–520.

Bogart, Dan. 2009. "Nationalizations and the Development of Transport Systems: Cross-Country Evidence from Railroad Networks, 1860–1912." *Journal of Economic History* 69: 202–237.

Boix, Carles. 2003. *Democracy and Redistribution*. Cambridge: Cambridge University Press.

Boix, Carles, and Sebastian Rosato. 2001. "A Complete Data Set of Political Regimes, 1800–1999." University of Chicago.

Bonica, Adam, Nolan McCarty, Keith T. Poole, and Howard Rosenthal. 2013. "Why Hasn't Democracy Slowed Rising Inequality?" *Journal of Economic Perspectives* 27: 103–124.

Boskin, Michael. 2000. "From Edgeworth to Vickrey to Mirrlees." Distinguished Address presented at the Forty-Seventh International Atlantic Economic Conference, Montreal, Canada, October 7–10, 1999.

Boucoyannis, Deborah. 2013. "The Equalizing Hand: Why Adam Smith Thought the Market Should Produce Wealth without Steep Inequality." *Perspectives on Politics* 11: 1051–1070.

Bowley, Arthur. 1930. *Some Economic Consequences of the Great War*. London: Butterworth's.

Bowsky, William. 1969. "Direct Taxation in a Medieval Commune: The *Dazio* in Siena, 1287–1355." *Explorations in Economic History* 7: 205–221.

———. 1981. *A Medieval Italian Commune: Siena Under the Nine, 1287–1355*. Berkeley: University of California Press.

Brandes, Stuart. 1997. *Warhogs: A History of War Profits in America*. Lexington: University Press of Kentucky.

Brownlee, Elliot. 1985. "Wilson and Financing the Modern State: The Revenue Act of 1916." *Proceedings of the American Philosophical Society* 129: 173–210.

———. 2004. *Federal Taxation in America: A Short History*. New York: Cambridge University Press.

Bureau of the Census (United States). 1913. "Wealth, Debt, and Taxation." Washington, DC: Government Printing Office.

Caillaux, Joseph. 1910. *L'Impôt sur le revenu*. Paris: Berger Lévrault.

Camerer, Colin, and Ernst Fehr. 2004. "Measuring Social Norms and Preferences Using Experimental Games: A Guide for Social Scientists." In *Foundations of Human Sociality*, ed. Joseph Henrich. Oxford: Oxford University Press.

Campbell, Andrea Louise. 2009. "What Americans Think of Taxes." In *The New Fiscal Sociology*, ed. Monica Prasad, Isaac Martin, and Ajay Mehrotra, 48–67. New York: Cambridge University Press.

Cappelen, Alexander, Astri Drange Hole, Erik O. Sorensen, and Bertil Tungodden. 2007. "The Pluralism of Fairness Ideals: An Experimental Approach." *American Economic Review* 97: 818–827.

Caramani, Daniele. 2000. *Elections in Western Europe since 1815: Electoral Results by Constituencies*. London: Macmillan Reference.

Carbonell-Nicolau, Oriol. 2009. "A Positive Theory of Income Taxation." *B.E. Journal of Economics* 9: 1–47.

Carbonell-Nicolau, Oriol, and Efe Ok. 2007. "Voting Over Income Taxation." *Journal of Economic Theory* 134: 249–286.

Carr, Michael, and Phil Melizzo. 2013. "Entitlement in a Real Effort Ultimatum Game." Department of Economics, University of Massachusetts–Boston.

Carrigan, Owen. 1968. *Canadian Party Platforms, 1867–1968*. Toronto: Copp Clark.

Carroll, Robert, and Alan Viard. 2013. *Progressive Consumption Taxation: The X Tax Revisited*. Washington, DC: American Enterprise Institute.

Cavaille, Charlotte, and Kris-Stella Trump. 2015. "The Two Facets of Social Policy Preferences." *Journal of Politics* 77: 146–160.

Chaunu, Pierre. 1977. "L'Etat." In *Histoire économique et sociale de la France. Tome 1: de 1450 à 1660*, ed. Pierre Chaunu and Richard Gascon. Paris: Presses Universitaires de France.

Clamageran, Jean-Jacques. 1868. *Histoire de l'impôt en France*. Paris: Librairie Guillaumin.

Cohen, G. A. 1989. "On the Currency of Egalitarian Justice." *Ethics* 99: 906–944.

Colm, Gerhard, and Helen Tarasov. 1941. "Who Pays the Taxes?" Washington, DC: U.S. Government Printing Office.

Conti, Elio. 1984. *L'imposta diretta a Firenze nel quattrocento (1427–1494)*. Rome: Istituto Storico Italiano Per Il Medio Evo.

Croissant, Aurel. 2002. "Electoral Politics in South Korea." In *Electoral Politics in Southeast and East Asia*, ed. A. Croissant, G. Bruns, and M. John (Hrsg.). Singapore: Friedrich Ebert Foundation.

Cronin, James E. 1991. *The Politics of State Expansion: War, State, and Society in Twentieth-Century Britain*. London: Routledge.

Darden, Keith. 2013. *Resisting Occupation: Mass Schooling and the Creation of Durable National Loyalties*. Cambridge: Cambridge University Press.

Daunton, Martin. 1996. "How to Pay for the War: State, Society and Taxation in Britain, 1917–24." *English Historical Review* 111: 882–919.

———. 2001. *Trusting Leviathan: The Politics of Taxation in Britain, 1799–1914*. Cambridge: Cambridge University Press.

———. 2002. *Just Taxes: The Politics of Taxation in Britain, 1914–1979*. Cambridge: Cambridge University Press.

Delalande, Nicolas. 2011. *Les Batailles de l'impôt*. Paris: Seuil.

Dell, Fabien. 2008. "L'Allemagne Inégale: Inégalités de revenus et de patrimoine en Allemagne, dynamique d'accumulation du capital et taxation de Bismarck à Schroder 1870–2005." Unpublished dissertation. Paris School of Economics.

de Saint Lambert, Jean-François (marquis de). 1765. "Luxe." In *Encyclopédie, ou Dictionnaire raisonné des sciences, des arts et des métiers*, ed. Denis Diderot and Jean le Rond d'Alembert. Volume 9. Paris: Briasson.

de Vries, Henry, and Berthold Hoeniger. 1950. "Post-Liberation Nationalizations in France." *Columbia Law Review* 50: 629–656.

Devereux, Michael P., Ben Lockwood, and Michela Redoano. 2008. "Do Countries Compete over Corporate Tax Rates?" *Journal of Public Economics* 92: 1210–1235.

Diamond, Peter, and Emmanuel Saez. 2011. "The Case for a Progressive Tax: From Basic Research to Policy Recommendations." *Journal of Economic Perspectives* 25: 165–190.

Dudley, Leonard, and Peter-Christian Witt. 2004. "Arms and the Man." *Kyklos* 57: 475–504.

Duff, David. 2005. "The Abolition of Wealth Transfer Taxes: Lessons from Canada, Australia, and New Zealand." *Pittsburgh Law Review* 3: 72–120.

Durante, Ruben, Louis Putterman, and Jol van der Weele. 2014. "Preferences for redistribution and perceptions of fairness: An experimental study." *Journal of the European Economic Association* 12: 1059–1086.

Du Rietz, Gunnar, and Magnus Henrekson. 2014. "Swedish Wealth Taxation, 1911–2007." Stockholm: Research Institute of Industrial Economics.

Du Rietz, Gunnar, Dan Johannson, and Mikael Stenkula. 2010. "The Marginal Tax Wedge of Labor in Sweden from 1861 to 2009." Stockholm: Research Institute of Industrial Economics.

Dworkin, Ronald. 1977. *Taking Rights Seriously*. Cambridge, MA: Harvard University Press.

———. 1981a. "What Is Equality? Part I: Equality of Welfare." *Philosophy & Public Affairs* 10: 185–246.

———. 1981b. "What Is Equality? Part II: Equality of Resources." *Philosophy & Public Affairs* 10: 283–345.

Edgeworth, Francis. 1897. "The Pure Theory of Taxation." *Economic Journal* 7: 46–70.

Eich, Stefan. 2013. "The Neglected Origins of Progressive Taxation." Working paper, Yale University, Department of Political Science.

Eichengreen, Barry. 1989. "The Capital Levy in Theory and Practice." NBER Working Paper 3096.

Engl, Christoph. 2011. "Dictator Games: A Meta Study." *Experimental Economics* 14: 583–610.

Fairfield, Tasha. 2015. *Private Wealth and Public Revenue in Latin America: Business Power and Tax Politics*. Cambridge: Cambridge University Press.

Farhi, Emmanuel, and Ivan Werning. 2009. "The Political Economy of Nonlinear Capital Taxation." Harvard University, Department of Economics.

Feldman, Naomi, and Joel Slemrod. 2009. "War and Taxation: When Does Patriotism Overcome the Free Rider Problem?" In *The New Fiscal Sociology*, ed. Monica Prasad, Isaac Martin, and Ajay Mehrotra. New York: Cambridge University Press.

Ferejohn, John, and Frances Rosenbluth. Forthcoming. *Forged Through Fire*. New York: W.W. Norton.

Fisman, Ray, Pamela Jakiela, and Shachar Kariv. 2014. "The Distributional Preferences of Americans." NBER Working Paper no. 20145.

———. 2014. "How Did Distributional Preferences Change During the Great Recession?" NBER Working Paper no. 20146.

Flora, Peter. 1983. *State, Economy, and Society in Western Europe 1815–1975: A Data Handbook in Two Volumes*. Chicago, IL: St. James.

Fong, Christina. 2001. "Social Preferences, Self-Interest, and the Demand for Redistribution." *Journal of Public Economics* 82: 225–246.

Frank, Robert. 2011. *The Darwin Economy*. Princeton, NJ: Princeton University Press.

Fritschy, Wantje. 1997. "A History of the Income Tax in the Netherlands." *Revue Belge de Philologie et d'Histoire* 75: 1045–1061.

Frydman, Carola, and Raven Molloy. 2012. "Pay Cuts for the Boss: Executive Compensation in the 1940s." *Journal of Economic History* 72: 225–251.

Ganghof, Steffen. 2006 *The Politics of Income Taxation: A Comparative Analysis*. ECPR publications.

Genovese, Federica, Kenneth Scheve, and David Stasavage. 2014. "The Comparative Income Taxation Database." Stanford University and New York University.

Giertz, Seth, Emmanuel Saez, and Joel Slemrod. 2012. "The Elasticity of Taxable Income with Respect to Marginal Tax Rates: A Critical Review." *Journal of Economic Literature* 50: 3–50.

Gilens, Martin. 1999. *Why Americans Hate Welfare: Race, Media, and the Politics of Anti-Poverty Policy*. Chicago, IL: University of Chicago Press.

———. 2012. *Affluence and Influence: Economic Inequality and Political Power in America*. Princeton, NJ: Princeton University Press.

Gillespie, Paul. 2006. *The Development of Precision Guided Munitions*. Tuscaloosa, AL: University of Alabama Press.

Gomel, Charles. 1902. *Histoire de la Législative et de la Convention*. Volume I. Paris: Guillaumin.

Grady, Henry Francis. 1968. *British War Finance, 1914–1919*. New York: AMS Press.

Graetz, Michael, and Ian Shapiro. 2005. *Death by a Thousand Cuts*. Princeton, NJ: Princeton University Press.

Graslin, J. J. Louis. 1767. *Essai analytique sur la richesse et sur l'impôt*. London: n.p.

Gros, Gaston. 1907. *L'impôt sur le revenu: essai d'économie financière*. Paris: L. Larose et L. Tenin.

Gross, Jean-Pierre. 1993. "Progressive Taxation and Social Justice in Eighteenth Century France." *Past and Present* 140: 79–126.

———. 1996. "Progressive Taxation and the Fair Distribution of Wealth." In *Fair Shares for All: Jacobin Egalitarianism in Practice*, ed. Jean-Pierre Gross. New York: Cambridge University Press.

Grotard, Sandrine. 1996. "Le Premier impôt sur les bénéfices d'entreprises en France. La contribution extraordinaire sur les bénéfices de guerre." *Etudes et Documents, Comité pour l'Histoire Economique et Financière de la France* VIII: 259–280.

Guicciardini, Francesco. ~1520 [1867]. "La decima scalata." In *Opere Inedite di Francesco Guicciardini: Ricordi Autobiografici E di Famiglia E Scritti Vari*. Firenze: Cellini, pp. 353–368.

———. ~1520 [1959]. "Two Discourses on Progressive Taxation of Land Incomes" (English translation by Elizabeth Henderson). *International Economic Papers* 9: 7–19. London: Macmillan.

———. ~1520 [1858]. "Del Reggimento di Firenze." In *Opere Inedite di Francesco Guicciardini*. Firenze: Barbera Bianchi.

———. ~1524 [1994]. *Dialogue on the Government of Florence*. Edited and translated by Alison Brown. Cambridge: Cambridge University Press.

Hacker, Jacob. 2008. *The Great Risk Shift: The New Economic Insecurity and the Decline of the American Dream*. 2nd edition. Oxford: Oxford University Press.

Haig, Robert Murray. 1929. *The Public Finances of Post-War France*. New York: Columbia University Press.

Hall, Peter, and David Soskice. 2001. *Varieties of Capitalism: The Institutional Foundations of Comparative Advantage*. Oxford: Oxford University Press.

Hall, Robert, and Alvin Rabushka. 1981. *The Flat Tax*. Stanford: Hoover Institution.

Hallerberg, Mark, and Scott Basinger. 1998. "Internationalization and Changes in Tax Policy in OECD Countries: The Importance of Domestic Veto Players." *Comparative Political Studies* 31: 321–352.

Haristoy, Just. 1918. *Finances d'après guerre et conscription des fortunes*. Paris: Félix-Alcan.

Hayek, Friedrich. 1960 [2011]. *The Constitution of Liberty: The Definitive Edition. The Collected Works of F.A. Hayek*. Volume 17. Chicago, IL: University of Chicago Press.

Hays, Jude. 2009. *Globalization and the New Politics of Embedded Liberalism*. Oxford: Oxford University Press.

Henrekson, Magnus, and Daniel Waldenström. Forthcoming. "Inheritance Taxation in Sweden, 1885–2004: The Role of Ideology, Family Firms, and Tax Avoidance." *Economic History Review*.

Henrich, J., J. Ensminger, R. McElreath, A. Barr, C. Barrett, A. Bolyanatz, J. C. Cardenas, M. Gurven, E. Gwako, N. Henrich, C. Lesorogol, F. Marlowe, D. Tracer, and J. Ziker. 2010. "Markets, Religion, Community Size, and the Evolution of Fairness and Punishment." *Science* 327: 1480–1484.

Hicks, J. R., U. K. Hicks, and L. Rostas. 1941. *The Taxation of War Wealth*. Oxford: Clarendon Press.

Hill, Joseph A. 1894. "The Civil War Income Tax." *Quarterly Journal of Economics* 8: 416–452.

Hines, James, and Lawrence Summers. 2009. "How Globalization Affects Tax Design." In *Tax Policy and the Economy*, ed. Jeffrey Brown and James Poterba. Cambridge: National Bureau of Economic Research.

Hochschild, Jennifer. 1981. *What's Fair? American Beliefs about Distributive Justice*. Cambridge, MA: Harvard University Press.

Hont, Istvan. 2006. "The Early Enlightenment Debate on Commerce and Luxury." In *Cambridge History of Eighteenth Century Political Thought*, ed. Mark Goldie and Robert Wokler. Cambridge: Cambridge University Press.

Huber, Evelyn, and John D. Stephens. 2001. *Development and Crisis of the Welfare State: Parties and Policies in Global Markets*. Chicago, IL: University of Chicago Press.

Hughes, Michael. 1999. *Shouldering the Burdens of Defeat: West Germany and the Reconstruction of Social Justice*. Chapel Hill: University of North Carolina Press.

Hui, Victoria Tin-bor. 2005. *War and State Formation in Ancient China and Early Modern Europe*. Cambridge: Cambridge University Press.

Hume, David. 1742 [1994]. *Of Taxes*. In *Hume: Political Essays*, ed. Knud Haakonssen. Cambridge: Cambridge University Press.

Ignatieff, Michael, and Istvan Hont. 1983. *Wealth and Virtue: The Shaping of Political Economy in the Scottish Enlightenment*. Cambridge: Cambridge University Press.

Ingenbleek, Jules. 1918. *La justice dans l'impôt*. Paris: Berger-Levrault.

Institute on Taxation and Economic Policy. 2013. "Who Pays? A Distributional Analysis of Tax Systems in All 50 States." 4th edition. Washington, DC.

Isaia, Henri, and Jacques Spindler. 1989. "1914–1940: L'impôt sur le revenu sous la IIIème République." In *L'Impôt sur le revenu en question*, ed. Jean-Claude Martinez. Paris: Litec.

Isenmann, Eberhard. 1995. "Medieval and Renaissance Theories of State Finance." In *Economic Systems and State Finance*, ed. Richard Bonney. Oxford: Clarendon Press.

Iversen, Torben, and David Soskice. 2006. "Electoral Institutions and the Politics of Coalitions: Why Some Democracies Redistribute More Than Others." *American Political Science Review* 100:165–181.

———. 2009. "Distribution and Redistribution: The Shadow of the Nineteenth Century." *World Politics* 61: 438–486.

Jha, Saumitra, and Steven Wilkinson. 2012. "Does Combat Experience Foster Organizational Skill? Evidence from Ethnic Cleansing during the Partition of South Asia." *American Political Science Review* 106: 883–907.

Johnston, Alexander. 1965. *The Inland Revenue*. London: George Allen and Unwin.

Jones, Charles. 2015. "Pareto and Piketty: The Macroeconomics of Top Income and Wealth Inequality." *Journal of Economic Perspectives* 29: 29–46.

Joseph, Richard. 2004. *The Origins of the American Income Tax: The Revenue Act of 1894 and Its Aftermath*. Syracuse, NY: Syracuse University Press.

Kahn, Otto. 1918. *Frenzied Liberty: The Myth of a Rich Man's War*. Extracts from address given at the University of Wisconsin–Madison.

Keen, Michael, and Kai A. Konrad. 2013. "The Theory of International Tax Competition and Coordination." In *Handbook of Public Economics*, ed. Alan Auerbach, Raj Chetty, Martin Feldstein, and Emmanuel Saez, 5: 257–328.

Kennedy, David M. 1980. *Over Here: The First World War and American Society*. Oxford: Oxford University Press.

Kenworthy, Lane, and Jonas Pontusson. 2005. "Rising Inequality and the Politics of Redistribution in Affluent Countries." *Perspectives on Politics* 3: 449–471.

Kleven, Henrik, Camille Landais, and Emmanuel Saez. 2010. "Taxation and International Migration of Superstars: Evidence from the European Football Market." *American Economic Review* 103: 1892–1924.

Kleven, Henrik, Camille Landais, Emmanuel Saez, and Esben Anton Schultz. 2013. "Migration and Wage Effects of Taxing Top Earners: Evidence from the Foreigners Tax Scheme in Denmark." University of California–Berkeley.

Klinkner, Philip, and Rogers Smith. 1999. *The Unsteady March*. Chicago, IL: University of Chicago Press.

Kopczuk, W., and Emmanuel Saez. 2004. "Top Wealth Shares in the United States: 1916–2000: Evidence from Estate Tax Returns." *National Tax Journal* 57: 445–487.

Kriner, Douglas, and Francis Shen. 2010. *The Casualty Gap: The Causes and Consequences of American Wartime Inequalities*. Oxford: Oxford University Press.

Kumar, Manmohan, and Dennis Quinn. 2012. "Globalization and Corporate Taxation." *International Monetary Fund Working Paper* 12/252.

Kuziemko, Ilyana, Michael Norton, Emmanuel Saez, and Stefanie Stantcheva. 2013. "How Elastic Are Preferences for Redistribution? Evidence from Randomized Survey Experiments." University of California–Berkeley.

Landais, Camille, Thomas Piketty, and Emmanuel Saez. 2011. *Pour une révolution fiscale. Un impôt sur le revenu pour le XXème siècle*. Paris: Seuil.

Leff, Mark H. 1984. *The Limits of Symbolic Reform: The New Deal and Taxation, 1933–1939*. Cambridge: Cambridge University Press.

———. 1991. "The Politics of Sacrifice on the American Home Front in World War II." *Journal of American History* 77: 1296–1318.

Levi, Margaret. 1988. *Of Rule and Revenue*. Berkeley: University of California Press.

———. 1997. *Consent, Dissent, and Patriotism*. Cambridge: Cambridge University Press.

Levy, Jack. 1983. *War in the Modern Great Power System, 1495–1975*. Lexington: University of Kentucky Press.

Lewis, Mark Edward. 2000. "The Han Abolition of Universal Military Service." In *Warfare in Chinese History*, ed. Hans van de Ven. Leiden: Brill.

Lieberman, Evan. 2003. *Race and Regionalism in the Politics of Taxation in Brazil and South Africa*. Cambridge: Cambridge University Press.

Lindert, Peter. 1994. "The Rise of Social Spending, 1880–1930." *Explorations in Economic History* 31: 1–37.

———. 2004. *Growing Public: Social Spending and Economic Growth since the Eighteenth Century.* New York: Cambridge University Press.

Litton, Leonard. 2000. "The Information-Based RMA and the Principles of War." *Air and Space Power Chronicles.* n.p.

Loewenstein, K. 1973. *The Governance of Rome.* The Hague: Martinus Nijhoff.

Lü, Xiaobo, and Kenneth Scheve. 2014. "Self-Center Inequity Aversion and the Mass Politics of Taxation." Stanford University.

Luttmer, Erzo. 2001. "Group Loyalty and the Taste for Redistribution." *Journal of Political Economy* 109: 500–528.

Mackie, Thomas T., and Richard Rose. 1974. *The International Almanac of Electoral History.* London: Macmillan.

Mallett, Bernard, and C. Oswald George. 1929. *British Budgets: Second Series 1913–14 to 1920–21.* London: Macmillan.

Mares, Isabela. 2003. *The Politics of Social Risk: Business and Welfare State Development.* New York: Cambridge University Press.

Mares, Isabela, and Didac Queralt. Forthcoming. "The Conservative Origin of Income Taxation." *Comparative Political Studies.*

Marion, Marcel. 1931. *Histoire financière de la France.* Volume 6. Paris: Rousseau.

Martin, Isaac William. 2013. *Rich People's Movements.* New York: Oxford University Press.

Martin, Isaac William, Ajay Mehrotra, and Monica Prasad. 2009. *The New Fiscal Sociology: Taxation in Comparative and Historical Perspective.* Cambridge: Cambridge University Press.

Martin, Lucy. 2014. "Taxation, Loss Aversion, and Accountability: Theory and Experimental Evidence for Taxation's Effect on Citizen Behavior." Yale University.

Mauro, Paolo, Rafael Romeu, Ariel Binder, and Asad Zaman. 2013. "A Modern History of Fiscal Prudence and Profligacy." International Monetary Fund Working Paper 13/5.

McAlister, Fiona, Debosis Bandyopadhyay, Robert Barro, Jeremy Couchman, Norman Gemmell, and Gordon Liao. 2012. "Average Marginal Income Tax Rates for New Zealand, 1907–2009." New Zealand Treasury Working Paper 12/04.

McCaffery, Edward, and James Hines. 2010. "The Last Best Hope for Progressivity in Tax." *Southern California. Law Review* 83: 1031–1098.

Mehrotra, Ajay. 2013. *Making the Modern American Fiscal State: Law, Politics, and the Rise of Progressive Taxation, 1877–1929.* Cambridge: Cambridge University Press.

Meidner, Rudolf. 1993. "Why Did the Swedish Model Fail?" *Socialist Register* 29: 211–228.

Meltzer, Allan, and Scott Richard. 1981. "A Rational Theory of the Size of Government." *Journal of Political Economy* 81: 914–927.

Meyer, Theodore. 1956. "The Reed-Dirksen Amendment." *National Bar Association Journal* 42: 44–45.

Mill, John Stuart. 1848. *Principles of Political Economy.* London: John W. Parker.

Milward, Alan. 1965. *The German Economy at War.* London: Athlone Press.

Mirrlees, James. 1971. "An Exploration in the Theory of Optimum Income Taxation." *Review of Economic Studies* 38: 175–208.

Mitchell, B. R. 1988. *British Historical Statistics.* Cambridge: Cambridge University Press.

———. 2007. *International Historical Statistics: Europe, 1750–2005.* Basingstoke: Palgrave Macmillan.

Moene, Karl Ove, and Michael Wallerstein. 2001. "Inequality, Social Insurance, and Redistribution." *American Political Science Review* 95: 859–874.

Molho, Anthony. 1996. "The State and Public Finance: A Hypothesis Based on the History of Late Medieval Florence." In *The Origins of the State in Italy, 1300–1600,* ed. Julius Kirshner. Chicago, IL: University of Chicago Press.

Morgan, Kimberly, and Monica Prasad. 2009. "The Origins of Tax Systems: A French-American Comparison." *American Journal of Sociology* 114: 1350–1394.

Murphy, Liam, and Thomas Nagel. 2002. *The Myth of Ownership: Taxes and Justice*. Oxford: Oxford University Press.

Murray, Williamson, and MacGregor Knox. 2001. "Thinking About Revolutions in Warfare." In *The Dynamics of Military Revolution, 1300–2050*, ed. Macgregor Knox and Williamson Murray. New York: Cambridge University Press.

Musgrave, Richard A. 1985. "A Brief History of Fiscal Doctrine." *Handbook of Public Economics* 1: 1–59.

———. 1994. "Progressive Taxation, Equity, and Tax Design." In *Tax Progressivity and Income Inequality*, ed. Joel Slemrod, 341–356. Cambridge: Cambridge University Press.

National Tax Association. 1917. "Memorial of Economists to Congress Regarding War Finance." *Bulletin of the National Tax Association* 2: 214–216.

Nelson, Eric. 2004. *The Greek Tradition in Republican Thought*. Cambridge: Cambridge University Press.

Newcomer, Mabel. 1937. *Estimates of the Tax Burden in Different Income Classes*. New York: Twentieth Century Fund.

Ober, Josiah. 2015. *The Rise and Fall of Classical Greece*. Princeton, NJ: Princeton University Press.

O'Brien, Patrick, and Phillip A. Hunt. 1993. "The Rise of a Fiscal State in England, 1485–1815." *Historical Research* 66: 129–176.

Ohlsson, Henry, Jesper Roine, and Daniel Waldenström. 2007. "Long Run Changes in the Concentration of Wealth: An Overview of Recent Findings." Stockholm School of Economics.

Onorato, Massimiliano, Kenneth Scheve, and David Stasavage. 2014. "Technology and the Era of the Mass Army." *Journal of Economic History* 74: 449–481.

Osborne. Robin. 2004. *The Old Oligarch: Pseudo-Xenophon's Constitution of the Athenians*. London: Association of Classical Teachers.

Oxoby, Robert J., and John Spraggon. 2008. "Mine and Yours: Property Rights in Dictator Games." *Journal of Economic Behavior & Organization* 65: 703–713.

Owen, Stephen Walker. 1982. "The Politics of Tax Reform in France, 1906–1926." University of California–Berkeley.

Palmieri, Matteo. 1429 [1982]. *Della Vita Civile*. Edited by Gino Belloni. Firenze: Sansoni Editore.

Peacock, Alan, and Jack Wiseman. 1961. *The Growth of Public Expenditure in the United Kingdom*. Princeton, NJ: Princeton University Press.

Perry, J. Harvey. 1955. *Taxes, Tariffs, and Subsidies: A History of Canadian Fiscal Development*. Toronto: University of Toronto Press.

Pesaran, M. H. 2004. "General Diagnostic Tests for Cross Section Dependence in Panels." Cambridge Working Papers in Economics, no. 0435. University of Cambridge.

Pierson, Paul. 1994. *Dismantling the Welfare State? Reagan, Thatcher, and the Politics of Retrenchment*. Cambridge: Cambridge University Press.

Pigou, Arthur. 1918. "A Special Levy to Discharge War Debt." *Economic Journal* 28: 135–156.

———. 1928. *A Study in Public Finance*. London: Macmillan.

———. 1941. *The Political Economy of War*. New York: Macmillan.

Piketty, Thomas. 1995. "Social Mobility and Redistributive Politics." *Quarterly Journal of Economics* 110: 551–584.

———. 2001. *Les hauts revenus en France au XXème siècle*. Paris: Grasset.

———. 2014. *Capital in the Twenty-First Century*. Cambridge, MA: Harvard University Press.

Piketty, Thomas, and Emmanuel Saez. 2007. "How Progressive Is the U.S. Federal Tax System? A Historical and International Perspective." *Journal of Economic Perspectives* 21: 3–24.

Piketty, Thomas, and Emmanuel Saez. 2013. "Optimal Labor Income Taxation." *Handbook of Public Economics* 5: 391–474.

Piketty, Thomas, and Gabriel Zucman. 2014. "Wealth and Inheritance in the Long Run." *Handbook of Income Distribution* 2B: 1304–1366.

Plagge, Arnd, Kenneth Scheve, and David Stasavage. 2011. "Comparative Inheritance Taxation Database." Yale University, ISPS Data Archive.

Pocock, J.G.A. 1985. *Virtue, Commerce, and History: Essays on Political Thought and History, Chiefly in the Eighteenth Century.* Cambridge: Cambridge University Press.

Pontusson, Jonas. 2005. *Inequality and Prosperity: Social Europe Versus Liberal America.* Princeton, NJ: Princeton University Press.

Posen, Barry. 1993. "Nationalism, the Mass Army, and Military Power." *International Security* 18: 80–124.

Poterba, James. 2001. "Estate and Gift Taxes and Incentives for Inter Vivos Giving in the US." *Journal of Public Economics* 79: 237–264.

Pratt, Edwin. 1915. *The Rise of Rail Power in War and Conquest 1833–1914.* London: P.S. King and Son.

Przeworski, Adam et al. 2000. *Democracy and Development.* Cambridge: Cambridge University Press.

Przeworski, Adam, and John Sprague. 1986. *Paper Stones: A History of Electoral Socialism.* Chicago, IL: University of Chicago Press.

Przeworski, Adam, and Michael Wallerstein. 1988. "Structural Dependence of the State on Capital." *American Political Science Review* 82: 11–29.

Quinn, Dennis. 1997. "The Correlates of Change in International Financial Regulation." *American Political Science Review* 91: 531–551.

Rawls, John. 1971. *A Theory of Justice.* Cambridge, MA: Harvard University Press.

Regent, N. 2014. "Guicciardini's La Decima Scalata: The First Treatise on Progressive Taxation." *History of Political Economy* 46: 307–331.

Rehm, Phillip. 2011. "Social Policy by Popular Demand." *World Politics* 63: 271–299.

———. 2014. *Risking Solidarity.* Unpublished manuscript.

Reuben, Ernesto, and Arno Riedl. 2013. "Enforcement of Contribution Norms in Public Good Games with Heterogeneous Populations." *Games and Economic Behavior* 122–137.

Ricca-Salerno, Giuseppe. 1881. *Storia delle dottrine finanziarie in Italia.* Atti della R. Accademia dei Lincei, Serie Terza, Roma. Coi Tipi del Salviucci.

Robbins, Lionel. 1932. *Essay on the Nature and Significance of Economic Science.* London: MacMillan & Co.

Roberts, Kevin. 1977. "Voting over Income Tax Schedules." *Journal of Public Economics* 8: 329–340.

Robin, Martin. 1966. "Registration, Conscription, and Independent Labour Politics, 1916–1917. *Canadian Historical Review* 47: 101–118.

Rodden, Jonathan. 2010. "The Geographic Distribution of Political Preferences." *Annual Review of Political Science* 13: 321–340.

Roemer, John. 1996. *Theory of Distributive Justice.* Cambridge, MA: Harvard University Press.

———. 1997. "Political-Economic Equilibrium When Parties Represent Constituents: The Unidimensional Case." *Social Choice and Welfare* 14: 479–502.

———. 1998. *Equality of Opportunity.* Cambridge, MA: Harvard University Press.

———. 1999. "The Democratic Political Economy of Progressive Income Taxation." *Econometrica* 67: 1–19.

Roine, Jesper, Jonas Vlachos, and Daniel Waldenström. 2009. "The Long-Run Determinants of Inequality: What Can We Learn from Top Income Data?" *Journal of Public Economics* 93: 974–988.

Roine, Jesper, and Daniel Waldenström. 2007. "Wealth Concentration over the Path of Development: Sweden, 1873–2005." Stockholm School of Economics.

———. 2014. "Long Run Trends in the Distribution of Income and Wealth." Uppsala Center for Fiscal Studies Working Paper 2014, 5.

Roland, Alex. 2003. "Once More into the Stirrups." *Technology and Culture* 44: 574–585.

Romer, Thomas. 1975. "Individual Welfare, Majority Voting, and the Properties of a Linear Income Tax." *Journal of Public Economics* 14: 163–185.

Rostas, L. 1940. "Capital Levies in Central Europe, 1919–1924." *Review of Economic Studies* 8: 20–32.

Rousseau, Jean-Jacques. 1755. "Discours sur l'économie politique." In *Oeuvres Complètes: Tome III Ecrits Politiques*. Paris: Gallimard.

Rueda, David. 2007. *Social Democracy Inside Out: Partisanship and Labor Market Policy in Advanced Industrialized Democracies*. Oxford: Oxford University Press.

Saez, Emmanuel, and Michael Veall. 2007. "The Evolution of High Incomes in Canada." In *Top Incomes over the Twentieth Century: A Contrast between Continental and English-Speaking Countries*, ed. Anthony Barnes Atkinson and Thomas Piketty, 226–308. Oxford: Oxford University Press.

Samuel, Herbert. 1919. "The Taxation of the Various Classes of the People." *Journal of the Royal Statistical Society* 82: 143–182.

Scheidel, Walter. 2005. "Military Commitments and Political Bargaining in Ancient Greece." Princeton/Stanford Working Papers in Classics.

Scheve, Kenneth, and David Stasavage. 2010. "The Conscription of Wealth: Mass Warfare and the Demand for Progressive Taxation." *International Organization* 64: 529–561.

———. 2012. "Democracy, War, and Wealth: Lessons from Two Centuries of Inheritance Taxation." *American Political Science Review* 106: 81–102.

Schnapper, Bernard. 1968. *Le Remplacement militaire en France, quelques aspects politiques, économiques, et sociaux du recrutement au XIX siècle*. Paris: SEVPEN.

Seligman, Edwin. 1908. *Progressive Taxation in Theory and Practice*. 2nd edition. American Economic Association Quarterly 9: 1–334.

———. 1911. *The Income Tax: A Study of the History, Theory, and Practice of Income Taxation at Home and Abroad*. New York: Macmillan.

———. 1925. *Essays in Taxation*. New York: Macmillan.

Seligman, Edwin R. A. 1919. "The Cost of the War and How It Was Met." *American Economic Review* 9: 739–770.

Sen, Amartya. 1980. "Equality of What?" In *The Tanner Lectures on Human Values*, ed. S. McMurrin. Salt Lake City: University of Utah Press.

Shayo, Moses. 2009. "A Model of Social Identity with an Application for Political Economy: Nation, Class, and Redistribution." *American Political Science Review* 103: 147–174.

Shirras, Findlay, and L. Rostas. 1943. *The Burden of British Taxation*. New York: Macmillan.

Shovlin, John. 2006. *The Political Economy of Virtue: Luxury, Patriotism, and the Origins of the French Revolution*. Ithaca, NY: Cornell University Press.

Shultz, William. 1926. *The Taxation of Inheritance*. New York: Houghton Mifflin.

Sidgwick, Henry. 1883. *The Principles of Political Economy*. New York: Macmillan.

Simons, Henry. 1938. *Personal Income Taxation*. Chicago, IL: University of Chicago Press.

Skocpol, Theda. 1992. *Protecting Soldiers and Mothers: The Political Origins of Social Policy in the United States*. Cambridge, MA: Belknap Press of Harvard University Press.

Slemrod, Joel. 2002. *Does Atlas Shrug? The Economic Consequences of Taxing the Rich*. Cambridge, MA: Harvard University Press and the Russell Sage Foundation.

Smith, Adam. 1776. *An Inquiry into the Nature and Causes of The Wealth of Nations*. London: Strahan and Cadell.

Snyder, Jack. 2000. *From Voting to Violence: Democratization and Nationalist Conflict*. New York: W.W. Norton.

Söderberg, Hans. 1996. Inkomstskattens utveckling under 1900-talet. *En vägvisare förskatteberäkningar åren 1921–1996*. Skattebetalarnas förening. Stockholm.

Sokoloff, Kenneth L., and Eric M. Zolt. 2006. "Inequality and Taxation: Evidence from the Americas on How Inequality May Influence Tax Institutions." *Tax Law Review* 59(2): 167–242.

Sorensen, Peter Birch. 2010. "Dual Income Taxes a Nordic Tax System." In *Tax Reform in Open Economies*, ed. Iris Claus, Normal Gemmell, Michelle Harding, and David White. London: Edward Elgar.

Soward, Alfred Walter. 1919. *The Taxation of Capital*. London: Waterlow and Sons Ltd.

Sprague, O.M.W. 1917. "The Conscription of Income: A Sound Basis for War Finance." *Economic Journal* 27: 1–15.

Stabile, Donald. 1998. *The Origins of American Public Finance: Debates over Money, Debt, and Taxes in the Constitutional Era, 1776–1836*. Westport, CT: Greenwood Press.

Steinmo, Sven. 1993. *Taxation and Democracy*. New Haven, CT: Yale University Press.

Swank, Duane. 2002. *Global Capital, Political Institutions, and Policy Change in Developed Welfare States*. Cambridge: Cambridge University Press.

Swank, Duane, and Sven Steinmo. 2002. "The New Political Economy of Taxation in Advanced Capitalist Democracies." *American Journal of Political Science* 46: 642–655.

Thiers, Adolph 1871[1896]. *Discours contre l'établissement d'un impôt sur le revenu*. Paris: Calmann-Levy.

Thorndike, Joseph. 2002. *Tax Justice: The Ongoing Debate*. Washington, DC: Urban Institute Press.

———. 2013. *Their Fair Share: Taxing the Rich in the Age of FDR*. Washington, DC: Urban Institute Press.

Tilly, Charles. 1975. "Reflections on the History of European State Making." In *The Formation of National States in Western Europe*, ed. Charles Tilly. Princeton, NJ: Princeton University Press.

———. 1990. *Coercion, Capital, and European States*. Cambridge: Blackwell.

Timmons, Jeff. 2005. "The Fiscal Contract: States, Taxes, and Public Services." *World Politics* 57: 530–567.

Titmuss, Richard M. 1958. "War and Social Policy." In *Essays on the Welfare State*. London: George Allen and Unwin.

Toma, Mark. 1992. "Interest Rate Controls: The United States in the 1940s." *Journal of Economic History* 52: 631–650.

Tooze, Adam. 2006. *The Wages of Destruction: The Making and Breaking of the Nazi Economy*. London: Allen Lane.

Tristram, Fréderic. 1999. "L'administration fiscale et l'impôt sur le revenu dans l'entre-deux-guerres." *Etudes et Documents* 11: 211–242.

van Creveld, Martin. 1977. *Supplying War: Logistics from Wallenstein to Patton*. New York: Cambridge University Press.

———. 1989. *Technology and War from 2000 B.C. to the Present*. New York: Free Press.

van Zanden, Jan Luiten. 1997. "Old Rules, New Conditions, 1914–1940." In *Financial History of the Netherlands*, ed. Marjolein 't Hart, Joost Jonker, and Jan Luiten van Zanden, 124–151. Cambridge: Cambridge University Press.

Velez, Juliana Londono. 2014. "War and Progressive Income Taxation in the 20th Century." University of California, Berkeley Working Paper.

Walker, Francis. 1883. *Political Economy*. New York: Henry Holt and Company.

Walker, Francis A. 1888. "The Bases of Taxation." *Political Science Quarterly* 111: 1–16.

Webb, Sidney. 1919. "National Finance and a Levy on Capital: What the Labour Party Intends." *Fabian Tract no. 188*.

Weinzierl, Matthew. 2014. "The Promise of Positive Optimal Taxation: Normative Diversity and a Role for Equal Sacrifice." Harvard Business School.

Weisman, Steven. 2002. *The Great Tax Wars*. New York: Simon & Schuster.

White, Lynn. 1962. *Medieval Technology and Social Change*. Oxford: Clarendon Press.

Witte, John F. 1985. *The Politics and Development of the Federal Income Tax*. Madison: University of Wisconsin Press.

Wolowski, Louis. 1872. *L'Impôt sur le revenu*. Paris: Guillaumin.

Young, Peyton. 1990. "Progressive Taxation and Equal Sacrifice." *American Economic Review* 80: 253–266.

———. 1995. *Equity: In Theory and Practice*. Princeton, NJ: Princeton University Press.

Zolt, Eric. 2009. "Inequality, Collective Action, and Taxing and Spending Patterns of State and Local Governments." *Tax Law Review* 62: 445–504.

INDEX

17x